Islam and AIDS

Islam and AIDS

Between scorn, pity and justice

EDITED BY

FARID ESACK AND SARAH CHIDDY

ONEWORLD

OXFORD

A Oneworld Book

Published by Oneworld Publications 2009
Copyright © Farid Esack and Sarah Chiddy 2009

ISBN 978–1–85168–633–9

Typeset by Jayvee, Trivandrum, India
Cover design by Design Deluxe
Printed and bound in the United States
of America by Thomson-Shore, Inc.

Oneworld Publications
185 Banbury Road
Oxford OX2 7AR
England
www.oneworld-publications.com

For
Shukria in Lahore,
Faghmeda in Cape Town,
and
Waheedah in Philadelphia

CONTENTS

ACKNOWLEDGMENTS

A Fall 2007 seminar course titled "HIV, AIDS and Islam, Between Scorn, Pity and Justice" at the Harvard Divinity School provided a wonderful forum where many of the contributions in this volume were first circulated and discussed. It was here that the idea of a truly collaborative partnership between professors, and students to produce material for this volume was developed. We are deeply grateful to all the participants in that seminar for contributing – if not in a formal submission in this anthology then with the willingness to think through all the issues and to be its amazing initial sounding board.

We are grateful to Dr Peter Piot, Under Secretary of the United Nations and Director of UNAIDS, for so kindly writing a foreword for this volume.

Invaluable research and editorial support were provided by Junaid Ahmad, Aziza Ahmed, Yousra Fazil, Kelly-Jo Fulkerson, Gola Javadi, Clara Koh, Laura McTighe, Nadeem Mohammed, Sam Prevatt, Carissa Sharp, and Rodney Christopher Yeoh. Trad Godsey helped with the final proofreading.

Professors Leila Ahmad and Kecia Ali reviewed early drafts and offered criticism of a number of submissions at a Contributors Seminar.

Professor Abdulaziz Sachedina's article is reworked from a contribution that first appeared in *Religion, Health and Suffering* (ed. John R. Hinnells and Roy Porter, London: Kegan Paul International, 1999), and some parts of Professor Hashim Kamali's article first appeared in *The International Islamic University of Malaysia Law Journal*. We are grateful to both these publications for permission to utilize these articles in this volume.

All the contributors to this volume offered the income from their work here to Positive Muslims, a South African organization that supports Muslims living with HIV and conducts research and awareness work around issues related to Islam/Muslims and AIDS. We (and Positive Muslims) wish to thank them warmly.

Sarah Chiddy wishes to thank Laura McTighe for two years of inspiration and refuge; Philippa Geddie for kindness and imagination across time and too much space; Leslie Kirsh for making it matter; and her parents, Frances and Peter, for everything that they have been for her and given her – including teaching her how to venerate the ornaments she manages to break.

FOREWORD

*Peter Piot, Executive Director of UNAIDS and
Under Secretary-General of the United Nations*

This anthology, *Islam and AIDS – Between Scorn, Pity and Justice*, is a significant contribution to the discussion on religion and AIDS in general and, more specifically, the discussion on Islam and Muslims and AIDS. It is part of a welcome trend among religious communities to reflect on the challenges presented by the AIDS epidemic and provide support to people living with HIV.

As the editors stress, this collection contains a wide variety of opinions. Each contributor is alert to the enormous intellectual, moral and theological challenges arising from this epidemic.

At UNAIDS we believe in the important role that religious communities and faith-based organizations have to play in responding to AIDS, and have a long and valued relationship with Positive Muslims, the initiators of this publication. There are five main reasons for this.

First, religion continues to play a pivotal role in many societies, and engagement with clergy and religious institutions is therefore vital to the work of those seeking to address significant social issues. The role of religion is particularly important when societies are confronted with new, "unfathomable" events. Often, people look to religious leaders to explain what is happening, and to provide a framework for dealing with it.

Second, religious institutions such as temples, mosques, and churches are traditionally respected as educators. In many parts of the world, religious leaders have played a key leadership role in their communities for centuries, connecting with their constituents once a week – a feat rarely attained by activists, academics, or politicians.

Third, AIDS presents a number of serious challenges regarding issues such as disease as divine retribution or grace, taboos, silence about sin, sex and sexuality. Religious thinkers and theologians need to ask what this means for their traditions, and what their traditions mean for AIDS.

Fourth, some forty percent of all AIDS care is provided by religious groups.

Fifth, many of those affected by AIDS have strong religious beliefs. Many people living with HIV report that the first thought that occurred to them was to run to God and demand to know "what sin they have committed." Others find much comfort and support in their religious belief and faith community

At UNAIDS, we try to bring science – including social and political science – together with religion, to strengthen and deepen our collective response to the epidemic. In April 2008 we held a consultation in Geneva with faith-based partners to reach new levels of effectiveness in addressing AIDS. At a regional and country level we have approximately sixty Partnership Officers working with regional and national interfaith networks, religious leaders, and non-governmental organizations with religious affiliations delivering AIDS services – often in remote rural communities.

One important focus of all our work is to eliminate the prejudice, stigmatization, and discrimination that still prevail in too many societies against people living with HIV.

Another is to take concrete action against the injustices and inequalities that fuel the spread of AIDS. It is shameful to discriminate against gay men, migrants, ethnic minorities, injection drug users, sex workers – people who often end up pushed out to the margins of mainstream society and therefore at higher risk of HIV. It is shocking that society continues to tolerate the suppression of women, and to do so little to protect them from violence – in the street and in the home.

Unless we get better at dealing with social vulnerability, and make it possible for these people to get the support they need, we will be hard-pushed to make lasting progress towards universal access to HIV prevention, treatment, care, and support. This is a theme that underpins all we do.

Religious leaders and institutions have, since the earliest days of the epidemic, played a remarkable role in providing care, services, and education for those who have been affected by it. The challenge now is to deepen this concern, to come up with effective, open, and non-judgmental responses.

One of the major themes that is evident from this collection of articles is that AIDS is not just an emergency, it is an issue that will be with us for decades to come, and something on which all sectors of society need to take action if we are to make any inroads on the epidemic. United Nations Secretary-General Ban-Ki Moon recently addressed some religious leaders, describing the continuing AIDS epidemic as a "moral scar on our conscience" and speaking of our shared "sacred duty" to take action. I hope this anthology will encourage more people to fulfil this duty, and heal that "moral scar."

INTRODUCTION

Saleem[1] of Rylands in Cape Town was certified HIV positive with
full blown AIDS. While still in the care of Groote Schuur Hospital,
his parents, two brothers and a sister rejected him. He was told not
to return home, and to find his own way. The hospital could do no
more for Saleem. He was taken in and cared for by a hospice run by
non-Muslim social workers. Repeated attempts by the social workers and Saleem to contact his family led to no response. Saleem was
so disgusted and felt so dejected by his Muslim family's attitude that
he decided to renounce the Islamic faith. He drew up a will in which
he stated that he wished to have his body cremated. By the time his
parents reached Goodall & Williams cremation centre in Maitland
to claim his body, they were offered Saleem's ashes in an urn. His
parents refused to pay for the urn, so the ashes were transferred into
a paper bag. His Muslim parents did not know what to do with the
paper bag of ashes. Saleem was only twenty-nine years of age.

(Ahmed, 2000, p. 1)

The above story was told in an early Positive Muslims (est. 2000)
publication by Abdul Kayum Ahmed, one of the organization's co-
founders. It was – and regrettably, remains – a not atypical story, as is
evident from a number of the articles in this volume. Mercifully, it is
a response to Persons Living with HIV (PLWHIV) that is becoming
less and less frequent among Muslims. This, in turn, is an indication
both of a growing trend towards greater compassion and of more
obvious indications of the reality of HIV in Muslim communities
and countries.

NOT US . . .

Like many others, Muslim societies, and those approaching the pandemic as Muslims, have responded to AIDS in a clearly discernable pattern: first ignorance and denial, then scorn and pity. For most of the decade after the virus was first detected in 1983, the vast majority of Muslims were simply unaware of the pandemic. More recently, a greater recognition of the prevalence of HIV among Muslims has been slowly spreading through many parts of the Muslim world. As information about the reality of AIDS and people living with it becomes more common, Muslims often respond by suggesting that it is still not "our problem." A few years ago, at a time when HIV was already becoming common in South Africa, an imam (religious leader), upon being asked what he knew about AIDS, replied "I once saw a story about it on TV when that actor [Rock Hudson] in Hollywood died of AIDS." The underlying message was that "it's on TV, not in real life; it was an actor, not an ordinary person; it was in Hollywood, not here." When the reality of the pandemic creeps closer to Muslims, the parameters of denial are pushed even further back: "It happens, yes, but to others, in other societies" (in "America" or "Africa"). When Muslims are actually living in America, the suggestion is often that it happens in "White America," "homosexual America," or to the "African-Americans" – certainly not *us*. When it becomes evident that AIDS actually *is* prevalent in these Muslim communities or countries, refuge is sought by confining it to "core groups" – an imagined sub-strata of society who are not "really Muslim": "immoral people", sex workers, drug addicts, prisoners, homosexuals, immigrants, migrant laborers, etc.

IT *IS* WITH US!

Before continuing with our reflections on the way Muslims have responded to the pandemic, let us make a few observations about HIV prevalence among Muslims. When looking at reported prevalence rates for predominantly Muslim countries, and the problems connected with reporting, we are wary of reductive explanations which attribute everything to the religious commitment of the majority. These countries are quite often at a particular place on a development trajectory, which means that while being Muslim may be a factor in how they are reporting or responding to the pandemic, an equally valid factor may be their socio-economic position. While there have been significant recent improvements, epidemiological surveillance in many Muslim countries remains limited (Obermeyer, 2006) and several Muslim countries, including Saudi Arabia, Kuwait, the United Arab Emirates, and Qatar, have no official statistics on HIV prevalence.

The Middle East and North Africa reported small numbers for HIV, with most infections occurring in men and in urban areas. While unprotected paid sex is a key factor in the HIV epidemics in most of the Muslim world, exposure to contaminated drug injecting equipment is the main route of transmissions in countries such as Afghanistan, Iran, Libya, Algeria, Morocco, Pakistan, and Syria (UNAIDS, 2007, 35). The country in South-East Asia with the fastest growing HIV epidemic is Indonesia – also the country with the largest Muslim population in the world – where most infections are due to the use of contaminated injecting equipment, unprotected paid sex, and, to a lesser extent, unprotected sex between men (ibid.). Similarly, HIV numbers are rising in the Muslim countries of central Asia such as Azerbaijan, Kazakhstan, Kyrgyzstan, and Tajikistan. Uzbekistan now has the largest epidemic in Central Asia, and, according to UNAIDS, "the epidemic is likely to continue to grow, given the high level of injecting drug use and sex with non-regular partners" (ibid.).

Relatively few studies have been undertaken to ascertain HIV prevalence amongst Muslims as a religious group, or on the definitive impact of Islam as a religion on sexual conduct that could increase or lessen susceptibility. What is also largely unexplored is the relationship between Muslim identity and HIV prevalence. To date, the most significant study is the much cited 2004 survey by Peter B. Gray of published journal articles containing data on HIV prevalence and religious affiliation in East Africa. This survey showed that six out of seven such studies indicated a negative relationship between HIV seropositivity and being Muslim (Gray, 2004). In Gray's study this relatively lower Muslim HIV seropositivity is attributed to the following factors: a) religious constraints on extra-marital sexual behavior, including homosexual sex; b) male circumcision; c) the Islamic prohibition on alcohol consumption; and d) personal hygiene (ibid., 1752).

BUT ONLY THE SINFUL ONES AMONG US . . .

Early ignorance of the modes of HIV transmission, its initial iden-
tification with homosexual activity, and its immediate association
with death contributed substantially to the anxiety with which
people responded to the pandemic and its modes of transmission. A
literature scan covering both the Internet and written sources clearly
indicates that the dominant, while not exclusive, Muslim voices that
have emerged in response to the AIDS pandemic argue that the virus
is a form of God's vengeance on a sexually perverse and/or immoral
group of people as punishment for their sins (Desai, 2004). While
the language of these voices is peculiarly Muslim, and the responses
– usually offered as "cures" or "solutions" – are framed in Islamic
terms, this response is not unlike the dominant voices from other
religious traditions.

A relatively early and insightful survey of some of the prominent
Islamic positions on HIV and AIDS is rendered in Ersilia Francesca's
article, "AIDS in Contemporary Islamic Ethical Literature" (2002).
The author includes perspectives by diverse Islamic voices such
as *Majallat al-Azhar*, the journal of the University of Al-Azhar in
Egypt, and the Jami'atul 'Ulama (Council of Religious Scholars)
of South Africa. Initially, all that could be found in Islamic literature was a condemnation of AIDS as a disease of homosexuals.
One statement, attributed to an anonymous US surgeon, parallels
the views of many a religious leader: "We used to hate faggots on an
emotional level. Now we have a good reason" (Allen, 2000, xviii).
Later, through the 1990s, extra-marital sexual practices – often por-
trayed as Western based promiscuity – were blamed as the cause
of AIDS amongst Muslims. Quite simply, as some put it, "those
people deserved to die." Their admonitions echo the words of
Thomas Dekker, who warned his fellow citizens in 1630, when
England was gripped by a bubonic plague, "Only this antidote apply:
Cease vexing Heaven and cease to die!" (cited in Allen, 2000, xx).

This line of argument has had a devastating impact on Muslims
like Saleem, whose story was recounted above, who are living with
HIV and fear rejection, isolation, and even violent reactions from
their fellow Muslims and families should they reveal their HIV positive status. Stigmatization and judgmentalism place an enormous
additional burden on those who are HIV positive, and contribute
immensely to the reluctance to disclose one's own positive status.

In the words of Faghmeda Miller, the first South African Muslim to disclose her HIV positive status, "I realised that in most cases it is not the virus that is killing the person but the stigma attached to it and the ignorance of our people" (cited in Heard, 2000).

There has regrettably been no shortage of glib "Islamic" reasons for being judgmental and withholding compassion. Scorn is often transformed into pity when people are in contact with someone who defies their preconceptions of the "usual suspects": when the person living with HIV emerges as a *hijab*-clad widow, or a young orphan, or at the end of a workshop where they have met, discussed, and had meals with an HIV positive person. Shukria Gul, a Pakistani Muslim woman, speaks of an imam she encountered at a workshop in Peshawar. Exasperated by the sympathetic tone of the discussion on persons living with HIV, he said "All HIV patients should just be shot, that'll solve the problem." "On the last day of the workshop," says Shukria, "when I revealed that I was HIV positive, he stood up and apologised to me for what he'd said" (http://news.bbc.co.uk/2/hi/south_asia/3239330.stm).

BEYOND PITY

While admittedly a much better response than wanting someone dead, pity is hardly an adequate response. It turns the other person into a victim, where we only see his or her HIV positive status. Pity is not about recognizing the fullness of the other person; it is not about how one's own life can be enriched by the other person; it is not about seeing our own weaknesses and frailty reflected in the other person. It often emerges from, and entrenches, patronizing others and is nearly always a smokescreen for feelings of superiority.

A number of Muslims engaged in HIV intervention work are increasingly speaking of a "theology of compassion" – a term first used in the literature of Positive Muslims in 2000 and, subsequently, in the material of the Malaysian AIDS Council. The most significant indication of the emergence of a compassionate approach as a new "mainstream" voice was the broad consensus reached at a UNDP conference of religious leaders held in Cairo in 2004, and an Islamic Relief Worldwide conference held in Johannesburg in late 2007. The

Cairo conference, held under the theme of "Compassion in Action," declared that "illness is one of God's tests; anyone may be afflicted by it according to God's sovereign choice. Patients are our brothers and sisters and we stand by them seeking God's healing for each one of them" (UNDP, 2005, 33). An approach rooted entirely in compassion is, however, not without its inadequacies.

The relationship is still primarily with the "other" as "victim." This ignores the heart of what makes us human: agency, the ability to take charge of and control our own lives. Thus compassion must simultaneously construct a discourse both of agency and of the rights of HIV positive persons. A mere appeal for mercy and compassion towards the "sick" or "diseased other" is itself dehumanizing, for it simply transforms people from being objects of medical surveillance (classification, examination, treatment, statistics, etc.) into objects of theological surveillance, objects who plead for mercy for the sins of the body, as if the bearing of the disease is a public confession that, once made, will entitle the sufferer to public compassion.

IT'S ALSO ABOUT JUSTICE

A number of essays in this volume argue for an Islamic response to the pandemic that transcends the personalist, individualist approaches and takes seriously socio-economic justice and the systemic roots of disease. While justice is a dimension to the AIDS pandemic that is still struggling to be born in the Muslim world, it is something deeply rooted in Islamic theology and is one of the characteristics of God. Justice is, indeed, one of the reasons why the universe was created: "And God has created the heavens and the earth in truth and [has therefore willed] that every human being shall be recompensed for what he/she has earned and none shall be wronged" (Q. 45:22). Blaming individuals and responding with solely moralistic and behaviorist solutions is relatively easy. Yet doing so ignores the fact that there is more driving this pandemic than simple moral choices. We must also ask how the structures of power in the world today – including the dominant economic system that reduces people to commodities and Black people and women to half the value of White people and men – contribute to the spread of viruses such as HIV. When we see the way in which the HIV pandemic is laying an entire continent to ruin, we must ask serious questions about the socio-economic conditions that allow the disease to spread and drive women onto the streets to sell their bodies to feed their starving children.

The AIDS crisis is at the extreme edge of a crisis of human health around the world. It will not be stopped or significantly slowed as long as we are controlled by economic systems that put profit and greed ahead of people. A global healthcare system that is truly consistent with a commitment to human rights is one in which the same treatment is available to all regardless of their race, religion, nationality, gender, sexual orientation, or ability to pay. Moreover, no matter what measures are adopted to stop one health crisis, the conditions which breed new crises – unemployment, poor sanitation, poor housing, lack of clean water, malnutrition – are continually being reproduced by economic systems that put profit ahead of people. So long as the obscenity exists whereby a minority can pay for good medical care while others cannot even find clean water, talk of a real solution is impossible. The resources for a global healthcare system that puts human needs first do exist today. The struggle for justice is a struggle to make these resources accessible to all.

A theology of compassion, responsibility, and justice must thus make the connections between compassion on the one hand, and power or, more appropriately, the lack of it, on the other. AIDS (or any other disease) is not an isolated entity; the pandemic is just as much about a crisis and collapse of all social security structures in society as it is about a crisis and collapse of the immune system in the body. In many ways, the actual disease is one tragic symptom of the major injustices in the world, particularly the growing gap between the rich and the poor. The context of our struggle to bring dignity to those living with this condition is part of a larger one where the obscured connections between disease and socio-economic conditions and processes are interrogated. This book seeks to do just that within a framework of Islam and being Muslim.

THE VOICES IN THIS COLLECTION

As with all anthologies, not all of the voices in this volume agree; indeed, some articles directly challenge each other. It is the nature of such a seminal project, however, to include such variety, and we hope that our selection manages to give the reader a fuller picture of the existing Muslim responses to HIV and AIDS while privileging a comprehensive response based on responsibility, compassion, and justice. What is unmistakable is that each contributor takes seriously both the severity of the pandemic and the need for Muslim individuals, communities, countries, and their allies to make a real contribution to solving this global problem.

In "Afflicted by God? Muslim Perspectives on Health and Suffering," **Abdulaziz Sachedina** considers two apparently contradictory understandings of the purpose of suffering found in the Qur'an and the *Sunnah* (Prophet Muhammad's precedent): the conviction that suffering is a test or an exercise to strengthen humans, and the conviction that suffering is punishment for disbelief or sin. These differing explanations of the theological reasons for suffering lead to conflicting approaches to how humans should respond to affliction. Professor Sachedina argues that contemporary Muslim biomedical ethics have come to accept both divine justice and moral agency, and that this involves a mandate to cure disease and care for the sick. He places the pandemic at the centre of this theological–ethical debate and finds hope in some of the responses of the Islamic medical community.

Malik Badri, one of the earliest and most widely-read Muslim scholars to address the AIDS crisis, exemplifies a widespread Muslim approach to the AIDS pandemic. From the early stages of our conception of this volume it was clear to us that it would be incomplete without a contribution from Professor Badri. His voice is important both because of his seminal work in the field and because we hope that the presence of his article will help the reader navigate other contributors' disagreements with his positions. The article as it appears here is a synthesis of Badri's main ideas and arguments, the most striking of which is his assertion that the pandemic is a sign of divine retribution for the (homo)sexual revolution in the West, and that the most effective response to this crisis in Muslim countries is to strengthen Islamic values. These are the claims that Norwegian social anthropologist **Sindre Bangstad** takes up in "AIDS and the Wrath of God." Dr. Bangstad offers a critique of Badri's work and reflects on him as a pioneer in the field of the "Islamization of knowledge," a project that sets itself up in opposition to what it regards as "Western modernity's infringement on 'Islam'."

One of the widely invoked proof-texts for the idea that AIDS is divine retribution for sexual promiscuity is a hadith (prophetic tradition) found in the collection of Ibn Māja, which suggests that when *fāḥishah* – often translated as fornication and/or homosexuality – is performed openly, new diseases and epidemics will become "widespread." In her article "When *Fāḥishah* Becomes Widespread: AIDS and the Ibn Māja Hadith," **Nabilah Siddiquee** calls this interpretation into question, interrogating the implications of divine collective punishment, and suggesting that *fāḥishah* may refer to a larger swathe of sins than simply transgressive sex. She offers an interpretation that grounds the hadith in the context of Islamic social justice, arguing that when it is read in full, the hadith offers Muslims a more "productive approach" to the pandemic. This close textual reading leads into **Mohammad Hashim Kamali**'s consideration of what Islamic Law might say about AIDS. While in modernist discourse the details of the Shari'ah and the maxims of the law may hold less significance, the vast majority of Muslims worldwide look to the Shari'ah as authoritative on how to answer the difficult questions that face our age. Professor Kamali's voice speaks clearly to the need to bring AIDS into conversation with normative traditional scholarly Islam.

The next four articles address the crucial topics of Islam, gender, and sexuality. Much attention has been given recently to the "feminization" of the AIDS pandemic. This is traceable both to the fact that women are biologically more susceptible than men to the HI virus, and to the gendered power imbalances that shape women's lives. **Clara Koh**'s article offers a broad introduction to these realities, highlighting attempts to downplay the impact of AIDS in Muslim societies, the volatile and contested terrain of the Muslim woman's rights, and the promise and the limitations of Islamic feminism. Koh's article is followed by a close look at the particular intersection of HIV, AIDS, gender, and patriarchy, and Islam in Malaysia. **Marina Mahathir** draws her expertise both from scholarly sources and from many years as an AIDS activist. She is critical in her evaluations of the world's obsessive interest in the state of AIDS in the Muslim world, adamant in her conviction that it is "poverty, denial, and social inequalities – not religion per se" that create the necessary conditions for HIV epidemics, and certain in her perspective that the human and patriarchal interpretations of Islamic law as enacted in Malaysia seriously compromise women's health and ability to protect themselves from the HI virus.

But where are men in this pandemic? **Trad Godsey**'s article faces this question, indicting forms of masculinity that hurt both women and men by glorifying male strength and power. Through an examination of Islamic sources, Godsey suggests that the Prophet Muhammad offers a very different – and mutually liberating – picture of masculinity.

As the articles written by Badri, Bangstad, and Siddiquee all demonstrate, AIDS has been associated with homosexuality in the public imagination since the early days of the pandemic. While it can no longer be argued that gay men and injecting drug users make up the majority of people with HIV worldwide, AIDS still equals homosexuality in many people's minds. Professor **Scott Siraj al-Haqq Kugle** and **Sarah Chiddy** explore the topic of what the Qur'an, *Sunnah*, and Islamic ethics might have to say about male homosexuality in a time of AIDS. Their article provides a sensitive navigation of difficult terrain and argues that any justice-based approach to the pandemic must take seriously the experiences of homosexual Muslims, and that addressing the stigma associated with them is an essential part of being able to speak honestly about the pandemic.

No serious consideration of AIDS can afford to ignore the power of silence and denial. Muslim societies – like many other tradition-based communities – have strong cultural taboos which suggest that speaking about illicit sexual activity is tantamount to condoning it. Drawing from her own scholarly and vocational experience negotiating religious ideals and daily realities in Catholicism, **Kate Henley Long** proposes a theological look at the questions of sin and silence. She considers the work of a performance troupe of Muslims in the Chitral region of Pakistan who, through their music, demystify and comment on some of the political tensions in the region. Long suggests that if storytelling emerges authentically from local communities, it can be an invaluable way to relieve some of the fear, anxiety, and stigma that AIDS evokes in many Muslims.

A thread that ties many of these contributions together is the devastating confluence of poverty with the spread of HIV, which invariably and disproportionately affects the most marginalized people throughout the world. These people often do not have access to basic health care, food and shelter, clean water, and reliable income, and it is in these circumstances that an HIV diagnosis is the most deadly. **Caitlin Yoshiko Buysse** and **Kabir Sanjay Bavikatte** both put the demands of economic justice at the centre of a Muslim response to the pandemic. Buysse points to the Qur'anic mandates for the right of the poor to wealth, the principle of distributive justice, and the prohibition of usury to suggest a powerful vision of how the Qur'an calls Muslims to respond to poverty. Her critique of the role of the pharmaceutical industry is an excellent introduction to Bavikatte's reflection on the largely economic structures that make certain people far more vulnerable to HIV and its attendant illnesses than others.

The final two articles in this volume turn the conversation to the most prevalent mode of HIV transmission in the Muslim world: injecting drug use. **Chris Byrnes'** article skilfully weaves personal narrative with UN facts and figures, NGO studies, and basic HIV science to speak sensitively about the risk for HIV transmission within drug using communities and beyond. Pointing to studies based out of Pakistan, Iran, Malaysia, Saudi Arabia, and Bangladesh, he dispels the myth that injecting drug use does not take place in Muslim countries, and points to a number of highly successful Muslim community responses.

This book is dedicated to three women on different sides of the globe – Faghmeda Miller in Cape Town, Shukria Gul in Lahore, and Waheedah El-Shabazz in Philadelphia. It is Waheedah's story that guides **Laura McTighe**'s compelling treatise on the power that an Islamic theology of liberation can bring to the world of HIV, addiction, and the fight against injustice. McTighe's article draws from and builds on the work of Islamic liberation theologians such as Ali Shari'ati (1933–1977), Asghar Ali Engineer, and Farid Esack, and is the first work to consider Islamic liberation theology seriously in an American context.

The conclusion to this volume is provided in the form of an Afterword by Professor **Kecia Ali,** who reflects on all of the articles and provides some of her own thoughts on the necessity and value of idealism as we struggle as Muslims to figure out responses to the AIDS pandemic.

In putting together this volume we were acutely aware of the very many dimensions to the question of Muslims, Islam, and AIDS. We have tried to cover some of them here and are cognizant of many inadequacies in our attempts – in terms both of the subjects covered and the people covering them. None of the authors, for example, are known to be HIV positive, and while many attempt to speak from the margins, their own privileged position in the academy or as inhabitants of the First World limit their ability to do so with authenticity. In the face of the enormous challenges presented to humankind by this pandemic, inadequacy is not a crime. Complacency and indifference are.

BIBLIOGRAPHY

Ahmed, Abdul Kayum 2000. "The Positive Muslim." www.positivemuslims.org.za/beinghiv.htm

Allen, Peter Lewis 2000. *The Wages of Sin – Sex, Disease, Past and Present.* Chicago, University of Chicago Press.

Desai, Muhammed 2004. "HIV/AIDS and Islam/Muslims – A Critical Survey of Available Resources, Networks, Organizations and Other Material." Unpublished term paper for the Introduction to the World of Islam Course, Xavier University.

Francesca, Ersilia 2002. "AIDS in Contemporary Islamic Ethical Literature." *Medicine and Law*, 21: 381–394.

Gray, Peter B. 2004. "HIV and Islam: Is HIV Prevalence Lower Among Muslims?" *Social Science & Medicine*, 58(9): 1751–1756.

Heard, Janet 2000. "Faghmeda's Story." *Sunday Times*, April 30, p. 17.

Obermeyer, Carla Makhlouf 2006. "HIV in the Middle East." *British Medical Journal*, 333, October 21: 851–854.

UNAIDS 2007. *Annual Report: Knowing Your Epidemic.* Geneva. http://data.unaids.org/pub/Report/2008/07_unaids_annual_report1_en.pdf.

United Nations Development Program (UNDP) 2005. *The Cairo Declaration of Religious Leaders in the Arab States in Response to the HIV/AIDS Epidemic, 23-12-2004.* Cairo, UNDP HIV/AIDS Regional Programme in the Arab States (HARPAS).

1

AFFLICTED BY GOD? MUSLIM PERSPECTIVES ON HEALTH AND SUFFERING[1]

Abdulaziz Sachedina

As we explore Muslim perspectives on health and suffering we must keep in mind that in the absence of an officially organized and recognized theological body, such as the Pope or the Vatican Council in Catholicism, it is well-nigh impossible to think of Islam in monolithic terms on any theological matter. Plurality in belief and practice is inherent in Islam, and Muslims invest the power of interpretation and decision-making in experts in religious matters, the *'ulama*. In this article, therefore, I will not attempt to identify particular views as strictly Sunni or Shi'i. As I shall demonstrate, it is not unusual even within a single school of thought to find very diverse views about freedom of will and predetermination which have ramifications for how suffering is understood.

In general, the Arabic term *musibah*, which signifies suffering or affliction caused by events that lead to some form of harm or loss (*darr* or *durr*), is discussed in the light of Muslim belief about the omnipotent and omniscient God. This belief is reflected in everyday expressions among Muslims which connect suffering to God's "permission" (*idhn*). It is very common to express one's sympathy for a loss, illness, or disaster by saying: *bi idhnillah* or *bi mashiyyatillah*, or *hakadha maktub* – that is, it happened with "God's permission", "God's will" or "thus it was written." However, such statements create a theological problem of imputing evil to God; it implicates a moral God in the dispute about the authorship of an action objectively described as bad or evil.

There are contradictory responses in the foundational sources of Islamic thought to the question of the existence of evil in the world. While the positive or negative estimation of evil among Muslims depends upon the way pertinent texts are interpreted by various scholars, the cryptic nature of some of the scriptural language about God's role in creating or permitting evil also lends itself to difficulty in explaining its purpose. Additionally, unofficial state theology was – and is – often at work in furthering unquestioning submission to the all-powerful God. There is overwhelming historical evidence to show that under the Umayyad rulers (C.E. 660–748), in order to contain growing discontent and opposition to the dynasty, the state policy was to perpetuate belief that the absolute will of God pre-determined all human action, including the evil conduct of those in power. On the basis of certain verses of the Qur'an, people were made to believe that human suffering as a form of God's punishment was caused by the divine will, and a good believer should submit to it without question.

SUFFERING IN THE QUR'AN

For Muslims the Qur'an is a foundational source for their belief system. Thus what it says about any religious or ethical issue is an authentic perspective on the Muslim creed. A careful examination of the Qur'an in its natural context reveals on the one hand the vulnerability of human life in the threatening conditions of living near the desert; and, on the other hand, it shows the complex interaction between the divine and human wills to overcome the effects of actual instances of suffering. In other words, the Qur'an juxtaposes a realistic treatment of suffering as part of what it means to be alive under severe life situations with suffering as a problem of theodicy, where it is ultimately faith in the transcendent God that can bring about confidence in divine wisdom.

Suffering is introduced in various forms (physical and mental) throughout the Qur'an to demonstrate the all-encompassing power of God. It is the Almighty Creator who causes it and "He [is the one] who answers the constrained, when he calls unto Him, and removes evil" (Q. 27:61). The Qur'an therefore frames suffering as a divinely ordained temporary situation, instead of an ethical problem for the just and compassionate God that needs vindication and rationalization. In some passages it clearly imputes the cause of suffering to humans who have been visited by "an affliction for what their own hands have forwarded" (Q. 4:63), requiring them to assess the positive role it plays in sharpening human awareness of God's continuous presence. In other passages it implicitly suggests that God has foreknowledge of suffering because "no affliction befalls in the earth or in yourselves, but it is in a Book, before We create it" (Q. 57:22). Most of the commentators on this latter verse regard affliction as value neutral, but they differentiate between natural catastrophes and the harm that touches human beings through injury, illness, death, etc. The latter occurs to summon humans to heed to the call of faith, requiring them to strive physically to make God's purposes on earth succeed.

A theological problem arises when affliction is written before it is created. This state of affairs implies God's omniscience. Does this omniscience require Muslims to believe that God has knowledge concerning things before they existed, from eternity? God's omniscience certainly led to the creedal statement in the majority of Sunni theological works that God has decreed and ordained everything, including suffering as a form of evil, and that nothing could happen either in this world or in the next except through His will, knowledge, decision, decree, and writing on the preserved table (*al-lawh al-mahfuz*).[2] However, this divine absoluteness is complicated by a declaration that God's writing is "of a descriptive, not of a decisive nature" (Wensinck, 1965, 190).

Another verse of the Qur'an admonishes human beings to endure patiently whatever visits them because "no affliction befalls, except by the leave of God" (Q. 64:11). "By the leave of God" – *bi idhnil-lah* – reinforces a Muslim cultural attitude of passiveness in the face of afflictions and pain when viewed as coming from God. Muslim theologians have debated the adverse ramifications of the phrase "by the leave of." How does it relate to the laws of causality which apparently govern human conditions? Does it imply that God's foreknowledge is the real cause of suffering? Or does it mean that God maintains the power to remove what impedes the realization of His salutary plan for humanity?

Suffering, the Qur'an asserts time and again, is in some sense purposeful. However, God's foreknowledge of imminent affliction raises a serious ethical problem about God willing an affliction to

occur despite His omnipotence to prevent it. If He *creates* affliction, divine authorship of harm contradicts His justice and boundless
benevolence. Reasonable people, some commentators argue, do not
consider a Being who has the power to prevent evil or harm and does
not do so to be a just and good God.

Other scholars question whether something called evil actually
exists in the world. They maintain that the evil of things is not a true
attribute but a relative one. This view suggests that when we encounter unpleasantness in our lives we often become unjustifiably upset
and term the causes of this discomfort "evil." However, good and
evil are not mutually exclusive categories in the order of creation.
Goodness is identical with being, and evil is identical with non-being;
wherever being makes its appearance, non-existence is also implied.
Thus the argument goes that when we speak of poverty, ignorance,
or disease we should not imagine that they are separate realities:
poverty is simply not having wealth, ignorance is the absence of
knowledge, and disease is the loss of health. Wealth and knowledge
are positive realities, but poverty is nothing other than the emptiness
of hand and pocket, and ignorance the absence of knowledge. They
are defined through the non-existence of other things.

The same is the case with afflictions and misfortunes that we
regard as the source of suffering, and therefore evil. They, too, are
a form of non-being and are evil only insofar as they are dependent
on the non-existence of something else. If afflictions did not entail
sickness and death, the loss and destruction of certain creatures, they
would not be bad. It is this loss and ruin that is inherently negative.

Apart from this, these scholars hold, nothing that exists can be
called evil, since the Qur'an regards everything as inherently good.
If something is evil, it is so only in connection with things other than
itself. The malarial mosquito is only evil insofar as it is harmful to
humans and causes disease. The existence of a thing in and of itself
is real and must derive its being from the Creator. The only things
and attributes that are real are those that exist outside the mind.
Relative attributes are created by the mind and have no existence
outside it, so the Creator cannot answer for them. From the vantage
point of God's wisdom, either the world must exist on the pattern
that is particular to it, or it cannot exist at all. A world without order,
lacking the principle of causality, where good and evil are not separate from each other, would be an impossibility and an illusion. It is
for this reason that there are relatively few references in the Qur'an

to suffering and they appear as inevitable concomitants of the real entities that give rise to them. The Qur'an sums up its treatment of suffering in the following verse:

> Surely We will try you with something of fear and hunger, and loss of wealth and possessions, death, and the loss of fruits of your toil. Yet, give glad tidings to those who are patient who, when they are visited by an affliction, say, "Surely we belong to God, and to Him we return." Upon those rest blessings and mercy from their Lord, and those are the truly guided. (Q. 2:155–157)

SUFFERING IN THE HADITH

When one considers the Muslim traditions collected in the books on the *Sunnah* (the prophetic paradigm), suffering in general and illness or loss of good health in particular are treated in light of theological positions about the divine and human wills. There are Hadith (traditions) that consider illness a form of divinely ordained suffering, assuming that God is the author of all that befalls human beings. Such traditions have been the major source of the skepticism in some quarters of Muslim society about seeking medical treatment. Here, God is regarded as the only Healer on whom a true believer should depend. Moreover, in these traditions illness is considered a form of divine mercy to expiate a believer's sins. According to a well known tradition, the Prophet is reported to have said: "No fatigue, nor disease, nor sorrow, nor sadness, nor hurt, nor distress befalls a Muslim, even if it were the prick he received from a thorn, but that God expiates some of his sins for that" (Bukhari, 371–372).

Some other traditions contradict this attitude of passivity. Here, since God is just, He cannot cause unremitting pain to His creatures. There is a strong emphasis on God's goodness and intentionality in all that He does. He intends only benefit. Reconciling this tenet with the suffering of the innocent has not been easy in Islam. Even when the general trend in Muslim piety has been to hold human beings accountable for their own pain and to recommend undertaking righteous acts to rid the world of suffering, it is particularly challenging to explain the affliction of infants and animals. The problem of infant suffering is also difficult to resolve from a juridical point of view. In Islamic jurisprudence, minors are not competent to assume religious or moral responsibility (*mukallaf*), so they cannot be punished for failing to carry out such obligations. Some Muslims try to explain such sufferings as admonitions for adults. In this interpretation, the sufferings of children serve as a sign and warning for the discerning. They provide a convenient means of putting parents to test. God then makes up in the hereafter for the unmerited sufferings of the innocent.

Even more difficult is the suffering of the animals, lesser beings, as an admonition to humans, higher beings. Although there are views among some Muslims that animals will be rewarded lavishly in paradise and even in this world in ways we humans cannot understand, the intricacies of divine Justice as regards the sufferings of the innocent are considered beyond human comprehension (Ormsby, 1984, 241–245).

The Hadith literature overwhelmingly regards illness as an affliction to be addressed by every possible legitimate means. In fact, in these traditions the search for a cure is founded upon unusual confidence generated by the divine promise reported in one of the early traditions: "There is no disease that God has created, except that He has also created its treatment" (Bukhari, no. 582). It is also because of this confidence in being cured by human efforts that a physician's role as a healer is regarded as spiritually and morally commendable and a collective duty; medicine is a religious necessity for society. Muslim physicians must treat illness not simply as a physical reality, but also as a psychological one, because in Islam medicine, hygiene, and regulations for healthy living together form the guidelines for living according to God's will. Like all human activity, medical practice can be both an act of worship and a source of divine testing. Medical doctors are exhorted to work sincerely under the guidelines of the religious law, to avoid all temptations to personal arrogance or riches, and to resist all kinds of social pressures, be they personal, political, or military. Medical caring and curing should therefore be practiced in a climate of piety and awareness of the presence of God (*Islamic Code of Medical Ethics*, 16–23).

Although some hadith are simply an elaboration of the Qur'anic views about suffering, a vast number of them are prophetic directives about the proper etiquette in dealing with illness and visiting the sick and bereaved. The following tradition provides the paradigm for the community to emulate the Prophet in what to say when visiting a patient. According to this tradition, the Prophet entered the home of a desert Arab to visit him. It was his custom when he visited the sick to say, "Don't worry. It is a [means of] purification, if God will," so he said to him, "Don't worry. It is a [means of] purification, if God wills." The man replied, "Never! Rather it is a fever boiling in an old man, which will send him on a visit to the graves!" The Prophet replied, "Very well, then be it so" (Bukhari, no. 566). In another tradition it is related that when a person fell ill the Prophet used to rub him with his right hand and then pray to God saying: "O Lord of the people, grant him health, heal him, for Thou art a Great Healer" (Muslim, no. 5432–5438). Other traditions recognize a religious purpose in illness and argue that its cause is God's trial and cleansing of the people. In one tradition the Prophet says that the patient earns merits under these trials and can attain the rank of a true believer. "When God intends to do good to somebody, He afflicts him with trials" (Bukhari, no. 373).

"*Asabahu bi maradin*" (He [i.e., God] afflicted him with disease or rendered him diseased), and its converse, "*asabahu bi sihatin*" (He rendered him healthy), are common articulations of God's activity in everyday human life. In a Muslim thanksgiving prayer, besides praising and thanking God for all his blessings, a believer affirms: "To You [O God] belongs praise for all the good affliction (*bala'in hasanin*) with which You have inured me" (Qummi, 1381, 405). The characterization of affliction as "good" in the above prayer suggests that suffering as such does not create a theological problem in Islam. Rather, it is treated in direct terms as part of the divine plan for humanity. When it occurs, it is identified and its impact reversed by the discipline of a person who truly affirms and submits to the will of God (*islam*). The Qur'an and the traditions provide an uncommon interpretation of suffering as a concrete human experience and an unavoidable condition of human existence. Suffering is not an evil and therefore not a problem that needs to be explained, since its author is the good God.

SUFFERING IN ISLAMIC THEOLOGY

As we move into theological evaluation of suffering, we directly encounter the problem of theodicy in Islam. Considering its preoccupation with the malicious polytheism of the Meccans in seventh-century Arabia, it is comprehensible that the Qur'an was more concerned with questions of belief and disbelief than those of suffering in human society. To be sure, in the Qur'an abandoning faith in God is both sinful and evil; here evil is nothing but the withdrawal of good, just as darkness is the withdrawal of light. Evil is comparable to a sin which has no essence. It is a state of moral inadequacy best described as "lack of good." If this explanation is applied to specific evil like illness, the illness cannot be regarded as truly evil. Rather, it is a trial from God, and although a form of tribulation and suffering, it fulfills a positive role in the lives of the faithful, revealing God's power to cure and to show His limitless compassion.

The question of whether God can inflict unremitting pain on His creatures is central to any theodicy and constitutes one of the most crucial and perplexing problems in human history (Eliade, 1995, 430–441). Muslims, like Jews and Christians, affirm God's goodness and the Divine Omnipotence and Almightiness over the entire creation. They must therefore defend God's justice and the Divine absolute power in the face of human suffering. Islamic theodicy is very much a feature of this ethical monotheism. Moreover, the religiously inspired ideals about a good society in Islam logically create an existential need to explain suffering and evil despite God's promises to the contrary. A theodicy is necessary in any religion where any God is regarded as invariably benevolent and omnipotent (Obeyesekere, 1968, 8). However, in Islam it would seem that its insistence on "submission" (one of the essential meanings of the term *islam*) to the divine will would remove untenable contradictions inherent in Muslim belief about the benevolent and omnipotent God and thereby reduce the centrality of theodicy. Islam's emphasis on God's transcendence from human moral judgment led Kenneth Cragg to observe that Islam "ignores or neglects or does not hear these questions [about the wrongs in life] . . . It does not find a theodicy necessary either for its theology or its worship" (Cragg, 1975, 16).

This oversight exists in Islam because of its rational theology founded upon human free will. In Muslim theology, as we shall see below, the free-will theodicy was constructed around the Qur'anic references to human agency and all-powerful divine will. The notion of evil as a necessary concomitant of good was an important theme in the theological, mystical, and philosophical literature of Islam.

Muslims endeavored to reconcile specific evils with God's attributes like All-knowing, All-powerful, and All-merciful. In view of God's regenerative mercy (*rahmah*) on all His creatures, regardless of belief, can one adequately explain illness by contending that it is nothing more than the lack of the good state of being that is health? The problem of theodicy is encapsulated in the tradition when God is made the sole agent of infectious disease. The Prophet is reported to have said:

> "There is neither contagion nor augury nor jaundice nor bird of evil omen." A Bedouin asked: "O Prophet of God, how is it then that my camels were in the sand [as healthy as] gazelles, and then a mangy camel mingled with them and made them mangy?" The Prophet replied: "Who infected the first (camel)?"[3]

God has Himself implanted the disease which causes suffering. There are verses in the Qur'an that can support a predestination theology that literally imputes evil to God (6:125, 61:5); however, there are other verses in which God plainly delegates responsibility for suffering to free creatures' abuse of their freedom (Q. 2:24). The Qur'an reminds human beings that "God will not wrong so much as the weight of an ant" (Q. 4:40). Moreover, the Qur'an, as previously discussed, also views suffering as a test of righteousness (Q. 29:1).

In the first half of the eighth century, debates about community injustices and how to redress them formed the basis of the earliest systematic theology, that of the Mu'tazilites (Hodgson, 1977, 384–386). The Mu'tazilites aimed to show that there was nothing repugnant to reason in the Islamic revelation. In defining God's creation and governance of the world, they sought to demonstrate the primacy of revelation. Simultaneously, their emphasis on human reason's ability to explain the ways of God revealed Hellenic influences. In the ninth century, translations of Greek philosophic and scientific treatises became available in Arabic, leading to a technical vocabulary and syntax pattern substantially similar to that of Judeo-Christian theodicies (ibid., 412ff.).

The Mu'tazilites championed human agency and developed a theodicy that emphasized an inseparable link between free will and divine justice. Divine justice was central to their conviction that human intellect is capable of recognizing good and evil without help from revelation. Human intuitive reasoning can discover the rational aspect behind each circumstance and event. Since all God's actions are for the well-being of individual creatures, it is necessary for human beings to discover and defend God's purposeful actions in the most apparently unseemly events (Hourani, 1985, 100ff.).

A reaction against the Mu'tazilite emphasis on free-will theodicy was bound to appear in the face of the apparently unmerited suffering of the just and the prosperity of the wicked. Even a vivid Qur'anic eschatology, where all the inequities will be corrected in the Hereafter, could not adequately explain the tribulations suffered by the innocent. "Whatever God does He does for the best" was a believer's way of accepting the hardships caused in this world, and it was this maxim that formed the Ash'arite theodicy based on a pre-destinarian position.

The Ash'arites, reacting to Mu'tazilite free-will theodicy, limited speculative theology to a defense of the doctrines given in the hadith reports attributed to the Prophet. These were considered more reliable than abstract reason. The Ash'arites emphasized the absolute will and power of God and denied nature and humankind any decisive role. Here, what humans perceive as causation is actually God's habitual behavior. They maintained that good and evil are what God decrees them to be, in an attempt to preserve the effectiveness of an omnipotent and omnibenevolent God who can and does intervene in human affairs. Accordingly, the difference between good and evil is found in the sources of revelation, like the Qur'an and the Prophet's paradigmatic conduct, the *Sunnah* (Hodgson, 1977, 440–441). God transcends the order of nature and divine transcendence directly determines all actions.

Ash'arite theological views remained dominant throughout Islamic history, well into modem times, and had profound effects upon scientific, and particularly medical, theory and practice among Sunni Muslims. The attitude of resignation, a by-product of belief in predestination, is encapsulated in the Sunni creedal confession: "What reaches you could not possibly have missed you; and what misses you could not possibly have reached you" (Wensinck, 1965, 103). Elaborating on this, the Ash'arites maintained that God directly wills whatever occurs in this world. It is He, and only He, who causes actions. Since good and evil are what God decrees them to be, it is presumptuous for human beings to judge God on the basis of human categories. In some cases, God creates a special quality of voluntary acquisition; here God wills the individual to be a voluntary agent and responsible. Of course, even with this limited human autonomy, divine agency still extends to all facets of human existence (sustenance, lifespan, pleasure, pain, etc.). In summary, the Ash'arite theodicy of determinism neither denies the evil aspects of pain, incapacity, illness or poverty, nor ignores the painful realities of existence. They are evils but they are not the result of social inequity, accident, or human wickedness. God intends poverty, pain, or disbelief for certain individuals, just as He intends wealth, well-being, and belief for others (Ormsby, 1984, 253ff.). This uncompromising belief in destiny was bound to have negative implications for some in Muslim society.

The Shi'ite theological and ethical doctrines, on the other hand, were based on the Mu'tazilite thesis about the Justice of God and the objective nature of moral values. In this world view, illness and suffering are considered to be caused by human excesses in exercising free will. Additionally, since Shi'ite leaders had suffered martyrdom in their cause, this minority considered tribulations as steps towards an eternal and blissful end. Their pious literature celebrating the martyrdoms of the Shi'ite Imams, especially the grandson of the Prophet Muhammad, al-Husayn (d. 680) and his family, describes the suffering of the innocent women and children as a divine blessing, the source of purification and preparation for the arduous spiritual journey to God. The Shi'ites maintain that, for the pious, this world is full of suffering and sorrow and conforming to this is how to attain God's mercy. Suffering is more than mere discipline; it is a choice made independently of rewards and punishments.[4] It is good in itself as a means of purification of the soul, and its patient endurance is the deepest way to express humility before God.

Muslim mystics, the Sufis, generally share the Ash'arite optimism about the divine wisdom in their understandings of human suffering, and regard it as a necessary part of their ascetic lifestyle (Ayoub, 1978, 25ff.). The inner life of the soul depends upon affliction to detach itself from the world and love God only. The goal is to gain control over one's passions, which cause pain and suffering. The Sufis aim to reach a level of consciousness where one's entire life is guided by the immediate will of God. This means giving up anything that does not bear the marks of divine blessing, however dire the consequences (Schimmel, 1975, 136ff.).

Muhyi al-Din ibn al-'Arabi (d. 1240), one of the great mystics of Islam, saw human affliction as an expression of divine mercy, as the heart of the mystic goes through inner purification at the hands of God:

> But the heart is between two fingers of its Creator, who is the All-Merciful. . . . Hence He does not cause the heart to fluctuate except from one mercy to another mercy, even though there is affliction (*bala'*) in the various kinds of fluctuation. But there lies in affliction's midst a mercy hidden from man and known to the Real, for the two fingers belong to the All-Merciful. (Cited in Chittick, 1989, 107)

In another place Ibn al-'Arabi speaks of affliction as an instrument used by God to measure whether a person can reflect on the divine purposes in creation:

> God afflicted man with an affliction with which no other of His creatures was afflicted. Through it, He takes him to felicity or wretchedness, depending upon how He allows him to make use of it. This affliction with which God afflicted him is that He created within him a faculty named "reflection." He made this faculty the assistant of another faculty called "reason." Moreover, He compelled reason, in spite of its being reflection's chief, to take from reflection what it gives. God gave reflection no place to roam except the faculty of imagination. God made the faculty of imagination the locus which brings together everything given by the sensory faculties. (ibid.)

CONCLUDING REMARKS

As we have seen, two contradictory evaluations of the purpose of suffering emerge in theological discussions in Islam. The first suggests that suffering is part of God's plan for the betterment of humanity. All forms of suffering, including illness, are either a form of punishment to expiate for a sin or a test or trial to confirm a believer's spiritual station. The second argues that suffering is the consequence of a free human choice to believe or disbelieve. Here, disbelief is the source of human misconduct which leads to suffering. This suffering serves an educational or disciplinary function: an absence of faith leads to afflictions. Correspondingly, there are two responses to whether one should attempt to alleviate suffering. The first position gives rise to a passive response: since God is testing human belief, one must endure suffering. In support of this position, the words of Abraham in the Qur'an are cited, saying that God is the only Healer on whom a believer should depend: "Lord of all beings who created me, and Himself gives me to eat and drink, and, whenever I am sick, heals me, who makes me die, then gives me life" (Q. 26:80). These are the grounds for skeptical attitudes towards medical treatment.[5]

The second position gives rise to an active response: since a human being is the cause of his/her own suffering, he/she should undertake righteous acts to rid the world of suffering. Good works negate suffering. This belief derives its strength from the Prophet Muhammad's oft-quoted advice to his followers: "O servants of God, seek a cure [from illness], because God did not create a disease without creating its cure, except for one disease, infirmity due to old-age."[6] Three assumptions support this position: health is preferable to sickness, "a strong (*qawiyy*) believer is preferred and better liked by God than a weak (*da'if*) believer", and seeking a cure does not contradict submission to God's decisions about humanity.

Theological–ethical debates on these responses are based on the two forms of Islamic theodicy: the determinist and free-will theodicies which both ground themselves in divine omnipotence and justice. In contemporary Muslim biomedical ethics, the free-will theodicy – founded upon divine justice and human moral agency – has gradually become the dominant approach in dealing with human suffering through illness. The result is evident in the startling human and financial investment in developing first-rate healthcare institutions in the Muslim world. God's abstract justice has found concrete expression in the health care provided to the destitute and downtrodden in society. Fair distribution of limited resources remains a distant goal in the corrupt political systems where socio-economic imbalances create a cynical attitude toward government-managed health care. It is remarkable, however, that religiously run Islamic hospitals and clinics, mostly staffed by volunteer or underpaid medical professionals, have often responded admirably to the medical needs of largely impoverished populations. A religious revival among pious professionals, both men and women, has found expression in serving the children of God – the destitute of the Muslim world – by dedicating their services to those who are most vulnerable: women and children.

The most striking example of this concern for women and children is seen in the changed attitudes toward AIDS and persons living with HIV. For a long time, AIDS was viewed as God's curse on those societies or individuals that had promiscuous sexual relations. There was also a denial of the presence of the disease in Muslim societies. In the recent (2007) AIDS awareness week in Iran, the government acknowledged the urgency with which human suffering caused by AIDS had to be combated with all possible medical and social programs, especially for women and children who suffered from the infection that they received from the male members of the family. AIDS is no longer regarded simply as God's punishment for immoral conduct. It is seen as a reality in Muslim societies which needs to be responded to actively and compassionately.

The changed attitude in many Muslim societies regarding the suffering caused by AIDS has ushered in a new understanding of affliction in the context of human spiritual perfection. In a Muslim thanksgiving prayer, besides praising and thanking God for all the blessings, a believer affirms: "To You [oh God] belongs praise for all the good affliction (*bala'in hasanin*) with which You have inured me."[7] The characterization of affliction as "good" in this prayer indicates that suffering as such does not create a theoretical problem in Islam. Rather, it is treated as part of the divine plan for humanity. When it occurs, as it does when diseases like AIDS or other epidemics affect large numbers of people, it is identified, and its impact is reversed by education and discipline in a true affirmation of, and submission to, the will of God (*islam*). The Qur'an and the traditions provide an uncommon interpretation of suffering as a concrete human experience, an unavoidable condition of human existence. They do not always regard suffering derived from natural evil as an evil and hence a problem that needs to be explained or vindicated because its author is the good God. Quite the contrary, its acceptance as a reality, like the acceptance of death as an existential reality, enables humanity to grow in spiritual and moral strength.

BIBLIOGRAPHY

Ayoub, Mahmoud 1978. *Redemptive Suffering in Islam: A Study of the Devotional Aspects of "Ashura" in Twelver Shi'ism.* The Hague, Mouton Publishers.
Chittick, William 1989. *The Sufi Path of Knowledge.* Albany, SUNY.

Cragg, Kenneth 1975. *The House of Islam*. Encino, Dickenson.

Eliade, Mircea (ed.) 1995. "Theodicy." In *The Encyclopedia of Religion*. New York, Simon Schuster Macmillan. Vol. 14, pp. 430–441.

Hodgson, Marshall G. S. 1977. *The Venture of Islam: Conscience and History in a World Civilization*. Chicago, University of Chicago Press.

Hourani, George F. 1971. *Islamic Rationalism: The Ethics of ʿAbd al-Jabbar*. Oxford, Clarendon Press.

Hourani, George F. 1985. *Reason and Tradition in Islamic Ethics*. Cambridge, Cambridge University Press.

Islamic Code of Medical Ethics, Kuwait Document. First International Conference on Islamic Medicine, Kuwait. Rabi al-Awwal, 1401 (January 1981).

Obeyesekere, Gananath 1968. "Theodicy, Sin, and Salvation in a Sociology of Buddhism." In E.R. Leach (ed.), *Dialectical in Practical Religion*. Cambridge, Cambridge University Press.

Ormsby, Eric 1984. *Theodicy in Islamic Thought: The Dispute over Al-Chazalr's "Best of All Possible Worlds."* Princeton, Princeton University Press.

Pelly, Sir Lewis 1979. *The Miracle Play of Hasan and Husayn*. 2 Vols, London, W. H. Allen & Co.

Qummi, ʿAbbas 1381. *Maflltrbal-jinan*. Tehran, Kitabfurushr-yi ʿIlmiyya-yi Islamiyya.

Rispler-Chaim, Vardit 1993. *Islamic Medical Ethics in the Twentieth Century*. Leiden, E. J. Brill.

Schimmel, Annemarie 1975. *Mystical Dimensions of Islam*. Chapel Hill, University of North Carolina Press.

Wensinck, A. J. 1965. *The Muslim Creed*. London, Frank Cass & Co. Ltd.

2

THE AIDS CRISIS: AN ISLAMIC PERSPECTIVE

Malik Badri

INTRODUCTION

The Western approach to HIV and AIDS is culturally patterned according to the new morality of the sexual revolution and follows the dictates of liberal secular Western society. This approach really aims to deal with the AIDS pandemic in a way that preserves Western civilization without in any way drawing upon the inner spiritual resources of Muslims or orientating Muslims towards a greater appreciation of their own moral and ethical values. Muslim health practitioners, educators, social workers, and other interested religious groups should be very skeptical about adopting these Western preventative approaches. These models are failing in their countries of origin, as AIDS has already become the prime killer of sexually active young Americans. They will surely be an utter failure in more spiritually and Islamically oriented societies. For prevention to attain any real success in these contexts, it must develop from Islamic roots.

There is an irreconcilable rift between the Islamic and the "liberated" Western perspectives on sex and sexuality. Opting for a genuine Islamic paradigm of prevention may, in the eyes of some, contribute to "a civilizational clash" and, as Muslims, we have no reason to apologize for this. This cultural conflict is most conspicuous when we compare what Islam as a religion and way of life teaches with what the extreme Western gay liberation movements and fanatic gender feminists say. American and European "preaching" of the new ethics of the sexual revolution with the zeal of missionaries is a clear example of Samuel Huntington's prediction that the coming century will be the century of a "clash between civilizations," wherein the West, at the peak of its power, struggles to subdue all other civilizations so that its worldview and secular values will rule the whole world (Huntington, 1997). Within the context of this clash of civilizations, one can understand why Western modernity pushes so hard to dominate other cultures and insist on its way of life as a "universal civilization that fits all men" and its secular and sexual values as those of the "world community." The West today is at the peak of its power. Looking only through the lenses of this power it insists that other cultures should cease looking back to any different moral traditions or contradictory religious teachings. The phrases "world community" and "universal civilizations" are Western inventions created to mislead the rest of the world into believing that the interests of Europe and America are also those of all the countries of the world.

This cultural clash is quite pertinent to the theme of this article, since AIDS prevention through Islamic measures would obviously make use of its strong family ties and ethical upbringing as well as the public psychological castigation of, and sanctions against, promiscuity and homosexuality; the Western paradigm, on the other hand, promotes the weakening of the family and the full acceptance of "alternative" cohabiting. The ultimate result of the Western paradigm is the disappearance of the traditional family and the absence of differentiation between heterosexuality and homosexuality.

Attempts to halt the AIDS pandemic in Muslim countries should not be left to alienated, Westernized WHO experts, lay public health practitioners who are willing to apply any "ready made" model of prevention, or brain-washed psychiatrists and social workers who are "auto-culture blind", unable to see the superior ethical values of their own religion and culture. They are so dogmatically Western-minded that they equate the usefulness of values and ideas with technological and material excellence. They should cease pretending that modernity's AIDS prevention, rooted in a worldview of sexual immorality, is the same as utilizing the latest laser medical technology or PET scanning.

AN ISLAMIC APPROACH TO HIV PREVENTION

There is a clear relationship between the way a society perceives sexuality and practices sex and the way it tries to prevent sexual deviations and sexually transmitted diseases. An Islamic approach to AIDS prevention must include new strategies evolved from Islam as a way of life and a worldview, such as its uncompromising position against fornication and drug and alcohol intake. Muslim health practitioners, specialists, and lay AIDS prevention personnel should therefore confidently and critically evaluate Western models from ethical, philosophical, psychological, cultural, and historical perspectives in order to develop their own Islamically oriented moral modes of prevention. I am not arguing for a limited and utterly ineffective "Islamization" of AIDS prevention, where boring radio lectures are delivered by traditional shaykhs of government religious departments, merely repeating shari'ah commandments while the active dynamic society continues its breathless parody of Western lifestyle. This spraying of new paint onto an old rusty car is not going to transform the Muslim *ummah* (community) in any way! The Islamization of AIDS awareness work in Muslim societies will only be effective if it is part of a comprehensive will and program to Islamize all of society.

The reader may well ask "What are the practical preventive strategies that the Muslim doctor, psychologist, teacher, or administrator needs to carry out in order to Islamize his work? What changes should he or she make as an AIDS prevention practitioner to Islamize his or her performance?" The answer to such questions cannot be precise, since different Muslim countries are so culturally divergent that no specific plan can be suitable or even acceptable to all Muslim societies. Islamized preventive methods applied in Iran, Sudan, or Afghanistan will not be suitable for Malaysia, the Maldives, or Muslims in South Africa and Europe. However, I shall try to give some broad practical suggestions. Some of these proposals may be more pertinent to some Muslim societies than others. Nevertheless, with genuine adaptations they could be useful to most Islamic countries.

Regardless of where the Muslim AIDS activist or medical practitioner may find him or herself, any program that he or she engages in should not adopt an ethically non-judgmental attitude or a stand which condones, or does not point out, the immoral aspects of promiscuity, homosexuality, and drug and alcohol intake. We must avoid the idea that we must not "preach" to our patients nor interfere in their "private affairs." Islam is about intervening in human affairs.

In the following few pages I want to a) outline some Islamic principles governing sex, particularly its affirmation of sex and sexuality, the prohibition of homosexuality and the use of drugs; b) examine how the five pillars of Islam can be utilized in combating the spread of AIDS; and c) reflect on the need for Muslims to consider this disease as a form of divine retribution while at the same time reaching out in compassion towards those who have been afflicted.

ISLAM, SEX, AND DRUGS: PREVENTION OF TRANSMISSION

Islam's valuing of sexuality

Islam, like Judaism and Christianity, prohibits adultery, sodomy, and other forms of fornication. However, unlike these religions, Islam does not condemn sex as an unavoidable pleasure for procreation but celebrates it as a great gift from God and a source of His pleasure and reward if practiced in the sanctioned manner. The Prophet emphatically asserts, "There is no monasticism in Islam; Do not impose austerities on yourselves so that austerities will be imposed on you, for people have imposed austerities on themselves and Allah imposed austerities on them. Their survivors are to be found in cells and monasteries." Then he quotes from the Qur'an, "Monasticism, they invented it; we did not prescribe it for them" (Abu Dawud, Book 41, No. 4886).

Pleasure and procreation are two sides of the same divine coin of grace. Islamic recorded literature is full of teachings and anecdotes about happy marriages and loving relationships between faithful Muslim spouses. The Holy Qur'an asserts God's mercy in creating spouses for the two sexes to provide them with love, mercy, and tranquility:

> And among His signs are that He created for you mates from among your wives so that you may dwell in tranquility with them and He has put love and mercy between your hearts. Verily in that are signs for those who reflect. (*Surah al-Rum*, 30:21)

These teachings and examples of gratifying love, spiritual peaceful-ness, and unwavering trust are still experienced in the life of many simple and rural Muslims all over the world. They fully enjoy each others' relations since their sexual urge is not satiated by promiscu-ity, their hearts are not tormented by fear and suspicion of being infected by their spouses, their minds are not pestered by thoughts of comparing their mates with other sex partners, their brains are not eclipsed by sexually dampening drugs and alcohol, and their heterosexual desire is not confused by gay preferences. They stand side by side as they humbly offer their five daily prayers in peace-ful, pleasurable bliss, and they lie side by side as they delight in the bounty of the flesh. Both are great gifts from Almighty God. There is no conflict between the spiritual and the physical; between body and soul; between the here and now and the hereafter. I have lived for many years amongst such happy people in Gazira State in Sudan, more intimately with the people of Rufa Town. I have, accordingly, felt much pity and sympathy for my many unhappy Western and Westernized patients who were referred to me because of marital and sexual dilemmas caused by their modern lifestyle.

Unlike other religions, the detailed Islamic teachings regard-ing sexual matters protect Muslims from HIV infection and other Sexually Transmitted Diseases (STDs). For example, Islam strongly prohibits two kinds of sexual relations between spouses. These are vaginal sexual intercourse during menstruation and anal intercourse at all times. To show how ugly it is, the Prophet describes anal inter-course with the wife as the "minor sodomy" (cited by Ahmad ibn Hanbal). A number of other Prophetic traditions speak about this repulsive practice as one of the greatest of sins. Early Muslim schol-ars and jurists such as Ibn Qayyim al-Jawziyyah (d. 1350), in his *Zad al-Ma'ad*, detailed the psychological and medical reasons for this forceful injunction. As confirmed by the modern behavioral point of view, these early Muslim scholars rightly argued that anal inter-course with the wife is minor sodomy since it can gradually lead a man to full-fledged homosexuality. This is so because of the identi-cal anatomy of females and males in this respect. A husband who gets used to anal intercourse with his wife may easily shift to boys and beardless men. Secondly, these scholars criticize the husband who engages in anal sex for his selfishness in pursuing his own plea-sure and denying his wife her Islamic rights to sexual satisfaction and procreation. They assert that the human rectum is not created by God for such a function. Finally, they remind such husbands that God prohibited vaginal intercourse during the wife's monthly period because it is harmful to both partners. The Holy Qur'an explicitly forbids vaginal sex during the wife's monthly flow and calls it a hurt or a pollution:

> They ask you concerning women's course; Say: They are a hurt and a pollution: So keep away from women in their courses, and do not approach them (by actual intercourse) until they are clean. But when they have purified themselves, you may approach them in any manner, time or place ordained for you by God. For God loves those who turn to Him constantly and he loves those who keep themselves pure and clean. (*Surah Al-Baqarah*, 2:222)

Homosexuality

Male homosexuality has been practiced to a greater or lesser degree in different Muslim countries, more in some Asian Muslim societies than in those of Africa. However, it is practiced in a concealed manner as a shameful sin. As they grow older, most homosexuals repent and settle with their wives. That is why homosexuality can still be banned and successfully combated as part of Islamic preventive measures. Accepting justifications for being gay, as modern Westerners do, will lead to a gradual downhill descent to homosexual marriages and the destruction of the family. It is lamentable that many Muslim colleagues in psychology and psychiatry have identified with the "Western model" provided by their American and European professors to the extent that some shamelessly condone sinful gay sexuality. Such opinions are obviously un-Islamic. They convey a very contradictory and unjust picture of God. If homosexuality is biologically determined, then it is God who created this "preference" in gays. If He then punishes them with mass destruction, as in Sodom, or severe sanctions, as in Shari'ah law, then no action can be more unjust than that. Western Christian thinkers and some high-ranking clergy have tried to resolve this problem by first declaring that homosexuality is neither sinful nor evil, and then that God wanted some of His slaves to be gay and so He created them this way.

Islam, however, still has a strong grip over the hearts and minds of its followers, so to copy Western approaches of "just enjoy your disposition" is utterly out of cultural tune. It will be of little or no temporary help, while psychologically damaging the guilt-laden gay Muslim patient who wants to get rid of his culturally and religiously shameful habit. Therapists who unthinkingly adopt a modern Western stand are out of touch with the real agony of a homosexual in a confirmed heterosexual, Islamically oriented society. His "orientation" is seen as scandalous by his family members, dishonorable by his colleagues, and hateful by the young generation of contemporary Islamic revivalists. Biological rationalism can only confuse their tragic situation. It is thus of paramount importance to AIDS prevention that this Islamic attitude should not be weakened by erroneous hereditary justifications for homosexuality.

The Qur'an clearly states that the townsfolk of Sodom were the first people on earth to adopt a homosexual lifestyle (*Surah al-A'raf*, 7: 80). It is thus a learned practice in which the deviant person allows his "libido" to flow into the wrong tributary. Just as peoples in various cultures learn distinct and sometimes contradictory standards of beauty for women, and different ways of heterosexually enjoying these pleasurable attributes, a group of deviant persons learn to restrict their eroticism to their own sex.

With a changed Islamic attitude towards therapy, psychiatrists, psychologists, and other mental health specialists should be able to cooperate with AIDS prevention bodies to launch a dynamic and effective program. Though this program ideally aims at eradicating the pathological consequences of homosexuality, promiscuity, and drug intake, everybody knows that no society on earth can be completely cleansed from these evils. We hope only to reduce their practice to a level below the "threshold" for STDs and epidemics such as AIDS to develop.

Drug and alcohol use

Another important area where the Muslim health worker can be of great help in Islamically changing the face of AIDS prevention is that of drug and alcohol intake. First, an effort should be made to rid this anti-drug campaign of the Western conception of "abuse." The ultimate aim of an Islamic approach to alcohol and drugs is to halt all intake. The use, or for that matter the misuse, of the term " abuse" in Western modernity is due to the assumption that total abstinence is unattainable or undesirable, and to campaign for it is neither realistic nor practical.

From my experience with drug and alcohol addicts I have come to see that in the vast majority of cases, the so-called reasonable "use" of drugs or social drinking is only a transient stage between abstinence and "abuse." I have also found that the great majority of Muslims who achieve abstinence are motivated by religion (Badri, 1976). Deterioration of health or economic status are mentioned far less often as reasons for sobriety. The importance of this deep spiritual dimension in the hearts of Muslims explains the success of even inefficient and partial campaigns in some Muslim countries, simply because the campaigners appealed to Islam. Accordingly, doctors and AIDS workers should confidently launch their Islamic campaign for total abstinence, and should make use of Islamic mass *'ibadat* (religious rituals) such as that found during Ramadan. This should particularly be directed towards injecting drug users, as they are at the greatest risk of HIV infection.

Alcoholic beverages are unrestricted in many parts of the world. Alcohol "dissolves" moral restraint so that, after a few drinks, people will not remember to use condoms or avoid risk groups. Drugs are even worse, since their intake by injection can directly infect. Another serious outcome of alcohol and drugs is their immuno-suppressive properties, which some scientists believe are the true cause of HIV infection. They support the view that the AIDS virus can be a real danger only when the immune system has already been weakened by other suppressants.

Islam sternly prohibits the intake of *khamr*, an Arabic word which literally means any substance which "covers" or curtails the mind. *Khamr* refers to anything that intoxicates its user, regardless of whether it is taken as a drink, inhaled, eaten, or smoked. For this reason, no practicing Muslim would take *khamr*, and even in the general population, modern Muslims have the lowest rate of alcohol abuse and the highest rate of abstinence with respect to all intoxicants.

INVOKING THE FIVE PILLARS IN AIDS PREVENTION

The Five Pillars of Islam form the basis of Muslim religious life. These duties are *Shahadah* (profession of faith), *Salah* (ritual prayer), *Zakah* (alms tax), *Sawm* (fasting during Ramadan), and

Hajj (pilgrimage to Mecca). Here we shall consider how they may become the core elements of a genuinely Islamic approach to AIDS prevention.

Faith in God: the cornerstone of Islamic AIDS prevention

An Islamic prevention program should make use of the deep belief that Muslims have in the absolute power and mercy of the Almighty God who creates and controls everything in this universe, from the tiniest electron to the largest galaxy. He knows every detail in human hearts. The Qur'an states "He knows your secrets and that which is even more hidden (in you than your secrets)" (*Surah Ta Ha* 20:7). This belief is deeply rooted in Muslim hearts and minds, whether they are saints or criminals, and it is for this reason that Muslims generally have the lowest percentages of HIV infections. This is quite clear in Muslim countries of the Middle East and North Africa, Pakistan, Afghanistan, Iran, and other societies of strong Islamic commitment. A successful AIDS prevention program would make use of these beliefs and seek the assistance of influential Muslim preachers who know how to tap them to change attitudes and sexual habits in order to avoid the spread of HIV infection.

Salah (prayer): an exercise in God consciousness and discipline

Iman (faith) is defined as that which is deeply anchored in one's heart, verified by one's deeds and actions. The most essential among these verifications is the performance of obligatory forms of worship and rituals. Chief among them are prayers and fasting. The practicing Muslim has to offer his five daily prayers. Though each prayer may take only a few minutes, it is a relaxing and highly spiritual and contemplative ritual which can take the faithful closer to God. This experience is especially moving when mass prayers are led by an imam who beautifully chants the inimitable poetry of the verses of the Qur'an. These prayers are nicely distributed during the day and early dark hours of the night, so that the Muslim can carry out his daily business and other responsibilities, but every few hours must return to the spiritual world. During these blessed times he is consciously and unconsciously reminded of his Islamic ethical standard and moral responsibility. Prayers, properly performed, strengthen the faithful's will-power against fornication, drugs, and alcohol. The

Holy Qur'an states: "Recite what is revealed of the Book to you and establish regular prayer: for prayer restrains from shameful and unjust deeds" (*Surah Al-'Ankabut*, 29:45).

Zakah

Zakah is often translated as charity. In reality it is an obligation that the wealthy owe to the less fortunate among us. The fact that in the Qur'an the duty of Zakah is often tied to Salah gives some idea of how our obligations towards our Creator are tied to our obligations towards each other. While we cannot really make a case for the role of Zakah in AIDS prevention, we can clearly see how it can play a significant role in supporting Muslims who are ill and require the support of the rest of the community. Indeed, a number of Muslim organizations in Uganda, Sudan, and South Africa are utilizing Zakah to support women and children who may have been widowed or orphaned as a result of a husband or parent's demise due to an AIDS related illness.

Fasting: the will to change

Fasting is another spiritually elevating, obligatory form of worship. For the entire blessed month of Ramadan Muslims resist eating, drinking, and any sexual activity from dawn to sunset. To this day, fasting is regularly observed by devout and sinful Muslims all over the world. Police records show an obvious decline in all forms of crime in this month in all Islamic countries. Similarly, abstaining from adultery, fornication, and sodomy can frequently be achieved during this month. An Islamically oriented AIDS prevention model should make use of the spiritual wealth of Ramadan in changing sexual attitudes and immoral pathological behavior. The combined influence of prayer and fasting can be a powerful incentive to a clean sexual life and freedom from risky behavior and drug intake. To do this is not to consider all kinds of sex sinful or "dirty." A practicing Muslim fully enjoys sex, for pleasure or procreation, but in doing so fully acknowledges that he is a slave of God and is guided by His moral rules. He is not a slave of his unruly insatiated lust, nor is he guided by his erogenous zones!

Prayers and fasting have another supporting aspect to the immune system. The steady spiritual invigoration, serenity, and peace of mind they create in the practicing Muslim enhance the immune system.

Modern research in psychosomatic and holistic medicine has repeat-edly confirmed this relationship between mind and body and it has become one of the established facts of modern medicine.

Hajj and 'Umrah: promoting AIDS awareness

The fifth pillar of Islam that can be very helpful in developing Islamically oriented AIDS prevention is pilgrimage, or the Hajj. Every year, millions upon millions of Muslims travel to Makkah to perform the holy rites of the Hajj and *'Umrah* (the lesser pilgrimage), and to Madinah to visit the holy grave of the Prophet Muhammad (peace be upon him) and to pray in his blessed mosque. The Hajj is an annual holy occasion in which more than two million Muslims every year voluntarily pay for their transportation and other expen-sive needs to visit the holy Ka'bah, carry out specified rituals, and congregate in the blessed valley of 'Arafah. All the pilgrims congre-gate in this vast valley from noon to sunset to engage in prayer, glori-fying Almighty God and begging Him for forgiveness and blessings. In spite of the hardships of overcrowding, high temperature, barren desert, and hot black mountains radiating heat like giant stoves, the experience is so moving and spiritually invigorating that most pil-grims return to their countries with completely different attitudes and spiritual orientations. In some Muslim societies, the esteemed title of "Hajj" (and "Hajjah" for a woman) is bestowed upon the per-son who performs this commandment. This impedes such a person from engaging in fornication, drug intake, or similar base practices associated with irreligious and good-for-nothing people, practices in which he might have indulged before his pilgrimage.

Utilizing the Hajj, millions every year could become aware of AIDS and how best to deal with it from an Islamic point of view. The message could be given in all the different languages spoken in the various Muslim countries, so that it could be widely propagated by these pilgrims when they return to their home countries.

DIVINE RETRIBUTION AND AIDS

The Western psyche greatly resents the idea of God's retribution. Western secularization denies the authority of divine sanctification and perceives its sanctions and punishments as opposed to human freedom and dignity, and to humanism. The Holy Qur'an tells us repeatedly that when punishment is directed to a whole group, as in the case of the people of *Thamud* and *'Ad*, the believers who live in the same community are always saved from this collective punishment. God not only punishes for sins in this world, but also selects some people to the exclusion of others. Islam offers a very optimistic, merciful, and rational conception of divine retribution. The Holy Qur'an clearly states that God's punishment in this world is meant to ward off more serious future pains and agonies, to coerce the sinful to repent and secure God's forgiveness: "And indeed We will make them taste the penalty (and pain) of this life prior to supreme penalty, in order that they may repent and return" (*Al-Sajdah*, 32:21).

Human anguish is a Divine test to wipe out sins and to elevate the spiritual position of the suffering person. As the Prophet Muhammad (peace be upon him) said, there is always a reward to the Muslim from God for even the slightest pain he incurs, even if it is the prick of a thorn (Bukhari[1]). Furthermore, the Islamic Shari'ah has specified penalties and punishments for theft, fornication, murder, and similar crimes. If modern man can give the state the right to punish with death those who break the law, it will indeed be most impertinent and arrogant not to give this right to God. These Islamic teachings about God's retribution and mercy convince Muslims that any misfortune befalling an individual is God's work for some sins he has committed, or because Allah wants to test and reward him. Divine retribution and punishment are always conceived within the context of God's mercy, wisdom, and justice.

Thus the general Islamic belief about the AIDS pandemic is that it is divine retribution for the immoral homosexual revolution of the West and its aping in other countries. This belief is firmly rooted in the Muslim mind because every child in his early school years has been thrilled by the Qur'anic story of the Prophet Lot (peace be upon him) and what God did to his homosexual people. This is further explained by a famous saying of the Prophet Muhammad (peace be upon him) where he appears to describe the contemporary phenomenon of AIDS. The famous hadith, quoted and authenticated by Ibn Māja and other early Hadith scholars, is translated as follows:

> If *fahishah* or fornication and all kinds of sinful sexual intercourse become rampant and openly practiced without inhibition in any

group or nation, Allah will punish them with new epidemics (*ta'un*) and new diseases which were not known to their forefathers and earlier generations. (*Sunan Ibn Māja, Kitāb al-Fitan,* Hadith 4019)

This hadith clearly implies the concept of mutation in the Prophet's use of the words "new diseases." The Prophet also states that these diseases will take epidemic proportions. This is explained by the Arabic word *ta'un*, which specifically means plague but is used generally in Arabic to stand for any epidemic. It is interesting to note that today AIDS is dubbed the "plague of the twentieth century." The hadith associates the new epidemic with rampant fornication which is practiced publicly and without shame or guilt.[2]

MUSLIM RESPONSIBILITY AMIDST THE PANDEMIC

I have argued that in a completely Islamic society there would be no sexually transmitted diseases, that these diseases are in fact a part of God's vengeance on the sexually promiscuous, and that our efforts as Muslims must focus on providing an Islamically rooted message of abstention from sex outside marriage. Does this mean that Muslims have no responsibility once the pandemic has already struck and we encounter persons living with the virus? I want to address this question in respect of the use of condoms and in relation to the question of compassion.

Condoms and Islam

A number of Muslim scholars and organizations, from Algeria to Indonesia, have spoken and written very strongly against the use of condoms, describing the practice as un-Islamic and as an invitation to promiscuity. Some influential Muslim scholars have even suggested that their use should be totally eliminated from any Islamically oriented prevention program. For example, Hasan Basri, the Chairman of the influential Indonesian Ulama Council was quoted by AFP (August 4, 1995) as saying that the Council opposes campaigns which advocate the use of condoms to prevent the spread of the AIDS virus. He described this as an open invitation to promiscuity and suggested that condoms should be sold only to married people who prove their marital status by showing their marriage certificate at the counter! Such an extreme position is not rational, practical, or Islamic. There is unmistakable evidence that, if used properly, condoms can help reduce HIV transmission. While condoms, even if used correctly, do not offer full protection, there is no doubt that they are much better than wearing nothing. It is unfortunate that the flood of information equating "safe sex" with the use of condoms has wrongly convinced many that by wearing one, a person can take any risks. The media has perpetuated such a hazardous belief.

Islamically, the use of condoms can be viewed within the general law of Fiqh or jurisprudence of *ikhtiyar akhaff al-dararain*, or choosing the lesser of two evils. If we apply this rule, on which there is general consensus among Muslim jurists, we could make the use of a condom obligatory for a fornicating Muslim who might expect HIV infection from his promiscuous practice. Fornication is a major evil, but endangering another person is definitely a much greater evil. According to Muslim jurists, there is a hierarchy of evils, and under duress one should choose the least harmful. Losing one's faith and religion is the worst of all catastrophes, followed by losing one's life. Next is the evil of losing one's mind, and then the loss of possessions. Lastly comes the issue of one's *'irdh* which concerns one's actual detestable deeds, like fornication. For a Muslim who fornicates there is still every possibility of repenting, and his earlier sins would be changed to good deeds, as the Holy Qur'an states.

Compassion

An important point about the Islamic concept of retribution is the difference between the way a punishment or test for a deserving group or society is understood and how Islam speaks of the individual in that society. When dealing with individuals in a state of distress such as an illness or catastrophe, even with those who were sinners or criminals, Islam very clearly preaches mercy, brotherly love, sympathy, and an optimistic attitude. Visiting sick people, praying for them, and raising their morale and hopes for improvement is one of the deeds very highly recommended by Islam in the blessed hadith and practices of the Prophet Muhammad (peace be upon him). Failing to care for the sick incurs the displeasure of God. In the well-known hadith *qudsi* – a prophetic saying wherein God is cited – the following conversation will take place between a Muslim and God in the Hereafter:

> Allah, the Lord of Honour and Glory, will say in the Day of Judgment: O Son of Adam! I was sick and you did not visit me! The man will submit and say: my Lord! How is it that I visit You and You are the Sustainer of the universe? And God will reply, "Didn't you know that My servant so and so was sick and you did not bother to visit him? Didn't you realize that if you had visited him you would have found Me with him?" (*Riyad al-Salihin*)

Another important aspect of visiting the sick and caring for them is to ask the visitor to make *du'a* or to pray for him or her. Since the afflicted person is being tested by God, his or her illness will purify him of his sins and his prayers are more likely to be fulfilled. The Prophet (peace be upon him) illustrates this purging of sins because of sickness by the tree which sheds its dry leaves (Bukhari). Thus the more serious the sickness, the purer the Muslim patient will be. These teachings are indeed a much needed consolation for the sick and a very useful instructive scheme for the counselors of HIV positive persons or persons living with AIDS in Muslim countries.

BIBLIOGRAPHY

Ibn Qayyim al-Jawziyyah n.d. *Zad al-Ma'ad fi Hadyi Khayr al-'Ibad*. Delhi, Idara Islamiyat-e-Diniyat.

An-Nawawi, Abu Zakariya Yahya bin Sharaf 2000. *Riyad al-Salihin*. Riyāḍ, Dār Ibn Khuzaymah.

Badri, Malik 1976. *Islam and Alcohol*. Takoma Park, MD, Muslim Students Association.

Huntington, Samuel P. 1997. *The Clash of Civilizations and the Remaking of World Order*. New York, Touchstone.

Māja, Ibn 1981. *Sunan Ibn Māja*. Istanbul, Cagri Yayinlari.

3

AIDS AND THE "WRATH OF GOD"

Sindre Bangstad

AIDS is, in fact, the wrath of God over the promiscuous sexual revolution sustained by the loose and liberal mores of Western civilization. (Malik Badri, 2000, 193)

INTRODUCTION

AIDS has been referred to as an "epidemic of signification" (Treichler, 1999, 11–42): throughout the world the epidemic has functioned as an additional vehicle for the "politics of accusation", through which regularly marginalized people, such as blacks, homosexuals, and the poor, are stigmatized. In many parts of the world the existence of popular discourses has been noted which attribute this global epidemic to various forms of "Western" conspiracies.

The work on AIDS of Malik Badri, a psychologist and Sudanese-born professor at the International Islamic University in Islamabad, as summarized in chapter 2, has been widely disseminated throughout the Muslim world by various Islamic Medical Associations (IMAs). Badri, a leading light in the movement to "Islamize" contemporary social sciences,[1] provides insights into how the moral and sexual anxieties of Muslims with Islamist leanings frame interpretations of HIV and AIDS. His work belongs to a subgenre of popular discourses of "Western" conspiracies found throughout the Muslim world, but in this case is provided with credence and legitimacy through its association with, and dissemination through, IMAs in various countries. Badri's discourse on HIV and AIDS exterior-izes the risk of HIV-infection among Muslims by constructing it as a product of "otherness" which appears in the form of "Western modernity" and the "Western sexual revolution". Badri constructs the "good Muslim" through opposition to "Western" modernities and their alleged sexual norms, shifts the valences of usual racial-ization of the epidemic, adopts dissident theories of causation of HIV, and places blame for this pandemic at the feet of "Western" homosexuals. Badri's book (2000) provides an example of popular Islamist understandings of HIV/AIDS, its aetiology and prevention, and indicates to what extent such popular Islamist understandings may contribute to further risks of HIV-infection among Muslims, and further stigmatization of marginal groups in Muslim societies. His work is an example of Occidentalism in the vein of Islamists such as Abu a'la Mawdudi (1903–1973) and Sayyed Qutb (1906–1966),[2] characterized by de-humanizing images of "the West" (Buruma and Margalit, 2004, 5), but one which interestingly closely mirrors and draws on a "Western" scientific lineage, as well as contemporary conservative Christian evangelical views on sexuality and morality, although both are denied in order to establish the "Islamic" creden-tials of his work.

HIV AND AIDS IN THE MUSLIM WORLD

HIV and AIDS awareness campaigns in the Muslim world have had limited success. Such campaigns are faced with considerable oppo-sition in as much as they bring sexual behavior and practices deemed to be transgressive of religious laws and cultural norms into the pub-lic sphere. This includes various forms of *zina* (adultery), such as pre- and extra-marital sex, and *liwat* (anal sex between men). It is an established principle of traditional Islamic law (*fiqh*) not to be overtly inquisitive about the private lives of one's fellow citizens. It would seem that this has historically provided one of the guidelines for the approach to, for instance, expressions of same sex sexuality in Muslim communities in many parts of the world. In effect, such expressions have historically been tolerated in many contexts, as long as they remained within the private domain. But in a globalizing era of identity politics and trans-national alliances based on homosexual identities, the private/public distinction on which traditional Islamic understandings of, and approaches to, the interpretation in which the presence of homosexual practice in Muslim societies was located, is increasingly redefined, and this often provokes virulent backlashes from religious scholars (the *'ulama*) and conservative and Islamist Muslim intellectuals.

HIV prevention campaigns have also been faced with the challenge of a public Muslim denial of the fact that HIV and AIDS affects Muslims just as it does non-Muslims. A common response throughout the world has been to exteriorize the epidemic by identifying risk with marginal groups such as homosexuals, sex workers, or people of another class or ethnicity than one's own. Among Muslims, the low registered HIV prevalence rates in the Middle East and North Africa are often seen as validating the notion that Muslims who practise their faith are not at risk of contracting the virus. Despite recent progress in surveillance efforts, the region still seriously lacks sufficient data to inform effective intervention policy (Sufian, 2004). UNAIDS and WHO estimate that 35,000 [16,000 – 65,000] people in the Middle East and North Africa acquired HIV in 2007, bringing the total number of people living with HIV to 380,000 [270,000 –500,000]. It is also estimated that 25,000 [20,000 – 34,000] died of HIV-related causes in the same year (unaids.org).

Malik Badri's *The Aids Crisis: A Natural Product of Modernity's Sexual Revolution,* first published in 1997 by the International Institute of Islamic Thought and Civilisation (ISTAC) in Kuala Lumpur, Malaysia, is currently (2007) in its third edition and has been translated into Swahili, Indonesian, and Arabic. Badri's book is one example of a popular genre of books in English and other languages purporting to explain *the* Islamic point of view on specific issues (assuming that there is a singular, monolithic Islamic view) to a Muslim audience often not conversant in Arabic. This genre is part of a modern development in which access to and the right of interpretation of religious texts has purportedly been democratized by mass literacy in the Muslim world. Traditional Islamic scholars have by and large become functionaries of the state, and Muslim public intellectuals, the majority of whom lack training in the religious sciences, often reduce the shari'a to a set of simple commandments (*akham*)[4] for facile public consumption in the form of books and pamphlets (see El Fadl, 2001, 171–172). Publishing in English or other trans-national languages reflects an aspiration on the part of such intellectuals to reach a mass readership and corresponding commercial successes. For this class of Muslim public intellectuals, whose contribution, according to Ebrahim Moosa (2005, 26), has led to a virtual "atrophy of knowledge" in the Muslim world, the provenance of an idea of practice often becomes more important than its substance. Respect for internal normative pluralism or dissent (*ikhtilaf*) within the Islamic tradition is thereby eroded.[5]

MALIK BADRI ON THE ORIGINS OF HIV AND AIDS

Dr. Malik Babikir Badri, a psychologist by training, is currently a professor at the International Islamic University in Islamabad after spending a number of years in Kuala Lumpur.[6] Born in Rufaʻa in the Sudan in 1932, he graduated from the American University of Beirut in Lebanon with an M.A. in 1958 and obtained a PhD from the University of Leicester in the U.K. in 1961, as well as a postgraduate certificate in clinical psychology from the University of London in 1967. His career as a psychologist appears to have spanned professional practice in several Muslim countries such as Saudi Arabia, Sudan, and Malaysia. He is a regular contributor on AIDS and mental health issues to the Yearbook of the Federation of Islamic Medical Associations (FIMA).[7]

For Badri, AIDS represents God's punishment for what he sees as immoral sexual behavior (Badri, 2000, 193). Although immoral sexual behavior was also prevalent among the Greeks and Romans of antiquity (ibid.), immoral sexual behavior in the modern age, according to Badri, has its origins in the sexual revolution which is described as a product of "Western" modernity (op. cit., xxiii). "Western" countries are, according to this theory, populated by "a promiscuous majority" (ibid., 29) who, spurred on by "the sexual revolution", engage in "rampant promiscuity" and "homosexual abandon" (ibid.). More specifically, he asserts that AIDS is caused by a mutation generated by anal sex among homosexuals.[8] Badri does not adopt the position of AIDS dissidents such as Peter Duesberg (whose argument that AIDS is caused by drug-induced immunosuppression has been discredited by medical scientists), but instead opts for an arguably even more untenable version of dissident science: namely that HIV originated as a "friendly virus" (ibid., 156) but in the course of the sexual revolution mutated through anal sex engaged in by homosexuals. Anal sex, he believes, results in suppression of the human immune system and subsequent outbreak of AIDS (ibid., 163).

It is therefore not promiscuous sex as such, but homosexual sex which explains HIV for Badri. Subsequently, AIDS has spread from "Western" homosexuals to other parts of the world (ibid., 159), for instance through "Western homosexual tourism." He suggests that Haitians infected by "American homosexual tourists" carried the virus to Africa.[9] The decline of religion in "Western" societies is directly linked to what he refers to as "the gay revolution." Badri denies the possibility of a genetic component to homosexuality and instead claims it is a socially learned sexual orientation made possible by the sexual mores of "Western" modernity. He supports this claim by arguing that if homosexuality were biologically determined it would have been practised "all over the world" (ibid., 286), but that there are communities in Africa where homosexuality is "totally absent" (ibid.). There appears to be an inherent contradiction in simultaneously asserting that homosexuality is a product of "Western modernity" and accepting that it existed in non-Western as well as premodern societies, as Badri does. According to him, homosexuality is a treatable "disorder" (ibid., 286), and since Muslims do not generally accept homosexuals, the psychologist who adopts "Western models" in dealing with homosexual clients is "out of touch with [the person's] real agony" (ibid., 286). Badri informs his readers that for motivated homosexuals it takes only "a few sessions of Islamically oriented behaviour and cognitive therapy" to turn a homosexual from his or her "sinful behaviour" into heterosexuality (ibid., 289). It is important to note that the view that homosexuality is a treatable mental disorder, and that there is no genetic component to homosexuality, was part of the standard repertoire of "Western" psychiatry until the early 1970s. The American Psychiatric Association (APA) classified homosexuality as a psychiatric disorder in its authoritative and much used international diagnostic guidelines, *Diagnostic and Statistical Manual of Mental Disorders*, until 1973, and the World Health Organisation (WHO) continued to classify it as such in its *International Statistical Classification of Disorders and Related Problems* until 1992. When viewed in this context, Badri's theories on homosexuality can be construed as less inherently "non-Western" and "Islamic" than Badri himself would have his readers think. His therapeutic repertoire in dealing with Muslim homosexual clients appears to include aversion therapy, such as giving Muslim homosexuals electric shocks whilst showing them homosexual images (ibid., 290).

While psychologists in the USA and Europe with an evangelical Christian orientation are less likely to go to such extremes as Badri appears to have employed in attempting to "treat" homosexuality (for fear of legal prosecution), there are a number of Christian evangelical churches and organizations, particularly in the USA, who advocate changing the sexual orientation of homosexuals through so-called "reparative therapy."[10] The observation that Islamists and conservative Christian evangelicals have more views in common than either one of them would like to admit, especially in the field of sexual moralities and HIV and AIDS, is not new, and Badri's example simply provides more evidence of this congruence. Badri recognizes the existence of homosexuals in Muslim societies, but qualifies this recognition by arguing that homosexuality is more common in some Asian Muslim countries than in African Muslim countries, and that most homosexuals "repent" as they grow older, and eventually settle down with their wives (ibid., 284). Elsewhere, he has advised Muslim men who fear that they may have a homosexual orientation to simply get married and discover the pleasures of heterosexual sex in marriage (Badri on Islam Online).[11]

Professor Badri vehemently denies the assertion that AIDS may have originated in Africa and among Africans. He is right to point to the fact that "Western" discourse on the origins of HIV has on numerous occasions had ethnocentric and racist connotations, and that locating the origins of the epidemic in the Great Lakes region may be a convenient way of displacing "Western" involvement in, and responsibility for, the epidemic. However, his idea that white colonizers brought homosexuality to Africa, and that the sexual mores of contemporary Africans are merely the product of "Western" sexual modernity (op. cit., 137), is made problematic by the recent work of Epprecht (2004), Delius and Glaser (2004), and Whitaker (2006). The fact that HIV was first diagnosed among homosexuals in New York and Los Angeles does not provide conclusive evidence that it originated among them.

Badri's target is not really "Western" homosexuals; rather his work is a frontal attack on the whole idea of "Western" sexual modernity, and on Muslims who "mimic" the "Western" model (ibid., 206) (again, assuming the existence of "one" "Western" model, "one" "Western" modernity and one set of sexual mores to which everyone adheres in the "Western" world) and refuse to "break the chains of mental slavery" (ibid., xxxiii). As a representation of Islamic opposition to "Western" modernities in popular literature in the Muslim world, Badri's book stands in the same tradition as the books of Abul A'la Mawdudi (1903–1977) and Sayyid Qutb (1906–1966), whose repulsion towards perceived "Western" sexual mores and specific elements of "Western" modernity[12] he largely shares. The fact that Badri's target is "Western sexual modernity" as such becomes clear when he asserts that social institutions in the "Western" world, such as academia and the popular media, advocate the "sexual" and "gay revolutions" and entice Western people to practice anal sex (ibid., 79, 84). Badri assures us that in all the university libraries that he has been to, he could not find a single author of "professional textbooks" "who has not enticed the reader to practice anal sex" (ibid., 84). Unfortunately, it appears that the professional textbooks he refers to are relatively few in number, and that many of these appear to be sex instruction manuals rather than academic works. Titles such as *Sex Without Guilt* (Ellis, 1975) and *Everything You Ever Wanted to Know About Sex* (Reuben, 1976) are unlikely to be considered part of the "Western" psychological canon by any professional scholar in that field. In much the same way, Badri attempts to claim that "Western" academics are also in the process of attempting to normalize pedophilia and incest through the mere fact that scholars are publishing studies about such phenomena in scholarly journals (ibid., 293). It is not only "Western" academia and media that spread the message of gay abandon and anal sex, according to Badri; non-governmental organizations (NGOs) in Western societies are "greatly influenced" by "homosexuals and lesbians" whose ultimate aim is the "total destruction of the traditional family" (ibid., 262) and the "absence of differentiation between heterosexuality and homosexuality" (ibid., 265). Gays and lesbians have also become powerful within the UN, an institution which has been "fully utilized by the United States and the West to culturally subjugate non-Western countries" (ibid., 269).

  Badri's use of statistics and citations is also somewhat problematic. He quotes extensively from the popular Malaysian daily *The Sun*, and in so doing sometimes in reality cites the press agency Reuters, which in turn is citing another "Western" newspaper. This may account for the apparent inaccuracy when Badri claims on page 60 of his book that a Scottish Anglican bishop, "Ritchard" [sic] Holloway, condones extra-marital affairs on the part of Anglican Church in Britain. (Badri's verbatim reference reads "*The Times*, as quoted by Reuters, as quoted by the Malaysian daily *The Sun*, May 18, 1995.") Unfortunately, Badri rarely quotes sources for his "statistics," which makes it difficult to assess the accuracy of his assertions. Thus, we learn on pages 170–171 that the median number of "lifetime sexual partners" of "the first hundred gay men to be diagnosed with AIDS" was "1120" (no source given), on page 107 that in the US "70 percent of the adult population take a special drug in parties" (source given, but appears to refer to alcohol rather than drugs), that "80 percent of the world's alcohol is consumed in Western countries" (ibid., 251, no source given), and that the young and sexually active Muslim "usually copulates 3 to 5 times a week" (ibid., 254, no source given).

MALIK BADRI ON PREVENTION OF HIV

Badri advocates *iman* or faith as the sine qua non of Muslim HIV prevention programs. For, he rhetorically asks, has not the very World Health Organization (WHO) found that Muslims have some of the "lowest percentages of HIV infections?" (ibid., 214). Badri accepts that there is a difference between ideal and actual sexual behavior even among Muslims, but to the extent that Muslims are at risk of HIV infection at all, it is all due to the influences of "Western modernity" and the "Western sexual revolution," the concomitant import of sexually "bizarre" homosexual practices, and Muslim males consuming alcohol, a substance which apparently makes them more prone to engage in extra-marital affairs. Since urban Muslim populations are exposed to "Western modernity" to a greater extent than rural populations, for Badri it follows that they are more at risk of HIV infection. In order to illustrate this, he introduces us to the peasants of his hometown of Rafa'a in the Sudan who, he claims, are untarnished by "Western" modernity to the extent that they cannot conceive of having sexual desires for persons other than their wives, let alone being "confused by gay preferences" (Badri, 2000, 49). One suspects this to be a somewhat reductionistic image of peasant life in the Sudan (unfortunately, the "simple and rural Muslim" peasant Badri invokes sounds more like a trope borrowed from Orientalist fictions); and it should be read as a Fanonian[13] inversion of discourses on black (Muslim) Africans and their sexualities, which replaces one image of sexual promiscuity, matrimonial instability, and patriarchal coercion, with another completely sanitized and a-historical image of social and sexual stability and bliss.

Badri also neglects to include an analysis of gender inequalities and the occurrence of coercive contexts of sexual relationships, which puts women at a greater risk than men of HIV infection in many parts of the so-called developing world. His assertion that prevention in Muslim societies "must develop from Islamic roots" to attain any success certainly has merit (ibid., 213). His problem is, of course, that there are a variety of opinions among Muslims as to what those Islamic roots have to say about an appropriate Islamic approach to the prevention of HIV. Countries like Brazil, Uganda, Senegal, and Thailand have managed to contain the epidemic by providing condoms to vulnerable and high risk groups such as sex workers, through working with them rather than condemning them.[14]

Malik Badri's suggestions with regards to actual Islamic prevention strategies are unfortunately spare. The Islamic approach to HIV prevention that he advocates is more than anything defined by opposition to an alleged "Western" prevention model, which according to him retains the values of the sexual revolution as he has previously defined it (i.e., "enticement to anal sex, sexual promiscuity and homosexuality"). "Western" prevention models, based more often than not on liberal notions of individual bodily and sexual autonomy (defined as the ability to exercise and negotiate "safe sex" practices), have their own particular weaknesses, but "enticing" people to engage in anal sex and sexual promiscuity has never been a central part of any known "Western" AIDS prevention program. For Badri the purported conflict between an Islamic HIV prevention model and a Western prevention model results in a "clash of civilizations" (ibid., 260), in the style of Samuel Huntington (1996), whom he cites approvingly, and it is through this model that he attempts to legitimize numerous exaggerations.

Badri advocates building on the abstention from sexual relations during Ramadan as a prevention strategy (ibid., 216), assuming that Muslims who engage in "adultery, fornication and sodomy" at other times of the year can be convinced to abstain from doing so by the example of Ramadan. As a prevention strategy, however, this does seem somewhat impracticable, given that those who do engage in "adultery, fornication and sodomy" are not likely to be identifiable to any Muslim prevention campaigner, precisely because these campaigners, according to Badri, ought to be religious teachers (ibid., 324). Additionally, Badri suggests that it is not advisable to speak openly to Muslim youths about being homosexual or bisexual, because references to "immoral or perverted sexual relations" can be "embarrassing" to them (ibid., 224), and because of his desire to build a society in which "the deviant few homosexuals and promiscuous can only practice their behavior in the secrecy of shame and guilt" (ibid., 238). As we have seen previously, however, it does not seem as if Badri himself considers it particularly embarrassing to talk about homosexuality and some of the sexual practices it might entail (in fact, he does so repetitiously and in great detail). Additionally, Muslim youths in many parts of the world are aware of the existence of homosexuals and are able to discuss the fact openly. We also learn about the findings of a somewhat mysterious study on the effects of fasting during Ramadan, which apparently demonstrated that immune cells showed greater "activity" in the bodies of a sample of Muslims fasting during Ramadan than in those who did not. This study does not appear to have been published in any peer-reviewed medical journal (Badri cites it from the Saudi monthly magazine *Ahlan Wa-Sahlan* or *Welcome*, an in-flight magazine rather than a medical journal). Badri informs us that the statistical significance of the findings was "a staggering 0.00009" (more *under*whelming than not), and was conducted by a "Dr. Qandil" at "the prestigious Harvard University" (ibid., 218).[15] Therefore one could conclude from this statement that prayer and fasting enhance the immune system of Muslims (ibid., 217) without mentioning precisely how praying and fasting prevent HIV transmission. Badri also advocates the washing of the genitals and the body *after* sexual intercourse (*ghusl*) as a means to prevent sexually transmitted diseases (STDs), and presumably HIV (ibid., 254). While it would be difficult to argue against the importance of intimate hygiene, there is little evidence to suggest that washing the body *after* sexual intercourse prevents transmission of HIV between sexual partners.

Badri's approach to Islamic prevention of HIV is holistic. Hence, he advocates the introduction of an Islamic state with shari'ah-derived punitive *hudud* laws for drug consumption and "fornication" (ibid., 336). Since he believes that the introduction of television, and "Western" films and television programs in rural parts of the Muslim world has led to "an obvious rise in crime and sexual offences, and in the way villagers dress and behave" (ibid., 309), the governments of Muslim countries ought to sharpen censorship dramatically (ibid., 310). The link between "Western" films and television programs and the alleged rise in sexual and criminal offences is an assertion which Badri is not able to document, but is allegedly based on "statistics" (ibid., 309). Badri has noted that the cost of providing for a wife and family has led many urban Muslims to postpone marriage into their thirties, which leads Muslim youths into engagement in pre-marital sex (ibid., 301–302), and he offers as a solution the simplification of marriage and a return to "early" and "traditional" Islamic ways (ibid., 301). Furthermore, one should consider opting for interpretations of the law which limit the Muslim husband's financial responsibilities to his wife and children (ibid., 304–305), an indication of Badri's flexiblility towards the selective application of Shari'ah. In this, he is quite characteristic of Islamist writers, who are often silent about the extent to which their models of the ideal society draw on or borrow from the very "Western" models of which they are so critical, and the exegetical violence their interpretations do to the plurality of interpretations of Islamic traditions.

Malik Badri on the use of condoms

Interestingly, with regard to the use of condoms, Prof. Badri adopts a less conservative position than many of the *'ulama*. Among the latter, condoms are often opposed, since they are believed to promote notions of sexual promiscuity among Muslim youth. Badri is careful to point out that condoms should only be used as a last resort, when one's "animalistic soul" becomes "too powerful to deter one from sinful behavior" (op. cit., 281). But unlike many of the *'ulama*, he takes the Islamic legal principle *ikhtiyar akhaff al-dararain* (the lesser of two evils) to mean that condoms should be used by Muslims who engage in *zina*, and who have reason to believe that they might be infected and infecting others with HIV (op. cit., 283).

CONCLUSION

Moral heterogeneity is one of the characteristics of modern societies (Asad, 2003, 186), and unease at this fact, and at sexual liberalization, has never been limited to the "Muslim world." It is worth
recalling that Badri's homophobia and emphasis on morality as the
only possible antidote against the spread of HIV is shared by many
Catholics as well as evangelical Christians. That opposition to supposedly "Western" modernities plays itself out on the contested
terrain of sexuality is not exactly something new in the history of
Muslim/non-Muslim relations. We should not be surprised to find
that for all the lurid Orientalist representations of Muslim otherness
and difference, there are parallel counter-images and inversions
which construct "Westerners" as sexually depraved.[16] The many
Islamist and Arab nationalist misappropriations and misreadings
of Said's *Orientalism* (1978)[17] may have generated the impression
that only "Westerners" engage in "othering."[18] Badri's work amply
demonstrates why "othering" should be seen as part of universal
human and social processes. The supposed different sexual mores
of "Westerners", and the need to oppose their imposition on Muslim
societies is a classical trope of much Islamist literature. It is an effective way of dehumanizing non-Muslim "Westerners" by reducing
"Western" sexual mores and "Western" modernities to simple for-
mulae, and by attributing social and moral changes to pernicious
"Western" influence through a simple line of causation.

Islamists like Badri in the Muslim world subscribe to the notion
of a Huntingtonian "clash of civilizations" chiefly because the invo-
cation of such binaries and inversions provides them with legitimacy inside and outside their own circles. A purported "clash of
civilizations" over sexual moralities provides them with greater
legitimacy than most other imagined and real clashes over values
and norms, because it involves issues of concern to a significant
number of Muslims beyond their immediate constituency.[19] In the
meantime, the classical bifurcation between the images of *dar al-
harb* ("the abode of war") and *dar al-islam* ("the abode of Islam"),
and between "Westerners" and Muslims, are made ever more obsolete by the real-time processes of globalization, which have led
to the increasing entanglement of the actual lives of Muslims and
"Westerners." Badri neglects to mention that Muslims have been
part of, and implicated in, the "Western" world for centuries. Badri's

statements seek to re-create an imaginary classical world of binary oppositions. "Westerners" happening to read this literature would, however, do well to keep in mind that the intended audience is primarily Muslim. The homophobia demonstrated by Badri's work is not exactly original – more often than not in Islamist literature of this kind, homosexuality and its recognition in Western liberal societies serve the function of a metonym for the perceived general depravity of "Western" sexual mores. Muslim conservatives and Islamists share these concerns, and the mere fact that it appeals beyond the confines of an Islamist readership makes its use appealing to authors like Badri.

So does it matter? Professor Malik Badri may not be the "reasonable scholar" of his imagination (ibid., 288) in "Western" eyes. His book is a virtual treatise on how to dehumanize non-Muslims as well as non-Muslim and Muslim sexual minorities, and furthermore it lacks scientific foundations in the way in which its author relates to basic issues of documentation and referencing. It is also noteworthy that Badri is in many ways a thoroughly modern polemical writer. He constructs his arguments on the basis of his own intuitions and on references to modern works of science, rather than on the basis of readings of works of classical *fiqh*. The paradox, which reveals some of the inherent limitations and contradictions of the notion of the "Islamization of knowledge", is, of course, as indicated by Badri's book, that this notion more often than not boils down to adopting a scientific paradigm which has been discredited and abandoned by modern "Western" science, and dressing it up to appear somehow inherently "Islamic." Badri's views on and prescriptions for eradication of homosexuality in Muslim societies are based on such a tactic.

I hope to have demonstrated in this article that there is nothing inherently or generically "Islamic" about knowledge that claims to be "Islamized" and is posited as an expression of radical non-"Western" alterity. More often than not, closer inspection reveals that such knowledge has as strong intellectual precursors and genealogies in the "West" as in the "East". We have no available information on how many Muslims may have read Badri's book, and what kind of impact it might have had. We would be wrong to consider Prof. Badri a marginal figure. This is attested by his association with Islam Online, Sheikh Yusuf al-Qaradawi, the Federation of Islamic Medical Associations, and by the fact that his book has been granted quasi-scientific legitimacy by its dissemination through the networks of Islamic Medical Associations in South Africa, the United States, Malaysia, and elsewhere. That Badri's work passes for intellectualism in some Islamic medical circles is perhaps the most perplexing and disturbing aspect of the story of Professor Malik Babikar Badri and his work on HIV and AIDS. One is not quite sure what to say about the intellectual state of such circles when they do in fact come in touch with the consequences of the pandemic on a daily basis.

BIBLIOGRAPHY

al-Attas, Mohammed Naquib 1978. *Islam and Secularism*. Kuala Lumpur, International Institute of Islamic Thought and Civilization (ISTAC).
al-Faruqi, Ismail R. 1982. *Islamization of Knowledge: General Principles and Workplan*. Herndon, Virginia, International Institute of Islamic Thought (IIIT).
al-Qaradawi, Yusuf 1982. *The Lawful and Prohibited in Islam*. New Delhi, Islamic Book Service.
Asad, Talal 2003. *Formations of the Secular: Christianity, Islam, Modernity*. Stanford, Stanford University Press.
Badri, Malik B. 2000. *The AIDS Crisis: A Natural Product of Modernity's Sexual Revolution*. 3rd edn. Kuala Lumpur, Meedena Books.
Buruma, Ian and Avishai Margalit 2004. *Occidentalism: A Short History of Anti-Westernism*. London, Atlantic Books.
Delius, Peter and Clive Glaser 2004. "The Myths of Polygamy: A History of Extra-Marital and Multi-Partnership Sex in South Africa." *South African Historical Journal*, 50: 84–114.
Ebrahim, Saad Eddin 2006. "Politico-religious cults and the 'end of history'." At http://www.opendemocracy.net/articles/ViewPopUpArticle.jsp?id=3&articleId=3523 (accessed May 19, 2006).
El Fadl, Khaled Abou 2001. *Speaking in God's Name: Islamic Law, Authority and Women*. Oxford, Oneworld Publishers.
El-Haj, Nadia Abu 2005. "Edward Said and the Political Present." *American Ethnologist*, 32 (4): 538–555.
El-Rouayheb, Khaled 2005. *Before Homosexuality in the Arab-Islamic World, 1500–1800*. Chicago, University of Chicago Press.
Ellis, Albert 1975. *Sex Without Guilt*. Chatsworth, California, Wilshire Press.
Epprecht, Mark 2004. *Hungochani: A History of Dissident Sexuality in Southern Africa*. Kingston, McGill-Queen's University Press.

Epstein, Helen, 2005. "God and the Fight Against AIDS." *New York Review of Books* 52 (7). At http://www.nybooks.com/articles/17963 (accessed December 10, 2005).

Esack, Farid 2004. *HIV, AIDS and Islam: Reflections Based on Compassion, Responsibility & Justice.* Cape Town, Positive Muslims.

Fanon, Frantz 1967. *Black Skin, White Masks.* New York: The Grove Press.

Farmer, Paul E. 1992. *AIDS and Accusation: Haiti and the Geography of Blame.* Berkeley, University of California Press.

Heywood, Mark 2005. "The Price of Denial." In M. Heywood (ed.), *From Disaster to Development: HIV and AIDS in Southern Africa.* Interfund Development Update 5 (3): pp. 93–122.

Hoffman, Murad Wilfried 1998. "Review: Malik Badri: *The AIDS Crisis: a natural product of modernity's sexual revolution.*" *Muslim World Book Review*, 18 (4).

Human Rights Watch 2003. *More than A Name: State-sponsored Homophobia and its Consequences in Southern Africa.* New York, Human Rights Watch. At http://www.hrw.org/reports/2003/safrica/safrig/hrc0303.pdf (accessed January 15, 2006).

Human Rights Watch 2005. *The Less They Know, The Better: Abstinence-Only HIV/AIDS Programmes in Uganda.* New York, Human Rights' Watch. At http://www.hrw.org/reports/2005/uganda0305/uganda0305.pdf (accessed January 15, 2006).

Huntington, Samuel P. 1996. *The Clash of Civilizations and the Remaking of World Order.* New York, Simon & Schuster.

Macfie, A. L. 2002. *Orientalism.* London, Longman.

Miles, Hugh 2005. *Al-Jazeera: How Arab TV News Challenged the World.* London, Abacus.

Moosa, Ebrahim 2005. *Ghāzāli & The Poetics of Imagination.* Chapel Hill, University of North Carolina Press.

Qutb, Sayyid, 1978. *Milestones.* Anonymous translator; Beirut, Holy Koran Publishing House.

Reuben, David 1976. *Everything You Ever Wanted to Know About Sex.* New York, Bantam Books.

Said, Edward W. 1978. *Orientalism.* New York, Pantheon Books.

Sardar, Ziauddin 2004. *Desperately Seeking Paradise: Journeys of a Skeptical Muslim.* London, Granta Books.

Shisana, Olive et al. 2005. *South African National HIV Prevalence, HIV Incidence, Behaviour and Communication Survey.* Cape Town, Human Sciences Research Council.

Sufian, Sandra 2004. "HIV/AIDS in the Middle East and North Africa: A Primer." *Middle East Report* 233, Winter 2004. At http://www.merip.org/mer/mer233/sufian.html (accessed December 10, 2005).

Tayob, Abdulkader 1995. *Islamic Resurgence in South Africa: The Muslim Youth Movement.* Cape Town, University of Cape Town Press.

Treichler, Paula A. 1999. *How to have Theory in an Epidemic: Cultural Chronicles and AIDS.* Durham, Duke University Press.

UNAIDS 2007. http://data.unaids.org/pub/EPISlides/2007/2007_epiupdate_en.pdf

Van der Vliet, Virginia 2004. "South Africa Divided Against AIDS: A Crisis of Leadership." In Kyle D. Kauffman and David L. Lindauer (eds), *AIDS and South Africa: The Social Expression of a Pandemic.* London, Palgrave Macmillan, 48–96.

Viswanathan, Gauri (ed.) 2005 [2001]. *Power, Politics and Culture: Interviews with Edward W. Said.* London: Bloomsbury.

Watanabee, Sabeena M. 1998. Review: Malik Badri: *The AIDS Crisis: A Natural Product of Modernity's Sexual Revolution. American Journal of the Islamic Social Sciences*, 15 (4).

Whitaker, Brian 2006. *Unspeakable Love: Gay and Lesbian Life in the Middle East.* London, Saqi Books.

4

WHEN *FĀḤISHAH* BECOMES WIDESPREAD – AIDS AND THE IBN MĀJA HADITH

Nabilah Siddiquee

INTRODUCTION

In much of the Muslim literature and rhetoric that explains AIDS as a form of divine punishment brought upon those who have sexually transgressed, one particular hadith consistently appears as authoritative support for this kind of divine retribution. The oft-quoted text is translated as follows:

> *Fāḥishah* [abomination][1] has never appeared amongst any people, which they commit openly, but an epidemic or disease that they have never encountered before became widespread amongst them.
> (*Sunan Ibn Māja, Kitāb al-fitan*, Hadith 4019)

This text is actually only the first of five parts of the hadith – the rest of the text rarely appears in this literature. Upon closer scrutiny, the hadith considered in its entirety raises a number of important questions of divine justice and "collateral damage" in Islam. With this problem in mind, this paper first investigates this hadith on its own grounds, in terms of both its traditional standing among hadith scholars, and its textual meaning in the context of divine justice in Islam. The main problem raised by the hadith is that of divine collective punishment in this world (as opposed to the Hereafter), which appears to punish the poor for the crimes of the rich, and entire communities for the transgressions of a few. Secondly, this paper investigates the hadith in terms of its use in the discourse on Islam and AIDS. Despite not featuring in the collection of the more authoritative Bukhāri and Muslim, this hadith is repeatedly employed to describe AIDS as a form of divine retribution for sex outside marriage and/or homosexuality.

In this analysis, I problematize the concept of divine collective punishment apparent in the hadith, in which an entire community may be punished in response to the faults of a few, by bringing in relevant verses from the Qur'an, I also argue that the "*fāḥishah*" referred to in the hadith may have a meaning other than just fornication and/or homosexuality. Based upon this analysis, I dispute the claim that the hadith in fact "explains" the AIDS crisis. I offer a reading of the text that is more in line with Islamic concepts of social justice than the one offered by a casual reading, a reading that is a more useful one for Muslims in approaching the AIDS epidemic.

Analyzing a hadith (pl. *aḥādīth*) is a complicated task. While always identified as secondary to the Qur'an, Hadith literature has traditionally been inseparable from it. Hadith literature offers elucidation of the Qur'anic text, and thus it is thought that a good portion of a Muslim's religion is drawn from it. However, the validation of hadith has long been a highly contested process, even within the *saḥīḥ* (correct) collections of Bukhāri and Muslim (referred to collectively as the *Saḥīḥayn*). Outside of these two collections, contestation runs even deeper. It is important to keep in mind that, generally, the way in which non-scholar Muslims choose to validate *aḥādīth* in their own belief systems often varies greatly from that of Muslim scholars. This paper examines the traditional methodology of examining a particular hadith as a starting point for studying it, in the belief that the opinions of the classical scholars continue to play an important role in how and when a particular hadith is employed in popular Muslim discourse.

HADITH METHODOLOGY

The systematic organization of hadith collections is usually dated to the middle of the second/eighth century. In the following two centuries hadith scholars traveled across the Muslim world gathering local knowledge of the prophetic traditions. The ensuing development of hadith studies centered on a methodology that sought to verify the accuracy and authenticity of the text. There are six major collections of *aḥādīth* that now constitute the major corpus of "hadith litera-ture." The *saḥīḥ* collections of Muhammad Ibn Ismāʿīl al-Bukhāri (d. 870) and Abū al-Ḥusayn Muslim ibn al-Hajjāj al-Nisapūrī (d. 875) were compiled in the third/ninth century. In addition to these two, there are the four *Sunan* collections compiled around the same time, including that of Abu Dāwūd Sijistānī (d. 275/888), Muḥammad ibn ʿIsa Tirmīdhī (d. 279/892), Ibn Māja Qazwīnī (d. 273/886) and Aḥmad ibn Shūʿayb Nasāʾī (d. 303/915). *Sunan* collections special-ize in legal *aḥādīth*, and the chapters are predominately devoted to practical rules (Kamali, 2005). While they are always deemed less authentic than the *Ṣaḥīḥayn*, the authority of the four *Sunan* was "almost universally" accepted over other collections by the sixth/twelfth century (*Encyclopaedia of the Qur'ān*, s.v. "Hadith").

In the third century, criticism of the existing prophetic traditions became an important part of the science of traditions (Goldziher, 1971, 135). For example, following this period there emerged a number of large works of criticism, including the *Kitāb al-Duʿafāʾ* ("Book of the Weak") by al-Nasāʾī. Any single hadith has two parts: the *isnād* (chain of transmission) and the *matn* (the body of the text). Traditionally, the *isnād* is the subject of criticism and analysis in these works:

> less attention is paid to the contents of the tradition itself than to the authorities in the *isnād* [. . .] belief in the authenticity of a hadith stands or falls with their reliability. Therefore the *isnād* could be called "the legs (*al-qawāʾim*) of the hadith," since the right to exis-tence of the utterances handed down rests upon it and without it they could not be sustained. (Goldziher, 1971, 134)

The focus was thus on determining the reliability of the transmitters comprising the chain of each hadith. The study of the biographies of hadith transmitters (referred to as *rijāl*) became a science called *ʿilm tārīkh al-ruwāt*, *ʿilm al-rijāl al-hadith*, or *asmāʾ al-rijāl*, which was formalized between the second and eighth, and fourth and tenth centuries (Kamali, 2005). A range of categories was used to evaluate the reliability of the persons in the chain. In the first order of reliabil-ity (in descending order) were *thiqah* (reliability), *mutqīn* (exact-ness), *zhabt* (strength), *hujjah* (admitted as evidence), *ʿadl* (truthful), *ḥāfiz*, and *ḍābit* (one who faithfully keeps and passes on what he has heard) (ibid., 135). In the second order were *ṣadūq* (saying the truth), *maḥalluhu al-ṣidq* (his position is that of truth), and *lā ba's bihi* (unobjectionable) (ibid.). Below this was *ṣāliḥ al-hadith*, and further below that were *ghayr kadhīb* and *lam yakdhib* (not a liar). Another classification assigned to a transmitter was *layyin al-hadith* (tender in respect of the hadith), referring to one whose reliability has been "wounded" but not fully disproved (ibid.). Less credible transmitters were characterized as *laysa bi-qawī* (not strong), and then *da'īf* (weak), *matrūk al-hadith* or *dhāhib al-hadith* (one whose hadith is left aside, or is invalid), and *kadhdhāb* (liar), etc. (ibid.).[2]

As mentioned above, the collectors of the *Sunan* were more liberal in their criteria than Bukhāri and Muslim, and included *aḥādīth* that did not meet the more stringent rules of the latter two. For example, while Bukhāri and Muslim omitted chains containing narrators who were disputed in reliability, Nasā'ī and Abu Dāwūd accepted *rijāl* as long as they were not unanimously rejected (Goldziher, 1971, 230). The following system for classifying the strength of hadith was used by Tirmīdhī for the first time: *saḥīḥ, hasan*, or *hasan ṣaḥīḥ* (232).

When did the Six Books attain canonized status? According to Goldziher, general recognition of the Six Books had "not yet pre-vailed" in the first half of the fourth century, but by the end of the fifth or beginning of the sixth century, al-Tirmīdhī and Ibn Māja were already included among the authoritative group (240). It was when Abū al-Faḍl Muḥammad bin Ṭāhir al-Maqdisī (d. 507 H) in the early sixth century A.H. included it as one of the "reliable works" on hadith, that the Ibn Māja collection became canonized as among the six collections (Kamali, 2005, 40). However, Ibn Māja's was the collection that took the longest time to gain general acceptance because it was widely regarded as containing numerous weak tra-ditions. For example, we find many references in the following centuries of only *al-ummahāt al-khams* (Ibn Khaldun, d. 808) that omit Ibn Māja (243). In the Western Islamic regions, classifications often replaced Ibn Māja with other collections, particularly with *al-Muwaṭṭa* of Mālik Ibn Anas (d. 796) (243).

THE SUNAN OF IBN MĀJA

Ibn Māja (Abū 'Abdullāh Muḥammad ibn Yazīd ibn Māja al-Rabī al-Qazwīnī) was born 209/824 in Qazwīn, in the region south of the Caspian Sea in present day Iran.[3] He died in 273/886 during the reign of the Abbasid caliph al-Muʿtamid.[3] Both Ibn Khallikān and al-Jazāri recognized his *Sunan* as the sixth authoritative collection of Hadith in the thirteenth century, after Bukhāri, Muslim, Tirmīdhī, Nasāʾī, and Abu Dāwūd (Abdul Ghaffar, 1986). In his lifetime, he is known to have studied in various places including Kufa, Basra, Egypt, the Shām, Baghdad, Rayy, Mecca, Medina, and Khurasān (ibid.). Regarding his works, Ibn Kathīr mentioned that he produced a work on *tafsīr* and a history, but neither survived. What did survive is his hadith collection, known as *Sunan Ibn Māja.*

There are a number of surviving classical commentaries on Ibn Māja's *Sunan*. Among them are those of ʿAlāʾ al-Dīn Mughaltay (d. 762 H) and Kamāl al-Dīn al-Damīrī (d. 808 H), as well as Ibn al-Hasan al-Hanafī's *Kifāyat al-hāja*, Ahmed ibn Abī Bakr's (d. 840 H) *Misbāḥ al-zujāj fī zawāʾid ibn mājah*, and Jalāl al-Dīn al-Suyūṭī's *Misbāḥ al-zujāj ʿala ibn mājah*. These commentaries are among those that will be referred to in analysis of the *isnād* and *matn* of the hadith below.

According to Fuʾād ʿAbd al-Bāqī, of the 4,321 *aḥādīth* in the collection, 3,002 are recorded in one of the other five collections. Of the remaining 1,339 unique to Ibn Māja (among the five authoritative collections), 428 have been deemed *ṣaḥīḥ*, 199 *ḥasan*, 613 *ḍaʿīf*, and 99 *munkar* or *makdhūb* (Abdul Ghaffar, 1986).[5] There are, of course, disputes among the commentators on these numbers. As was stated above, because the collection includes some fair and weak (*ḥasan* and *ḍaʿīf*) *aḥādīth*, it was not included among the authoritative collections in the initial centuries of the hadith movement. Even after attaining status as the sixth collection by the early sixth century, Ibn Māja was still sometimes omitted in favor of *al-Muwaṭṭa*, particularly in North Africa and among the Māliki school of law. However, the reason Ibn Māja's collection was recognized over others, mostly in the East, may have been because it included many additional *aḥādīth* not found elsewhere (Kamali, 2005). In his own time, Ibn Māja apparently showed his collection to Zurʿa al-Rāzī, (d. 878) who was impressed with it, but added that it may have contained *aḥādīth* weak in *isnād* (ibid., 40). Ibn Hajar al-ʿAsqalānī also spoke of Ibn Māja's *Sunan* in a similar way, and confirmed the existence of weak *aḥādīth* in it (ibid., 40). Ibn al-Jawzī, a major critic of the authenticity of *aḥādīth* in Ibn Māja, concluded in his work *al-Mawḍūʿāt*, that many of the *aḥādīth* on the merit of individuals, tribes, or towns, particularly from Ibn Māja's hometown Qazwīn, were fabricated (ibid., 40–41).

The *Sunan* of Ibn Māja has been noted for being well planned and easy to use (Abdul Ghaffar, 1986). Ibn Māja would also often point out a specific area where a particular hadith was well-known or specifically relevant. Shihāb al-Dīn Abū Bakr al-Buṣīrī's (d. 840/1446) *Zawā'id ibn Māja* was a full volume on additional *aḥādīth* of Ibn Māja, explaining the weak ones among them. The contents of this book are now preserved in a work by Abu al-Ḥasan Muḥammad bin 'Abd al-Hādī al-Sindī (d. 1138/1725) (ibid.). Ibn al-Jawzī (d. 597 H) was a harsh critic of the *aḥādīth* in Ibn Māja, and pointed out 34 as "spurious" in his *al-Mawdu'āt* (ibid.). Suyūti, however, defended many of those "spurious" *aḥādīth* in his works, *al-Qawl al-ḥasan fī al-dhabi 'an al-sunan* and *al-Ta'aqqubāt 'ala al-mawdu'āt* (ibid.).

HADITH ANALYSIS: *ISNĀD*

The *isnād* of the particular hadith in discussion, the one used to invoke the idea of AIDS as punishment from God, includes six individuals before being traced back to the Prophet:

> Maḥmūd ibn Khālid al-Dimashqī narrated from Sulaymān ibn 'Abd al-Rahman Abu Ayyūb who narrated from Ibn Abī Mālik (Khālid ibn Yazīd) who narrated from his father (Abū Mālik) who narrated from 'Atā' ibn Abī Ribāḥ who narrated from 'Abd Allāh bin 'Umar [who said] said . . . (*Sunan Ibn Māja*, Hadith 4019)

From the commentary of Al-Sindī' (d. 1138/1725) in *Sunan al-Mustafa*, we learn that al-Buṣīrī (in *al-Zawā'id*) deemed this hadith "*ṣāliḥ al-'amal bihi*" (appropriate to act upon). The same is accounted in the analysis by Fu'ād 'Abd al-Bāqī. The strength of the chain, however, is disputed. Al-Buṣīrī reported that it was disputed on account of Ibn Abī Mālik and his father (al-Sindī, 488–489). In a commentary by Bashshār 'Awwād Ma'rūf, the *isnād* is deemed weak (*ḍa'īf*), again upon the weakness of Ibn Abī Mālik, whose full name was Khālid bin Yazīd bin 'Abd al-Rahmān (Vol. 5, *Kitāb al-Fitan* (36): Bāb al-'Uqūbāt (22), 490–491). However, in a commentary by Maḥmūd Muḥammad Maḥmūd Ḥasan Naṣṣār, the hadith is deemed *ḥasan* (ibid., Part 4). He writes further that according to al-Ḥākim in *al-Mustadrak*, by way of 'Aṭā' bin Abī Ribāḥ, the hadith was deemed *ṣaḥīḥ* of *isnād* and *ṣāliḥ al-'amal bihi*. But also according to him, the reliability of Ibn Abī Mālik and his father was disputed. Ibn Abī Mālik was deemed trustworthy by Abū Zar'a al-Dimashqī, and Abū Zar'a al-Rāzī. He was deemed weak by Aḥmad bin Ṣāliḥ al-Maṣrī, Ibn Mu'ayyin, al-Nasā'ī (in *al-Du'afā' wa-l-mutrikīn*), and al-Dāraquṭnī. Ibn Abī Mālik's father, a *qaḍī* of Damascus and among the successors (*tābi'īn*), was deemed trustworthy by Ibn Mu'ayyan, Abū Zar'a al-Rāzī, Ibn Habān, al-Dāraquṭnī, and al-Burqānī. Naṣṣār also includes Ya'qūb bin Sufyān's statement that in the hadith of the two (the father and the son) is "tenderness" (*fī ḥadīthihimā līn*). As was mentioned above, this characterization suggested doubt in the reliability of the transmitter, who is weakened but not completely discounted. Additionally, he stated that Ibn Māja is unique in this *isnād* (*Tuḥfat al-ashrāf* no. 7332). Based upon the commentators' disagreement on the reliability of Ibn Abī Mālik and his father, and given that the *isnād* varies from *ṣaḥīḥ* to *ḍa'īf*, it should be clear that the strength and authenticity of this *isnād* is not unanimously accepted.

HADITH CONTENT ANALYSIS: *MATN*

The text of the hadith is translated as the following:

> The Messenger of God came to us saying, "O *Muhājirūn* (community of exiles)! There are five things when you are tested by them, and I seek refuge by Allah that you should [ever] experience them:
>
> 1 *Fāḥishah* has never appeared amongst any people, which they commit openly, but an epidemic or disease that they have never encountered before became widespread amongst them;
> 2 Cheating in weighing will result in a crisis of poverty and tyranny;
> 3 Unwillingness to pay *zakāt* [wealth tax] will result in an extended drought, without rain so much so that if it were not for [God's mercy on the] cattle, it would not rain at all;
> 4 Damaging the bond between God and his Prophet will result in the appearance of an enemy; and;

5 Leaders refusing to base laws on the Book of God will cause dissension within their ranks." (*Sunan Ibn Māja*, Hadith 4019)[5]

In the classical works, commentary on the meaning of the text is limited. Most of the notes offered by al-Sindī are clarifications of a few words and points of grammar. It is important to note that al-Sindī interpreted *fāḥishah* as *zina* (fornication), and in the following commentaries, it is this interpretation that is quoted. The meaning of the word *fāḥishah*, and thus the meaning of the first section of the hadith, will be explored in further detail later.

There are a number of concepts introduced in this text that are deeply problematic to a justice-seeking reader. In each of the five points, a form of divine collective punishment is promised in response to the crimes of a specific part of the population. For example, if the crime of *fāḥishah* is committed openly amongst a people, we know that it is impossible that every person in that community is engaged in the crime. Why is the divine response an epidemic or disease, something that will necessarily afflict those not guilty of *fāḥishah* as well as those who are guilty? Next, if there is cheating in weighing, then there is also one who is cheated. Why should those at the receiving end of dishonesty suffer poverty and tyranny as a result of the crimes inflicted upon them? Both poverty and tyranny afflict people indiscriminately, and primarily harm those who are economically and socially disadvantaged. If there is tyranny in a community, there is necessarily a tyrant who is not harmed or oppressed. If there is poverty, the previously wealthy can afford to flee, while everyone else must remain. Next, the hadith states that the failure to pay *zakāt* results in extended drought. But why should the unwillingness of the wealthy to pay *zakāt* to the poor result in a drought that will necessarily punish the poor as well as the wealthy? Those without wealth have nothing to do with paying or not paying the wealth-tax. In this case, more sympathy is placed on the cattle than on the suffering poor, who seem to be completely omitted from God's consideration. Finally, dissension in the ranks amounts to a punishment not just for the leaders, but also for the people of the country who rely upon the protection of those leaders. Why should the people suffer for the misdeeds or corruption of their leaders, even if those leaders happen to be elected by the people? This point is even more obvious when considering that in most cases, leaders are not chosen by the people, nor do they enjoy the approval of the people.

Fāḥishah

In order to further investigate the meaning of the hadith, we now look at the meaning of the word *fāḥishah*. Given that it is the first part of the hadith that is usually cited, and that here it is the word *fāḥishah* that is often interpreted to be sexual transgressions that lead to AIDS, it will be useful to investigate the precise meaning of the term, which is left un-translated above because of the ambiguities involved. The argument made here is that in the hadith the word does not necessarily mean *zina* (although al-Sindī concluded such), nor is it specific to homosexuality. As it appears in the Qur'an, the word refers generally to "transgression" or "abomination." This transgression often refers to sexual transgression, in the context of the social norms of that time period, but not always. Additionally, we should note that in the hadith there is emphasis on the public nature of the *fāḥishah*, implying that the publicity of these transgressions is something new. It is this widespread publicity and newness, not just the existence of the *fāḥishah* alone, that warrants the punishment (plague, or *ṭāwūn*) never seen before by the forefathers.

According to Lane's Arabic-English lexicon, the definition of *fāḥishah* is "an excess, an enormity, anything exceeding the bounds of rectitude: a thing excessively, enormously, or beyond measure, foul, evil, bad, abominable, or unseemly . . . gross, immodest, lewd, or obscene" (Lane, 1893/2003, 1:2345). It also means "anything not agreeable with the truth . . . a sin, or crime, that is very foul, evil, bad, etc.," and, "anything forbidden by God . . . any saying, or action, that is foul, evil, bad, etc" (ibid.). A variation of the word from the same root is *faḥshā'*, which is synonymous. The word can also mean, particularly, "adultery and fornication." According to Lane, in verse 4:23 of the Qur'an and in other instances, *fāḥishah* is a woman's going out without permission, or using foul language against her husband's relations, "by reason of the sharpness of their tongues." *Faḥshā'* can also particularly mean "niggardliness, tenaciousness, or avarice" in the payment of the poor rate (*al-Baqara* (2), 271). In this definition we can see clearly that the word does not always refer to sexual transgression.

Toshihiko Izutsu, who has studied words in the Qur'an in the context of their "semantic fields," goes into some depth in discussing the meaning of the root *f-ḥ-sh* in the context of the Qur'an. The forms *faḥshā'*, *fāḥishah*, and the plural of *fāḥishah* (*fawāḥish*) appear. According to Izutsu, *fāḥishah* signifies "anything foul and abominable beyond measure" (Izutsu, 2002, 233). The word is often used in conjunction with other words of similar meanings, such as the root *s-w-'* in the forms *sū'* and *sayyi'āt*. The words *sū'* and *fahshā'* have almost synonymous meanings, as apparent in the verse, "Follow not Satan's footsteps: for, verily, he is your open foe, and enjoins upon you naught but *sū'* and *fahshā'*" (al-Baqarah (2), 168– 169). *Fāḥishah* is "essentially descriptive" rather than classificatory, while *sayyi'ah* is more "evaluative" than descriptive (Izutsu, 2002). While the word *fāḥishah* can have many meanings, it sometimes carries a specific meaning in the Qur'an. For example, in the following verses, again in conjunction with *sū'*, *fāḥishah* clearly refers to fornication:

> And come not near to *zina* (fornication). Verily, it is a *fāḥishah* and an evil way. (*al-Isra* (17), 32)

> She [the wife of the Egyptian Governor] desired him passionately, and he [Joseph] would have desired her too, had it not been that he saw [just then] a proof of his Lord. Thus did We turn away from him *sū'* and *fahshā'*. (Yusuf (12), 24)

> Draw not near to fornication; verily it is a *fāḥishah*; it is evil (*sā'a*, a verbal form from SW') as a way. (*al-Isra* (17), 32)

In other cases, *fāḥishah* has a particular meaning other than fornication. On one occasion, it refers to a specific pagan custom of marriage which is forbidden: "Marry not women your fathers married, except bygone cases, for it is surely abomination (*fāḥishah*), a hateful thing (*maqt*), and an evil way (*sā'a sabīlan*)" (*al-Nisā* (4), 22). The word *fahshā'* is sometimes used in a more general sense. The following verses establish a connection between *fahshā'* and Satan. *Fahshā'* happens by the instigation of Satan, and in express opposition to God:

> O believers, follow not the footsteps of Satan, for upon those who follow the footsteps of Satan, verily, he enjoins *fahshā'* and *munkar*. (*al-Nur* (24), 21)

> Satan promises you poverty and enjoins upon you *fahshā'*, while God promises you forgiveness from Himself and bounty. (*al-Baqarah* (2), 268)

> We have made the Satans patrons of those who believe not. And whenever they commit a *fāḥishah*, they say, "We found our fathers

practicing it, and God bade us do it." Say, "God does not enjoin upon you *faḥshā'*. Do you say against God that which you know not?" (*al-A'rāf* (7), 28)

Verily, God enjoins justice (*'adl*) and kindness (*iḥsān*) and giving to kinsfolk, and forbids *faḥshā'* and *munkar* and insolence (*baghy*). (*al-Nahl* (16), 90)

In these cases, the exact nature of the transgression is not specified, but it is placed in opposition to God and to justice. Izutsu also indicates a relationship between *faḥshā'* and *kufr* (commonly translated as "disbelief"). *Kufr* is *dhanb* (sin), which includes *faḥshā'* and *ẓulm* (oppression):

God loves the good-doers (*muḥsinīn*) who, when they commit a *faḥishah* or wrong (*ẓalamū*) themselves (*ẓulm al-nafs*), remember God and ask forgiveness for their sins (*dhunūb*) – and who forgives sins save God? – and persevere not knowingly in what they did. (*al-Imrān* (3), 135)

In other cases, *faḥishah* is not specifically defined, but has been interpreted by commentators to mean a specific thing. The story of the Prophet Lut is a good example of this. The Lut story appears in a number of segments, in which Lut's people are punished for committing *faḥishah* and *sayyi'āt* (*Hud* (11), 78). Lut questions his people, "What, do you commit such *faḥishah* as no one in all the world has ever committed before you? Verily, with lust you approach men instead of women: nay, but you are people given to excesses!" (*al-A'rāf* (7), 80).[6] He calls on his people to be conscious of God, and stop assaulting his guests (*Hud* (11), 78). Interpreters have often read *faḥishah* here to mean same-sex acts, and so the Lut story is commonly claimed as evidence that the Qur'an forbids homosexuality. The word *faḥishah* in this story may seem particularly relevant to its appearance in our hadith, because there is a similar theme of divine retribution in response to *faḥishah*. However, this interpretation is contested, and there has been some study in the interest of more carefully defining the *faḥishah* of Lut's people. Elsewhere in this volume, Scott Siraj al-Haqq Kugle and Sarah Chiddy have argued that the people of Lut were punished for disregarding God in a number of ways, not for the homosexuality of their actions. Their transgressions included miserliness, greed, and disregard for the ethic of hospitality characteristic of the Prophets. They argue that the sexual transgression denounced in the Lut story is that of violence and rape, not of sexual orientation or fulfilling same-sex desire.

DIVINE RETRIBUTION AND JUSTICE

The hadith is problematic for a justice-seeking reader, on the grounds described earlier, only if we understand divine collective punishment in this world, in which the innocent suffer along with the guilty, to be incompatible with an Islamic conception of justice. Is it actually unjust, according to the Qur'an and Hadith?

First, does God punish people in this world? One only needs to consider the numerous prophetic stories in the Qur'an to see that divine collective punishment *is* referred to in the text. Unbelievers and evildoers can be both punished on earth and suffer eternal chastisement in the hereafter, according to God's will. This conclusion is drawn from the frequent occurrence of divine punishment stories in the Qur'an, which serve as warnings to those who reject God. In these stories, a Prophet is usually sent to a people, who proceed to reject him and scorn God. In light of this rejection, God responds with various forms of punishment on earth.[7] This intervening role of God in the affairs of this world introduces questions on the nature of divine punishment.

> There is an acknowledgement of the destructive power of some events and processes. Consequently, theological reflection takes up the question of the cause of human calamities, attributing them variously to natural explanations and acts of divine judgment. This question presents a tension that is central to the Qur'ānic view of humankind's relationship to the divine. (*Encyclopedia of Islam*, s.v., "Chastisement and Punishment")

There are a number of punishment stories in the Qur'an that are meant to warn people. It would appear that divine punishment usually comes after God has given the people an opportunity to reform, but they persist in transgression (*Encyclopedia of the Qur'ān*, s.v., "Reward and Punishment"). In these stories, it seems that the very nature of divine justice rests upon God's ability to intervene in this world and punish those who have transgressed without repentance.

Thus there is scope for interpreting divine punishment in this world as part of divine justice. Prophetic stories seem to indicate that this has happened in the past – whether or not one argues that these stories are rhetorical and/or need to be contextualized is a separate issue.

The Lut story is probably the most widely known and referenced example of earthly divine punishment in the Qur'an. As mentioned above, the story is particularly relevant to Hadith 4019 in Ibn Māja because it constructs God's response to *fāḥishah* in a similar manner. However, the difference between the punishment in the hadith and the punishments in the Lut story and other Prophetic stories in the Qur'an is that chastisement in the latter comes directly in response to rejection of a messenger. The moral justification for divine punishment comes not from "negligence" or from the disbelief itself, but from "reckless disregard" for the truth expressed by a prophet of God (*Encyclopedia of Islam*, s.v., "Crime and Punishment").

Secondly, do the innocent suffer along with the guilty in divine retribution? A few considerations lead us to answer in the negative. Within the punishment stories above, it is sometimes expressed that God's retribution affects specifically the guilty, and that the innocent are saved from the punishment.

> And in the course of time, We brought out [of Lut's city] such [few] believers as were there: for apart from one [single] house, We did not find there any who had surrendered themselves to Us. (*al-Zāriyat* (51), 35–36)

In this verse, the "single house" refers to Lut's family, who were saved from God's punishment. Here and in other places, we can see that in the story of Lut's people, there is emphasis that the chastisement of "stone-hard blows" fell specifically upon the evil-doers (*Hud* (11), 82–83). The idea that the innocent suffer along with the guilty also conflicts with the ethic enshrined in the following verse:

> Who receiveth guidance, receiveth it for his own benefit: who goeth astray doth so to his own loss: *No bearer of burdens can bear the burden of another*: nor would We visit with Our Wrath until We had sent an apostle (to give warning). (*al-Isra* (17), 15)

It is clearly stated that no individual will be made to bear the burden of another or the consequences ("burdens") of another's acts.

Additionally, the verse promises that there is no divine punishment without the sending of a warner (apostle) ahead of time. However, another verse must be considered here: "And fear tumult or oppression (*fitna*), which affecteth not in particular (only) those of you who do wrong: and know that Allah is strict in punishment" (*al-Anfāl* (8), 25, trans. Yusuf Ali). Pickthall's translation is as follows: "And guard yourselves against a *chastisement* which cannot fall exclusively on those of you who are wrong-doers, and know that Allah is severe in punishment."[8] The verse identifies a form of "tumult or oppression" (alternatively chastisement or retribution) that harms the guilty as well as the innocent.

Does the verse contradict the earlier verse which states that no one will be made to carry the burdens of others? Not necessarily. First, a relevant question is whether the "burden" in the first verse is found in the present world or in the Hereafter. Second, is the *fitna* referred to in the second verse a punishment ("chastisement") from God, or rather a "tumult" or "oppression" brought about by evil deeds of other people, such as an oppressive ruler? While everything happens or does not happen according to the will of God, we know that there are some troubles that are considered to be initiated by man, not God. For example, if a murderer kills an innocent person, we do not view that person as the subject of divine punishment, but as the victim of a murderer and of societal ills. Is the verse simply warning us that the evils we commit may harm entire societies, including the innocent, this having nothing to do with divine retribution?

SPEAKING OF THE AIDS EPIDEMIC

This hadith, as stated earlier, looms large in Muslim attempts to establish a causal relationship between sexual transgression and the AIDS epidemic, in which the suffering of persons living with HIV is a form of divine punishment in response to transgression. This kind of argument is found in popular literature on the subject, easily accessed on the Internet, which suggests that it is the growing "normalization" of homosexuality and extra-marital sexual activity between men and women that is at the heart of God's current wrath, manifested in AIDS. The "public" nature of the *fāḥishah* as referenced in the hadith is primarily linked to the "permissiveness" of Western societies, which is slowly permeating other societies. A number of these articles argue that because in the past there has been no known mention of another plague-like disease hitting these particular societies, the AIDS virus must be that plague prophesied by the hadith. The reader may detect in these writings a sense of awe at how a 1,400-year-old hadith has prophesied this contemporary epidemic and explained its causes:

> Is the AIDS pandemic not a warning to the transgressors? More than 1,400 years ago, the Prophet Muhammad (*sallallahu 'alayhi wa-sallam*) . . . had already admonished mankind of the consequences and dangers of promiscuous sexual relationships: "Whenever sexual permissiveness spreads among the people until it becomes declared, infections and killer diseases, as well as illnesses not previously found in their ancestors will also spread among them."
>
> The AIDS problem, which is reaching pandemic proportions, is due largely to sexual permissiveness. Thus, the divine punishment (*ḥudūd*) for these social ills is certainly for the good of the entire humanity. Although the AIDS problem is currently affecting largely those indulging in sexual promiscuity, many innocent individuals, including doctors, nurses and children, have been victimized by this social carnage. (Mamarinta Umar P. Mubabaya, "Islamic Solutions to the World's Social Problems")

Here, the harm suffered by the "innocent" doctors, nurses, and children is the fault of those who indulged in sexual promiscuity and thereby instigated God's punishment. On a website of the Ahmadiyyah Muslim Community, Mirza Ghulam Muhammad (d. 1908), its founder, is quoted as also having prophesied a plague, now specifically identified as AIDS, that was to be specific to Europe and other Christian countries. This claim is supported with the Prophet's prediction, utilizing the same hadith from Ibn Māja.

> The word *faḥshā'* means "permissiveness" with the connotation of audacity and shamelessness, resulting in open display of sex. It should be noted that mere permissiveness does not warrant so severe a chastisement from Allah; but when it exceeds all bounds and is acknowledged as a commonly accepted social behavior, then that society is affected with some completely new sex-related disease as a sign of God's displeasure. (Mirza Tahir Ahmed, "The Aids Virus")

CONCLUSION

In conjunction with the earlier content analysis, we can see that the manner in which this hadith has been employed in the Muslim discourse on AIDS is problematic. As indicated above, the authenticity of the *isnād* for this hadith is disputed among the classical commentaries on Ibn Māja. While one scholar deemed the *isnād* strong, others considered it weak. Further, all of the commentators acknowledged that there was doubt regarding the reliability of two transmitters, Ibn Abī Mālik and his father. Even if the hadith is to be taken into consideration, interpreting it to mean that God punishes the "sexually deviant" by sending AIDS, a plague that may affect all people indiscriminately, is not justifiable. Such a conclusion is problematic to the Islamic ethic that "no bearer of burdens can be made to bear the burdens of another" (*al-Isra* (17), 15). Further, it is incorrect to interpret *fāhishah* as only *zina* and/or same-sex acts, as the word can have other meanings, or a more general meaning. Based on the weakness of the hadith, the use of this text to demonize all persons living with HIV does injustice to the text, as well as to these people.

Is there an alternative reading of the hadith? Is there a better way to employ it in the AIDS discourse? When the text is taken in its entirety, we can see that God establishes serious punishments for the powerful and the wealthy who disregard their responsibilities to the poor and the public in general. God threatens to punish those who fail to pay *zakāt* to the poor, as well as the leaders who fail to consider the interests of the public when governing. One might even conclude that the warnings of punishment are meant to be symbolic ones, elucidating the importance of God-consciousness, ethical conduct, honesty in trade, paying the wealth tax, and responsible leadership. In this light, one might read the hadith as a serious defense of the rights of the underprivileged, emphasizing the social responsibilities of all. When we pause and recognize that persons living with HIV in many parts of the world are among the most marginalized and oppressed, we can see how these themes are relevant and could be better applied as we engage with the AIDS crisis.

BIBLIOGRAPHY

al-Dhahabī 1988. *al-Mujarrad fi asmā' rijāl ibn mājah*. Commentary by Bāsim Faysal al-Jawābarah. Riyad, Dar al-rāya.

Al-Sindī. *Sunan al-Mustafa*, vol. 2.

Abdul Ghaffar, Suhaib Hasan 1986. *Criticism of Hadith among Muslims with Reference to Sunan Ibn Maja*. 2nd edn. London, Ta-Ha Publishers, Inc.

Ahmed, Mirza Tahir n.d. "The Aids Virus." Al.Islam.org: Revelation, Rationality, Knowledge, and Truth. At http://www.alislam.org/library/books/revelation/part_6_section_6.html.

Al-Hashimi, Al-Sayed Ahmad. *Selection of Prophetic Hadiths & Muhammadan Wisdoms*. Trans. Salma al-Houry. Beirut, Dar al-Kutub al-Ilmīyya.

Goldziher, Ignaz 1971. *Muslim Studies*, Vol. 2. Trans C. R. Barber and S. M. Stern. London, George Allen & Unwin Ltd.

Ibn Mājah, Muḥammad ibn Yazīd 1998. *Sunan Ibn Mājah*. Taḥqīq Bashshār 'Awwād Ma'rūf. Beirut, Dār al-Jīl.

Izutsu, Toshihiko 2002. *Ethico-Religious Concepts in the Quran*. Montreal, McGill-Queen's University Press.

Kamali, Mohammad Hashim 2005. *A Textbook of Hadith Studies: Authenticity, Compilation, Classification and Criticism of Hadith*. The Islamic Foundation.

Lane, Edward William Lane [1893] 2003. *Arabic English Lexicon*. Online edition. At www.laneslexicon.com.

Mubabaya, Mamarinta Umar P. n.d. "Islamic Solutions to the World's Social Problems." At http://www.islamawareness.net/Islam/solution.html.

5

A SHARI'AH PERSPECTIVE ON AIDS[1]

Mohammad Hashim Kamali

INTRODUCTION

In the absence of any direct comment in the Shari'ah on the subject of AIDS, we can look at some of its general principles and guidelines in order to develop an Islamic legal perspective of some related issues. Because of the diversity of issues associated with AIDS and the lack of direct precedent, I have taken an exploratory approach which involves some speculation, in the hope of making a contribution that might eventually prove worthwhile. AIDS is not a monolithic theme and some of its related issues have ethical and sociopolitical implications far beyond the strictly medical context. The issues that we face are wide-ranging, and although Islamic law may help to provide some answers, public education and cultural attitudes are equally, if not more, important in addressing and overcoming AIDS-related dilemmas.

THE LEGAL MAXIMS

The legal maxims of *Fiqh* (Islamic Jurisprudence) refer to a set of principles and guidelines which have derived from the Qur'an and the *Sunnah* (the Prophet's precedent). They basically consist of the work of Muslim jurists who have formulated a set of guidelines on various legal themes which convey the general message and purpose of the Shari'ah in reference to their subjects. These collected maxims often consist of extracts from the detailed legal evidence on a subject and help to provide the reader with insight into the general objectives (*maqasid*) of the law. In an attempt to ascertain a Shari'ah perspective on AIDS we can refer to some of these maxims on the subject of *darar* (harm or injury). These rank among the most prominent of the one hundred legal maxims that appear in the introductory section of the *Ottoman Mejelle*, the civil code of the Ottoman Empire in the late nineteenth and early twentieth centuries which still represents the most widely accepted codification of the Shari'ah.

The first of these simply declares that "harm must be eliminated (*al-darar yuzal*)" (article 20). This maxim is deliberately worded in the broadest of terms so as to comprise all *darar* regardless of its nature, origin, or cause. There is no reference in the text to how harm should be fought, nor to the scale and *darar* itself, the prevailing circumstances, and the capacity of the combatant. By common acknowledgement, this is one of the most comprehensive of all legal maxims, so much so that it can encompass the whole of the Shari'ah.[2] The message here is clearly one that supports and encourages action and openness to diverse ways and means to prevent and eliminate *darar*. Although this maxim does not specify any type of harm, our understanding of the basic value structure of Shari'ah suggests that priority should be given to fighting harm that threatens the safety of the five essential values (*al-daruriyyat al-khamsah*) of faith, life, intellect, property, and lineage (article 20).[3]

In relation to AIDS, efforts towards eliminating harm that threatens the essential values must be stepped up and continued. Since AIDS awareness is about protecting at least two of the essential values (those of life and lineage), and the harm that we face is undoubtedly destructive, it becomes the Shari'ah-ordained responsibility of every Muslim, indeed anyone who values human life and the survival of the family, to join hands and play a role in whatever capacity they can to make this campaign all-embracing and effective.

The maxim above should be read together with another one: "a *darar* may not be eliminated by its equivalent" (*al-darar la-yuzal bi-mithlih*) (article 25), i.e., fighting one *darar* should not cause the onset of another equivalent *darar*. For example, if two people are equally in need of a certain medicine which is in the hands of one of them, the latter may not be deprived of it in order merely to satisfy the need of the former, since doing so would mean eliminating one *darar* by its equivalent. According to yet another legal maxim, "harm is to be prevented to the extent that is possible" (*al-darar yudfa'u bi qadr al-imkan*) (article 31). This maxim carries to its logical conclusion the basic message of the Qur'anic text, which declares that "Allah does not impose on a soul a burden beyond its capacity" (Q. 2:286). The campaign that is waged against *darar* must thus be reasonable and effective, utilizing all the available resources. This campaign should not, however, expect what is unfeasible, since unrealistic demands will exhaust everyone's energies. On a similar note, we would expect the state to make an adequate contribution to the struggle to combat AIDS. Whenever we are engaged in fighting one *darar*, the campaign should not be such that would give rise to a greater one. But if the fight against a *darar* entails what may be seen as a lesser, and inevitable, prejudice, then that may well be tolerated. This is the main message of yet another legal maxim which proclaims simply that "a lesser *darar* may be tolerated in order to eliminate a greater *darar*" (*al-darar al-ashadd yuzal bi al-darar al-akhaff*) (article 27). A comparative evaluation of one *darar* against another can be complex at times and may well involve a margin of error, but a judgment may nevertheless have to be made. For example, in the case of protecting the confidentiality of a person living with HIV on the one hand, while protecting a potential employer's interest on the other, it may not be easy to determine which involves the stronger of the two *darars*. The answer may lie in some compromise and partial protection of both interests. It would, on the other hand, be arbitrary if a Person Living with HIV involved in an accident was deprived of medical services for fear of transmission of disease. Here the perceived *darar* is merely a fear, not a genuine *darar*, since it can be averted with proper precautionary measures.

In the event of a conflict between private/personal and public/social interests, *darar* to the former may be tolerated in order to protect the latter. Thus according to another legal maxim, "a particular *darar* may be tolerated in order to prevent a general one (*yutahammal al-darar al-khass li-daf' al-darar al-'am*)" (article 26). For example, should a conflict arise between the interests of an individual, or a group of individuals, and that of the community at large, the latter must prevail. This, however, does not allow a total disregard of the minority interest. We follow the public interest as a matter of priority but protect the private interest as much as possible under the circumstances. Imam Abu Hamid al-Ghazali (d. 505 AH/1111 CE) has given an extreme example of such a clash of interests: the safety of a ship on the high seas that seemingly depends on throwing off some of its passengers in order to save the rest from imminent danger. Ghazali rejects this option simply because the choice here involves total destruction of the lives of the selected few. When we speak of interest (*maslahah*) and of *darar*, Ghazali added, we usually speak in relative terms, but death is so final that it leaves no room for reconciliation and compromise of interests. Ghazali concluded that God alone will decide and we should leave the matter to *tawakkul* (trust) in Him (Ghazali, n.d., 247–249).

We can also envisage a conflict of interests in regard to the question whether a written consent should be a prerequisite of HIV testing in cases relating to what are commonly perceived as high risk or particularly vulnerable groups: prostitutes, drug addicts, and prisoners. The question of compelling HIV testing can perhaps be determined in the light of the legal maxim before us. Since the issue is primarily one of public interest, it would be for the government to decide. In my opinion, bearing in mind the nature of the pandemic facing us, overriding the individual right of consent is, in some cases at least, a sacrifice that has to be made if we are to protect the public against the spread of HIV.

All of these maxims on *darar* are in turn founded on the authority of the following hadith: "Harm is neither inflicted nor reciprocated in Islam" (*la darar wa la dirar fi-al-Islam*) (Ibn Māja, no. 2340; see also *The Mejelle*, article 19). This hadith provides basic textual authority for almost all the legal maxims on the subject of *darar*. Its message is far-reaching and it has been widely utilized as a basis of many a legal ruling of the Shari'ah. Its immediate message is that no one may inflict a harm on another (note that the text of the hadith is not even confined to human beings), but when a harm is inflicted, whether by accident or design, then the injured party must not reciprocate it. While the victims of *darar* are, of course, entitled to seek judicial relief, they must not reciprocate harm by way of personal vendetta and retaliation. It is equally clear from this hadith that *darar* should neither be tolerated nor condoned and that we need to be vigilant and alert in the face of all *darar* that threaten the safety of the five essential values, as noted above.

In the event that *darar* amounts to what may be seen as an emergency situation, a calamity that may be overwhelming, debilitating, and dangerous for everyone, there comes a point where the normal rules of law may be abandoned in order to wage an effective campaign against it. This is the exclusive subject of another legal maxim, which simply declares that "necessity makes the unlawful lawful" (*al-darurat tubih al-mahzurat*) (article 21). The principle here reflects some of the Qur'anic *ayat* on the subject of necessity (cf. *Surah al-Baqarah* 2:173; *Surah al-Ma'idah* 5:3) and represents an indisputable guideline of the Shari'ah. The substance of this maxim is to treat emergency situations and the stress on necessity on their own grounds: to give a suitable response which is in the best interest of the people, to prevent or contain *darar* as far as possible, and to assist those who are afflicted in the true Islamic and humanitarian spirit of compassion (*rahmah*). Some conditions need to be observed, as are discussed below, but essentially any measures that are taken in pursuit of this response will be in harmony with the objectives of Shari'ah and its goal of protecting human life, eliminating *darar* in all of its manifestations, and safeguarding the essential values which are the sine qua non of normal life and order in society.

Darurah (necessity) and *darar* (harm) are derived from the same root word, *darra* (to face adversity); they are interrelated in the sense that situations of necessity are often those where one is faced with fighting or preventing a *darar* (Mubarak, 1998, 28). Necessity is defined as a situation which presents:

> fear of destruction or substantial harm to one of the essential values involving oneself or another human being; the fear is perceived either with certainty or strong probability in such a way that the destruction or damage will occur, either immediately or later, if action is not taken to prevent it. (ibid.)

The jurists have drawn a distinction between necessity of the first degree (*darurah*) and that of the second degree (*hajah*) and added that this distinction holds good in respect of individuals but in respect of the community as a whole the two become one and necessity of the second degree is elevated to that of the first rank (Ibn Taymiyyah, 1965, vol. 29, p. 64). For example, to make penicillin available to someone suffering from a non-lethal illness may be ranked as *hajah* but to have penicillin available in the market-place and hospitals is a *darurah* of the first rank.

Darurah in individual cases is often related to life-threatening situations, in which case what is forbidden may be done to the extent necessary: to eat forbidden substances in order to prevent death from starvation, to cure a patient with a medicine that consists of impure substances, to carry out an autopsy on human remains, and abortion in advanced stages of pregnancy in order to save the life of the mother – these are all typical examples of *darurah* in individual cases. With reference to preventive measures designed to protect the public against the spread of HIV, the two degrees of necessity we have distinguished are likely to become one. We do not normally anticipate that this campaign will entail violation of the commands and prohibitions of Shari'ah. Should there be a case of direct clash, however, where observing a strict rule of Shari'ah means abandoning the campaign, even in a partial sense, then the prohibition may be ignored. If the campaign against HIV means, in the case of an individual, that some of his rights are violated, this may also be allowed on an exceptional basis. It should be noted, however, that the law generally advises a restrictive, as opposed to a liberal, approach toward the rules of necessity which lead to neglect of the rights and liberties of people.

Another legal maxim concerning necessity has it that "necessity must be measured in accordance to its true proportions" (*al-darurat tuqdar biqadriha*) (article 22). This obviously means that once the state of necessity has come to an end then recourse must be had to normal rules. The exceptional concessions that are granted on grounds of necessity cease to apply. For instance, a sick person is allowed to perform the *salah* (daily prayers) while sitting, but when he or she recovers, whether after a week or a month or any length of time, he or she is expected to perform the *salah* in the normal manner as of that time. Similarly if someone has to consume forbidden food in order to avert starvation, he or she should do so to the extent necessary but no more. It is recommended that the person should himself do whatever he can to terminate indulgence in prohibitions on grounds of necessity (Mubarak, 1998, 366). Applying this maxim to the issue before us, one might say that certain concessions that might be granted to the PLWHIV in the areas of working hours, choice of work, or matters of worship should be in accordance with his or her condition and individual needs, and should be ended when no longer needed. To take an overly exaggerated and phobia-driven view of AIDS on the one hand and to disregard the reasonable needs of the PLWHIV on the other would both be against the rational advice of the legal maxim we have just reviewed.

In response to the question as to who is qualified to invoke *daru-rah* in a particular situation, the jurists have envisaged two possibilities. In the event where the decision concerns the community in general, only the lawful government is authorized to make it. It is thus stated that during the time of the Caliph 'Umar al-Khattab (d. 644) when famine became widespread, the Caliph made a decision to suspend the implementation of the *hadd* punishment for theft. In personal matters where *darurah* concerns individuals without it having a direct bearing on public interest, it is for the individual to exercise his best judgment and make a decision himself (Abu Sulayman, 1993, 62). *Darurah* often represents a conflict between two interests and involves a decision as to which should take priority over the other. In matters involving indulgence in *haram* (prohibited acts) on the ground of *darurah* it is important to carry out an exhaustive enquiry into the possibility of a lawful alternative which would avert indulgence in *haram*. If a lawful alternative can be found then it must be taken as a matter of priority (Mubarak, 1998, 302).

Four conditions must be observed in the determination of *darurah*.

First, given that *darurah* aims at vindicating the basic objectives (*maqasid*) of the Shari'ah, recourse to *darurah* must also be consistent with these objectives. The *maqasid*, in other words, provide the general framework for the application of *darurah*. This also implies that complete reliance on rationality without any reference to the value structure of the Shari'ah is not recommended. As already noted, *darurah* often involves two interests or objectives, both of which are recognized Shari'ah values, one of which is given preference over the other. A person may thus not indulge in "sexual gratification and indecency (*al-fawahish*) in the name of *darurah*, despite some claims to the contrary" (al-Jawziyyah, 1961, 241–242; Mubarak, 1998, 306–307). The question has arisen, for example, whether *darurah* can be invoked in support of distribution of condoms among prisoners in order to prevent the spread of HIV. There are two weak links here, one of which is the question of certainty as to whether distribution of condoms will actually result in their proper use and therefore achieve the purpose, and the other is that one of the two sides in the equation violates the stated objectives of Islam in regard to preserving the moral integrity of the community. There are uncertainties, to say the least, and in my opinion *darurah* is not the best frame of reference for the question raised.

Second, *darurah* must be a present reality as opposed to a mere expectation, and unless it has actually occurred, recourse to it is not recommended. Although some jurists have accepted strong probability (*al-zann al-qawi*) as a substitute for certainty, most of the examples that occur in juristic works relate to starvation and disease which are actually present (Mubarak, 1998, 312).

Third, acting on *darurah* must not lead to an evil equal to, or greater than, the one averted by it. The substance of this condition is in fact confirmed by the maxim cited earlier, that a lesser harm is to be tolerated in order to prevent a greater one but not vice versa (Abu Sulayman, 1993, 65; Mubarak, 1998, 319).

The fourth and final condition is that acting on *darurah* must be only to the extent of averting the danger, and *darurah* comes to an end when that danger is no longer present. The substance of this condition has also been covered in a separate legal maxim, discussed above, that "necessity must be measured in accordance with its true proportions" (Abu Sulayman, 1993, 66).

TOWARDS A THEOLOGY OF COMPASSION

Whenever we note a reference in the Qur'an and the *Sunnah* of the Prophet to illness and disease, there is a parallel reference to the importance of showing sympathy, compassion, and support to those afflicted with disease. It is equally evident that no attempt is made to exclude any particular type of patient or disease from the scope of that invitation and advice. *All* patients remain entitled to these things, and Persons Living with HIV are no exception. It would indeed be arbitrary, and contrary to the moral norms of Islam, to discriminate against any unwell person with regard to the help society and state may be able to give them. If there is any background of deviant behavior or injustice they may have done to themselves – which does not amount to crime – that must remain a matter between the individual and his or her Creator. As we learn from the clear messages of the hadith, God will show mercy to those that suffer from illness. With regard to the Islamic duty towards the PLWHIV, we read a definitive statement in a widely reported hadith: "a Muslim is one from whose tongue and hand other Muslims are safe" (*Bukhari*, vol. 1, book 2, no. 9). The word "Muslim" could here be read as a substitute for "human being" without altering the spirit of the message conveyed. This attitude has, in turn, been directly linked with the essence of Islam when we read in another hadith that "none of you is a (true) believer unless you like for your brother what you like for yourself" (Muslim, hadith no. 69).

The Shari'ah advises care and compassion for the sick and disabled and grants them special concessions with regard to daily religious duties. They are accordingly allowed to take a dry ablution (*tayammum*) instead of an ablution proper (*wudu'*), and then to perform the prayer in an easier variation such as sitting instead of standing, to combine two prayers at the same time, to postpone or abandon the fasting of Ramadan, and so forth (cf. al-Zuhayli, 1990, 135). It is highly recommended for friends and relatives to visit the patient as a gesture of sympathy and support. The noble Prophet was diligent in visiting the sick and when he laid down in a hadith six rights that Muslims have over one another, he included "returning a greeting, visiting the sick, responding to invitations, giving sincere advice (*nasihah*)" (Muslim, cited in al-Nishaburi, 1984, hadith no. 1418), and made no distinction whatsoever as to the type or origin of illness. When sick people are no longer able to earn a living and are in need of support, it becomes the duty of their close relatives to provide them with maintenance during illness. In the event of people having no relatives to support them, the duty falls on the state to provide them with basic necessities including medical treatment, and service in the case of those who are disabled (Abu Zahrah, n.d., 147).

There is no room whatsoever for prejudice and discrimination in this attitude, and when it comes to medical assistance and treatment, PLWHIV are no different to other unwell people; they are all entitled to equal treatment, compassion, and service, without any reference to the origins and causes of their condition.

As long as AIDS remains incurable, preventive measures through health education must remain the primary target of the campaign against it. As for those who are already infected with the virus, the main focus of the campaign can no longer be on preventive measures. As far as the PLWHIV is concerned, the focus of the anti-AIDS campaign must be on developing an effective support system within the family, the health services, and the community at large. This is precisely where the community needs to pool its resources and renew and revise its strategy from time to time in order to develop an effective support network for PLWHIV, and this is also where the religious bodies and religious leaders can play an important role. It is by no means an exaggeration to say that correct and purposeful religious advice and education remain one of the main challenges in developing an effective support system for the PLWHIV.

The main task facing religious leaders, religious bodies, and religious education in this campaign is to try and eliminate negative social attitudes toward AIDS and the people living with HIV. These negative attitudes are extremely debilitating and serious when we learn that PLWHIV are often stigmatized and avoided even by their own family and friends. These people can barely cope with the torment involved in being afflicted with an incurable disease, and still they are confronted by what for many must amount to insurmountable prejudice and stigma. This is contrary to the advice of compassion, understanding, and support that lies at the heart of Islamic teachings.

The only valid course and advice for those facing a health condition for which there is no currently available cure is to try, within the limits of their capacity, not to sink into total despair and to remain hopeful for the grace of their Merciful creator – and for the rest of us to support them in every way that we can. This is the clear and unambiguous advice of Islam, and the profound validity and strength of this advice is even more evident in our own times. The effort on the part of the victims of the (incurable) disease to keep the ray of hope alive in themselves will provide each person with the incentive to follow correct advice and offer a constructive response to expert assistance and support. We need to understand our position, both as Muslims and as caring individuals: in our treatment of the ill and the afflicted we are not dealing with a sin – we may not even know whether there has been a sin committed at all – but with a human tragedy that calls for sympathy and support, not revulsion and disdain. To keep our attitude clear between these two diametrically opposite responses, which are prone to confusion, is a part of our responsibility as sensitive and caring individuals.

Our health education policy should be in keeping with the moral values of Islam and the customs and culture of our society, yet we should avoid the temptation of turning that policy into a chapter on moral education. As we learn from the teachings of our Prophet, "religion is sound advice – *al-din al-nasihah*" (Muslim, 2/37). Sound advice and religion both tell us that in combating calamity and *darar* our priority must be to try and be as relevant and effective as possible. This would imply that we need to take affirmative action and address issues on their own grounds. This, I believe, should be the essence of good advice, one which is in total harmony with the rules of Shari'ah relating to *darar*. We must try to be realistic and affirmative while acting in harmony with the moral and cultural values of our society. In the event of a conflict between the two, and in places where fighting a lethal *darar* entails unavoidable sacrifice of our moral and religious values, then fighting *darar* takes priority over conformity to religious rules. This is the essence of the realism in Islam which favours efficiency and rational advice, and which should be reflected in our heath education and disease prevention strategies.

CONCLUSION

Prejudice and stigma are undoubtedly among the major obstacles and challenges of this campaign; they remain insidious, and can be expected neither to disappear nor to be totally eliminated. This essay has for the most part been expressive of concern for the protection of the essential values of faith, life, intellect, property, and family – and has explored some of the resources of Islamic law that could be utilized toward that end. The values we have discussed are upheld not only by Islam, but by civilized society and almost all the great traditions of the world. The specific themes and principles of *darurah* (necessity), *darar*, and the value of compassion have identified the avenues we can take to relate the Shari'ah to the anti-AIDS campaign, educate the public, and provide advice and support both for the PLWHIV and the community at large. I may add, on a more general note, that to make this campaign effective, to muster the resources of the community in order to avert prejudice, and to further the ideals of a caring society are all admirable objectives which are also in harmony with the teachings of Islam.

BIBLIOGRAPHY

Abu Sulayman, 'Abd al-Wahhab Ibrahim 1414/1993. *Fiqh al-Darurah wa Tatbiqatuh al Mu'asarah*. Jeddah, al-Ma'had al-Islami li-al-Buhuth wa al-Tadrib.

Abu Zahrah, Muhammad n.d. *Tanzim al-Islam li al-Mujtama'*. Cairo, Matba'ah Mukhaymar.

Al-Ghazali, Abu Hamid n.d. *Shija'al-Ghalil*. Ed. Hamd al-Kabir. Baghdad, Gh Matba'ah al-Irshad.

Al-Jawziyyah, Ibn Qayyim. *Ighathah al-Lahfan min Maka'id al-Shaytan*. Ed. Muhammad Anwar al-Balataji. Cairo, Dar al-Turath al-'Arabi.

—— 1961. *Al- Turuq al-Hukmiyyah fi al-Siyasah al-Shar'iyyah*. Cairo, al-Mu'assasah al-'Arabiyyah li al-Tiba'ah.

Al-Maqdisi, ibn Qudamah 1401/1981. *Al-Mughni*, III. Riyad, Maktabah al-Riyad al-Hadithah.

Al-Nishaburi, Muslim bin Hajjaj 1984. *Mukhtasar Sahih Muslim*. Ed. Muhammad Nasir al-Din al-Albani. Beirut, Dar al-Maktab al-Islami.

Al-Zuhayli, Wahbah 1990. *Al-Darurah al-Shar'iyyah*. 4th edn. Beirut, Mu'assasah Dar al-Fikr.

Ibn Taymiyyah, 1965. *Majmu' Fatawa Shaykh al-Islam Ibn Taymiyyah*, vol. 29. Ed. 'Abd al- Rahman ibn Qasim. Beirut, Mu'assasah al-Risalah H.

Ibn Māja 1981. *Sunan Ibn Māja*. Istanbul, Cagri Yayinlari.

Kamali, M.H. 1989. "*Siyasah Shar'iyyah* – on the Policies of Islamic Government." *The American Journal of Islamic Social Sciences*, 6, 59–81.

Mubarak, Jamil Muhammad 1408/1998. *Nazariyyah al-Darulralr al-Slar'iyyalr*. Cairo, Dar al-Wafa'li'l- Taba'ah wa'-Nashr.

Taj, 'Abd al-Rahman 1953. *Al-Siyasah al-Shar'iyyah wa al-Fiqh al-Islami*. Cairo, Matba 'ah Dar al-Ta'lif.

The Mejelle 1967. Trans. C.R. Tyser. Lahore, Law Publishing Co.

6

GENDER JUSTICE, ISLAM, AND AIDS

Clara Koh

INTRODUCTION

AIDS first appeared in the West as a disease of men. Despite early data indicating infection amongst female hemophiliacs, injecting drug users, female partners of men in those categories, and poor women in developing countries, women's vulnerability to HIV was distorted and ignored in scientific and popular discourse in the West. Recent statistics on global HIV infection reveal that forty-eight percent of adults living with HIV are women (UNAIDS, 2006) – a sharp increase from thirty-five percent in 1985 (UNAIDS, 2004). Among young women between the ages of 15 and 24, that percentage jumps to a startling sixty percent (UNAIDS, 2004). If one notes that ninety-three percent of new HIV infections occur in developing countries, it becomes clear that the face of AIDS in the twenty-first century is one of poor women (Farmer, 2000, 40).

Since 1985, Muslim ethical literature has construed AIDS as an illness pertaining to the Western homosexual world (Francesca, 2002, 381). The early response of most Muslim countries was one of denial and presenting the pandemic as a consequence of the decadent sexual morals of "other" countries (Obermeyer, 2006, 851). When presented with supposedly "clearly innocent victims" such as children, the suggestion was usually they were "undergoing a divine trial for the sins of a perverted society" (ibid., 381). In particular, Muslim authorities have neglected to address women's vulnerability to HIV infection.

Current research on gender, HIV, and AIDS has reiterated that women are both biologically and socially more susceptible to infection, in the context of consistent patterns of gender inequality and poverty worldwide (Gupta, 2000; Türmen, 2003, 411–417; UNAIDS, 2004). According to Rao Gupta, president of the International Center for Research on Women (ICRW), "[t]he unequal power balance in gender relations that favors men translates into an unequal power balance in heterosexual interactions, in which . . . men have greater control than women over when, where, and how sex takes place" (Gupta, 2000, 2). This hampers women's ability to negotiate safer sex, even within marriage, and protect themselves from HIV infection. In the words of Marina Mahathir of the Malaysian AIDS Council, "It is a fact not repeated enough that 90% of women who have been infected with HIV have only ever slept with one man in their lives, their husbands" (cited in Barnett and Whiteside, 2002, 185). These data seriously challenge the view that Muslim sexual regulations render Muslims immune to HIV infection. What is desperately needed is an honest critique of the patriarchal conservatism in religious fundamentalism that undergirds women's vulnerability to HIV.

Islamists have consistently propounded that Islam provides women with rights and gender equality, albeit different from "Western" paradigms. Nonetheless, language of "equality" and "rights" often obscures patriarchal tendencies to control and restrict women's social, economic, sexual, and reproductive autonomy. This rhetoric, however, needs to be contextualized in a larger global discourse of identity politics, wherein essentialized categories of the "West" and "Islam" are pitted against each other. In this "clash of civilizations", both parties use women's rights to elevate their own chivalry and point out the misogyny of the "Other". This has meant that debates surrounding Muslim women's rights have not materialized into substantive change; instead, they have led to more restrictive conditions for women through the "War on Terror" and political Islam.

Paul Farmer points out that "[e]sssentialist notions of [. . .] 'otherness' [tend to] reinforc[e] a hazardous tendency to conflate the outcomes of structural violence and cultural differences" (Farmer, 2000, 66). Conservative Muslim rhetoric, in maintaining that AIDS is a disease of the West and that (Western) women's rights lead to sexual promiscuity and AIDS, activates categories of "otherness" to avoid seriously engaging with the exigencies of the pandemic.

Similarly, Western discourses turn a blind eye to local epidemics to scrutinize the "exotic" and peculiar sexual practices of non-Western cultures (ibid., 66). Both use identity politics to overlook the structural poverty and gender inequality that transcend the boundaries of nation, religion, or culture, and which lay the groundwork for the spread of AIDS. Perhaps most grievous in this battle of discourses is the objectification of Muslim women as each party tries to culturally emasculate the other – all this at the expense of women's security and well-being in an era of AIDS.

WOMEN'S VULNERABILITY TO HIV

A host of biological factors make women more susceptible to HIV infection than men. Some studies have found that the rate of male-to-female transmission of HIV is between two and four times more efficient than its opposite (Türmen, 2003, 412). This can be explained by the greater concentration of HIV in seminal fluids than in vaginal secretions, as well as the extensive convoluted lining of the vagina and cervix which allow the virus to more easily enter the bloodstream (Farmer, 2000, 47). However, "[w]hat appear to be [merely] biological differences in disease and clinical manifestations may, in fact, be a reflection of gender inequalities in society" (ibid., 47). In early first coitus, young women are especially vulnerable to infection since the immature reproductive tract experiences genital trauma in the absence of adequate cell layers and secretions. For the same reason, cultural practices that privilege male pleasure such as dry sex render mature women susceptible to infection. Co-infection with other sexually transmitted diseases (STDs), which again disproportionately affect women, further increases the risks of HIV infection in women and girls. Since gonorrhea and syphilis are asymptomatic in fifty to eighty percent of women, but only ten percent of men, women are less likely to seek treatment (ibid., 50). However, even if women recognize STDs, social stigma and lack of finances and facilities may deter them from receiving treatment.

In discussing women's vulnerability to HIV, Rao Gupta highlights that structures of gender inequality are intimately linked to social constructions of sexual behavior and norms (Gupta, 2000, 2–3). Whereas variations in gender roles exist across cultures, studies persistently indicate that women possess less control over resources than men. This inequality and imbalance of power is reflected in the dynamics of heterosexual interaction, wherein men's sexual pleasure supersedes that of women, and men control the circumstances of sexual intercourse. This power imbalance is secured by cultural norms and expectations that govern gender and sexual relations, institutionalizing women's sexual subordination and, subsequently, their vulnerability to HIV. Societal conventions that demand women's sexual ignorance and prize women's virginity put women at risk of infection. These contexts, coupled with a pervasive lack of education for girls, leave women uninformed about sex, reproductive health, or HIV/AIDS (UNAIDS, 2004). To avoid suspicion about their virginity, regardless of their actual status, women are unable actively to solicit information or seek treatment in the event of contracting STDs. In a 2004 UNAIDS report, about eighty percent of young women globally did not have "sufficient" knowledge about HIV or AIDS. In regions such as South-East Asia and sub-Saharan Africa, up to fifty percent of young women are unaware that the condom is an effective means of prevention. Nonetheless, even if women are aware of preventive measures, they often do not have the negotiating power to insist on safer sex. Emphasis on men's sexual pleasure make it difficult for women to insist on monogamy or refuse dangerous sex that they believe is pleasurable for their male partners (Gupta et al., 1996, 342). In addition, lack of education or access to formal employment and laws that deny women the right to inherit, own, or manage resources make women economically dependent on men. As a result, women are unable to refuse high-risk sexual intercourse for fear of economic dispossession. For instance, in a study in Mumbai women saw the financial consequences of leaving a high-risk relationship as far worse than staying in it (George, in Gupta, 2002, 183).

Gender violence, affecting ten to sixty-nine percent of women worldwide, is considered the leading cause of HIV infection in women (UNAIDS, 2004). Studies have also shown that one-third to one-half of physically abused women also experience sexual violence (Heise, Ellsberg, and Gottemoeller, 1999, quoted in Gupta, 2000, 3). According to a study carried out in Dar es Salaam, Tanzania, HIV positive women were more than two times as likely to have experienced partner violence than HIV negative women (Maman, 2002, 1333). This same study found that cultural norms on masculinity legitimate partner abuse: up to forty-one percent of women participants justified at least one incident of violence on the basis of disobedience, infidelity, and non-completion of household work. Further, no less than forty-four percent of female participants agreed that women do not have the right to refuse sex after being beaten by their partner.

Undergirding women's susceptibility to infection is poverty. Studies carried out in Africa, Haiti, India, and South-East Asia indicate that high rates of AIDS are "intimately linked" to histories of under-development and worsening inequality (Farmer, 2000, 56). Indeed, poverty compounds biological and social inequalities, exacerbating women's vulnerability to infection. In countries affected by Structural Adjustment Programs of the World Bank and International Monetary Fund, rollbacks on government spending and the privatization of social services have acute consequences upon the poor. In particular, women and girls become the "shock absorbers" of the restructured economy and care providers in households on the verge of survival (Wamala and Kawachi, 2007, 172). Among the complex factors that make women in these circumstances vulnerable to infection is their entry into the informal labor sector, which may include or be supplemented by sex work, thereby putting them at high risk of infection (Kirmani and Munyakho, 1996, 333–350).

The above discussion underscores the various ways in which biological factors, gender inequality, and poverty work together to make women susceptible to HIV infection. Although women's rights discourse looms large in the international arena, the challenge of gender justice faces a political obstacle where Islamist groups have been increasingly active. The issue of Muslim women has historically been a cause célèbre within identity politics between the "West" and "Islam." Today, women's rights discourse continues to be embedded in this larger exchange, posing considerable challenges to realizing any real gender justice for Muslim women.

THE POLITICS OF MUSLIM WOMEN'S RIGHTS

The 2006 UN epidemiology report on the Sudan highlights a generalized HIV epidemic in the country. Decades of war and massive social dislocation and insecurity for women and children have facilitated the rapid spread of the disease. For instance, HIV prevalence as high as 4.4% has been found among displaced adults along the Ugandan border. A 2007 *New York Times* article reports fears of escalating numbers of HIV infections in Afghanistan, a country that is emerging from conflict. Socio-economic upheaval, migration of refugees and foreigners, and a resurgent drug economy have rendered Afghans extremely vulnerable to the epidemic. While little data on HIV/AIDS has come out of Iraq, its virtually non-existent security, societal disruption, and rising levels of prostitution and sexual assault on women may also place Iraqis at increased risk (Al-Ali, 2005, 755–756; Al-Ali, 2007).

Amidst these vulnerabilities, the US and its allies in the "War on Terror" proclaim "liberation" for Muslim women from under an "oppressive Islam." Likewise, Islamist groups and conservative religious authorities continue to reject "Western" paradigms for women's rights, touting an Islamic gender "equity" while remaining silent about the violence enacted upon Muslim women in the Sudan and elsewhere, by Muslims and Islamists alike (Abd El-Hadi, 1996, 47–54). These contradictions bespeak the hypocrisy behind discourses on Muslim women's liberation, and their instrumentality in identity politics between the "West" and "Islam." In this section, I will examine the politics of Muslim women's rights and argue for the need to transcend categories of "West" and "Islam" in order to empower women in the context of HIV and AIDS.

The construction of the opposing categories of the "West" and "Islam" can be traced back to the colonial period, and has found recent popularity in the "clash of civilizations" narrative. In this Manichean system, "Islam and Muslims have become the foils for [Western] modernity, freedom and the civilized world," while the Muslim woman represents the boundary between the two competing identities (Zine, 2006, 2). According to the West's myth of its superiority, Muslim women are oppressed by Islam and can only be liberated through Western norms and values. This myth, ignoring complex structures of injustice such as poverty and conflict, in which Western countries are complicit, reduces the cause of women's problems to a misogynist Islam. Thus, this myth functions to produce public consent for the capitalist, expansionist enterprises of Western nations into Muslim lands. This also allows Western countries to overlook its own acts of misogyny within its borders and without, the latter brought about through global schemes that restructure economies and undermine social security in Third World countries.

The policing of the boundary (and hierarchy) between the "West" and the "Other" is performed on the bodies of Muslim women. From colonial times to the current wars in Iraq and Afghanistan, the veil has figured prominently in discourses on Muslim women's rights. In the colonial period, colonists combined European feminist narratives with imperialist agendas, producing narratives of "colonial feminism" that served to justify the West's civilizing mission in the Middle East (Ahmed, 1992, 151). Focusing on the oppression of the veil, the colonists signified women's liberation in the act of unveiling. Evidently, this trope continues to serve in the interest of the current "War on Terror", which was initially construed as a war to liberate Afghan women in *burqa* (Abu-Lughod, 2002, 785–786). However, the pure instrumentality of this rhetoric is exposed when one considers the sexual politics undergirding early colonial efforts and the current war. In the former, the Muslim woman's body was an allegory for her land and people, and was rendered pliable to military conquest and domination in European literature and artwork: the elusive, veiled Muslim woman, frustrating the male colonizer's gaze, was to be unveiled and presented in the nude in pornographic postcards that circulated during the colonial period (Zine, 2006, 6).

The process of feminizing the "Other" is the modus operandi of militarism, which is inherently masculine and antagonistic to the feminine. As such, one should not have been surprised to learn of US soldiers sexually humiliating prisoners at Abu Ghraib, through role plays in which Muslim men were made effeminate. Nor should one be shocked that pornography was used as a primer aboard the USS John F. Kennedy for US bombing missions over Iraq (ibid., 6–7). Herein lies the contradiction between the rhetoric of liberating Muslim women and the misogyny that turns women into sexual objects made amenable for masculinist projects for domination.

Muslims also participate in regulating the boundary between the "West" and "Islam," manipulating Muslim women's bodies to that end. For Islamists, Muslim women are guardians of faith and honor, and need to be protected from the seduction and corruption of Western morals (ibid., 11). In Iraq, heightened local sentiments of opposition to Western invasion and occupation have positioned Iraqi women as the vanguard against Western cultural and political imposition (Al-Ali, 2005, 741). The issue of women's honor has become an obsession, and honor killings have been on the rise, creating a climate of fear for women and girls in Iraq. Increasingly, radical Islamist groups have demanded that women wear the headscarf, physically harassing uncovered women in the streets. Anti-West emotions have also led many Iraqis, who might have been sympathetic to or supportive of women's empowerment in different circumstances, to view women's equality negatively as an intrusion of Western values into Iraqi society.

Feminist scholars and activists have long identified and underscored the impact of identity politics upon women. In particular, they have sought to draw attention to the manipulation of gender roles in statecraft for the purpose of nationalism prior to engaging in conflict. Within these processes, women are valorized as reproducers of the nation and the nation's culture, while men are glorified as the protectors of the feminized nation. Concerning women's role, "[t]he patriarchal family, microcosm of the nation, governs women's behaviour because only their sexual containment guarantees the purity of the bloodline and the honour of the family" (Cockburn, 1998, 43). The construction of Muslim women in Islamist identity politics is no different. The discourse of authenticity and purity in returning to the fundamentals of religion, unsullied by Western modernity, also coincides with greater control over women's autonomy and sexuality within the patriarchal state and family. Ayesha Imam presents several examples in Afghanistan, Algeria, Bangladesh, Iran, Nigeria, and the Sudan, wherein the management of Muslim women's sexuality and fertility (e.g. abortion and use of contraception) was brought into the hands of men and the state. In some extreme cases, women's defiance of imposed rules led to violent punishment and even death (Imam, 2000, 128–132).

This brief discussion highlights how identity politics are obstacles to realizing women's equality and empowerment in Muslim societies. It is crucial to recognize that Islamist and Western discourses on Muslim women's rights are two sides of the same coin, the former reacting against the latter's denigration of Islam as misogynist and backward. In the context of HIV and AIDS, the rejection of women's rights places women at risk of a debilitating disease that makes no distinction between the "West" and "Islam."

ISLAMIC FEMINISM

Islamist misogynist discourses, however, have not gone uncontested. Scholar-activists for gender justice have reinterpreted religious texts to challenge the dominance of patriarchal interpretations of Islam, while departing from the identity politics of the "West" and "Islam." In the following section, I shall discuss the work of Islamic feminism, and attempt to evaluate the promise and limitations this movement brings to gender justice in the context of HIV and AIDS.

Muslim women have historically been producers of feminist[1] discourses and active participants in feminist movements in the Middle East and elsewhere. Islamic feminists engage in the dual task of challenging patriarchal elements within Islamic tradition and practice and contesting neo-colonial feminist discourses in Islam that construe Islam as inherently misogynist (Shaikh, 2003, 155).

Islamic feminists take their mandate for gender equality and justice from the Qur'anic message of radical equality amongst all human beings. They insist that women's rights are not inimical to Islam, and ground their scholarship-activism in Qur'anic concepts such as *'adl* (justice), *tawhid* (unity of God), *ihsan* (benevolence), and *rahmah* (compassion) (Wadud, 1999, 25–26; Engineer, 2001, 112; Barlas, 2002, 13). Traditional Islamic methodologies of *ijtihad* (independent reasoning) and *tafsir* (exegesis) are employed to re-engage with theology (e.g. Hosni Abboud), shari'ah (e.g. Azizah al-Hibri), hadith (e.g. Fatimah Mernissi) and Qur'an (e.g. Amina Wadud, Riffat Hassan). Traditional methodologies are complemented with the social sciences, such as linguistics, literary criticism, sociology, anthropology, and history. Islamic feminists argue that the discrepancy between the Qur'an's message of gender equality and patriarchal tendencies in Muslim practice and tradition is a consequence of flawed, human interpretation of the Qur'an. Wadud cites two reasons for the distortion of the Qur'an's egalitarian vision: 1) interpretation of the text was exclusively a male activity, and 2) the socio-political context of the male interpreters was andocentric (Wadud, 1999, 1).

Using hermeneutical keys that are found in the Qur'an, Islamic feminists seek to retrieve the Qur'an's message for radical human equality to debunk the dominant patriarchal narrative. Asma Barlas, for example, relies on the Qur'an's "auto-hermeneutics" of "Divine

Self-Disclosure" to direct her rereading of the text (Barlas, 2002, 25). For Barlas, the "Divine Ontology" constitutes the three principles of Divine Unity (*tawhid*), Justness (God cannot commit *zulm* or harm), and Incomparability (ibid., 13). Arguing from the precept that God does not commit *zulm* (broadly defined as "injustice resulting from transgressing against another person's rights" (ibid., 204)), Barlas contends that God's speech cannot teach *zulm*. It therefore follows that readings of the Qur'an that justify sexual inequality – clear infringements upon women's full human dignity – are misunderstandings of God's intent. Relying on the principle of *tawhid*, Barlas argues that assertions for father- or husband-rule are inconsistent with the indivisibility of God's sovereignty. For Wadud, the Qur'an's *Weltanschauung* constitutes "concepts of justice towards humankind, human dignity, equal rights before the law and before Allah, mutual responsibility, and equitable relations between humans" (Wadud, 1999, 63). Accordingly, Wadud contends that the Qur'an affirms that a woman is "primordially, cosmologically, eschatologically, spiritually, and morally a full human being," equal to all who profess faith in Islam (ibid., ix–x).

However, the Qur'an is not without its difficult passages that appear to conflict with this message. Many Muslim feminists rely on the hermeneutics of Fazlur Rahman to engage with this issue. This approach accepts the specificity of revelation in particular contexts while affirming that the Qur'an proposes moral values that are "extrahistorical" and "transcendental" (ibid., 29). Thus, underlying particular injunctions and principles is the Qur'anic intent or meaning, which undercuts the specificity of the revelation, allowing this meaning to be adaptable to new environments and ethical standards for gender justice. In this hermeneutical approach, the Qur'an is understood to set out "a logical progression with regard to the development of human interactions, morality, and ethics" (ibid., 63). Accordingly, this system takes into account why certain misogynistic practices, such as female infanticide, were immediately abolished, whereas others, such as polygamy and marital violence, were only modified (ibid., 9). For Wadud, this gradual reform of patriarchal practices was to meet man at the level of his depravity: "God's permissibility only showed man's cruel heart [. . .] Had it not been for the viciousness in his mind [. . .] God would not have granted him then such allowances that He disliked and which were meant to vanish with time" (ibid., 82).

Similarly, Engineer recognizes that "[t]he Qur'an was certainly mindful of what was just in the era when it was revealed and what ought to be just in the transcendental sense" (Engineer, 2001, 124). It is this dynamic between "is" and "ought," or between history and eternity, that informs the spirit of the Qur'an. Thus, when the Prophet permitted a Muslim wife retaliation against her husband as a measure of justice, the Qur'an overruled him and permitted a measure of conditional male dominance (Q. 4:34), since the Prophet's recommendation would not have been accepted in that society. With respect to the fact that a daughter inherits only half of what a son receives (Q. 4:11), Engineer reminds his readers that this verse was revolutionary for its time, since daughters in pre-Islamic society did not inherit at all. This verse, though bestowing favor on the son, is actually "cautious reform" on the part of the Qur'an (ibid., 126). Understood against other provisions for women such as the *mahr* (dower) and the fact that wives are not required to maintain their husbands financially, Engineer suggests that this verse ultimately does no injustice to women. Barlas argues that "justice consists not only in treating like cases alike but also in treating them differently," so at times different treatment in the Qur'an serves to protect the interests of women, and not to justify male privilege (Barlas, 2002, 132, 197–198).

ISLAMIC FEMINISM: PROMISE AND LIMITATIONS

Islamic feminists, who are reinterpreting religious texts and challenging patriarchal traditions, have been "discredited and maligned" by the conservative and patriarchal forces in the global *umma* (Badran, 2006). Despite this opposition, it is becoming increasingly difficult to square Islamic notions of justice and equality with patriarchal beliefs and practices endorsed by conservative male religious authorities. As such, even as the messenger and her authority are attacked, the new gender-sensitive scholarship is gradually becoming authoritative in the global *umma*. Ziba Mir-Hosseini has identified shifts in feminist scholarship in Islam which she argues will have crucial tactical import (Mir-Hosseini, 1999, 4–7). Conventionally separate and hermetic strands of feminist discourse, which she calls "*shari'a*-based" and "feminism-based," have begun a rapprochement. In particular,

Mir-Hosseini cites the example of Fatimah Mernissi and compares two of her publications: *Le harem politique* (1987) and *Beyond the Veil: Male-Female Dynamics in Muslim Society* (first published in 1975). Mir-Hosseini notes that, while the earlier work conformed to the feminism-based genre by exposing the patriarchal logic of Islamic texts, the later work fits more with the shari'a-based genre in that it seeks to discover new and egalitarian readings of sacred texts. According to Mir-Hosseini, Mernissi is one among many scholars from both genres who have begun to take seriously the other's arguments and approaches.

Despite the positive outlook projected by proponents of Islamic feminism, criticisms of Islamic feminist methodologies outline the limitations of the movement for achieving gender justice. Critics highlight that the Qur'an is so threaded with patriarchal norms that interpretations for radical equality between women and men are only possible through "hermeneutical acrobatics" or distortions of the text. As Ebrahim Moosa says, "[M]odern Muslim interpreters, especially Muslim feminists, make too much of a few verses of the Qur'an that suggest reciprocal rights and duties between unequal spouses and then hasten to suggest that the Qur'an advocates egalitarianism as norm" (Moosa, 2003, 125).

Kecia Ali, for example, observes that there exists a systematic incompatibility between contemporary requirements of mutuality and consent for good sex, and those of classical scholars, who have derived their rulings from the Qur'an and *Sunnah* (Ali, 2006, 151). According to Ali, injunctions and regulations concerning marriage and sex are founded on the concept of *milk*, or male ownership, and are thus associated with the institution of slavery (*milk al-yamin*). This foundation, evident in the Qur'an, hadith, and classical jurisprudence, structurally contradicts contemporary standards of equity and mutuality between women and men. While some feminist or reformist strategies appeal to the andocentrism of the medieval scholars while leaving the Qur'an blame-free, Ali affirms the accountability of the Qur'an in its endorsement of gender inequality (e.g. the unilateral right of the *talaq*). She highlights that the Qur'an presents conflicting views in simultaneously exhorting mutuality (Q. 30:21), and hierarchal and andocentric provisions for marriage and sex (Ali, 2006, 152).

Apologetic tendencies on discourses relating to gender justice often overlook this incongruence in the Qur'an, with potentially fatal consequences, Ali contends. This oversight precludes fruitful discussions and clear discernment of root causes. It may also obscure or excuse certain injustices found in Islamic law. Moreover, Ali and Moosa suggest that Islamic feminist hermeneutics, which claim to "retrieve" the Qur'an's message of gender equality, veer near to the "text fundamentalism" practiced by conservative and Salafi groups. According to Moosa, those who practice text fundamentalism perpetuate the fiction that "the text actually provides the norms, and we merely 'discover' the norms," thereby allowing several competing agendas to claim the voice of Islam (Moosa, 2003, 125). In other words, Ali and Moosa caution feminists against adopting the very tools utilized by opponents of gender justice, and insist on critical hermeneutical approaches to the Qur'an which acknowledge the patriarchal and andocentric elements within the text.

In speaking from the context of the Iranian Islamic feminist movement, Valerie Moghadam adds that despite the good and necessary work of religious reinterpretation, there are limits and pitfalls with such endeavors (Moghadam, 2002, 38). She argues that working exclusively within religious frameworks distracts attention from socio-economic and political concerns, while focusing on "correct" Islamic interpretations of texts or theological argumentation. Thus, Moghadam contends that international standards for human rights, such as the United Nations Convention on the Elimination of All Forms of Discrimination Against Women (UN-CEDAW), should be a point of reference for Islamic feminists – not the Qur'an.[2] Moosa and Ali seem to concur. Moosa highlights that the Qur'an (meaning "recitation") prefigures a community of listeners and participants, so that the text ceases to be the Qur'an without its audience (Moosa, 2003, 124). Thus, he insists that Muslims depart from always finding justification in the past, in a text, or in the practice of a founder, and embrace the ethical norms of the present. This hermeneutical move was not alien to earlier scholars who produced interpretations that were, at times, contrary to verses in the Qur'an in order to meet the standards of ethical norms of the time (ibid., 126). Ali recommends historicizing the Qur'an in order to distinguish between historical precedence and individual conscience. This way, the Qur'an can be regarded as a *starting point* for ethical reflection, and not constitutive of a comprehensive system of universal ethics. Ali affirms that Muslims, as earthly vicegerents, have to take responsibility for acts of interpretation in the process of keeping Islam relevant to shifting cultural values: Muslims need genuinely to interrogate their actions rather than simply insist that what they do is "what 'Islam' requires" (Ali, 2006, 156–157).

CONCLUSION

Women and men are affected differently by HIV. Women are at a greater risk of infection because of biology, pervasive and entrenched gender and sexual inequality, and poverty. Despite the great need to empower women and affirm their rights in a time of AIDS, identity politics frustrate and stymie the realization of these rights. The "War on Terror" and the 1995 Beijing Conference on Women and its aftermath have both been international arenas in which discourses on women's rights were exchanged and contested. However, neither situation brought about real and positive changes for women. In fact, stated concerns for gender equality and women's liberation merely functioned to garner popular support and moral legitimacy for specific power agendas. Islamic feminism situates itself within these contestations for power, but aspires to a multiple critique of identity politics in its struggle for gender justice. Although some scholars are optimistic about the positive changes Islamic feminism will bring for gender justice, others posit the limitations of the movement unless a hermeneutical shift occurs. This shift entails a more critical approach to the Qur'an which acknowledges the historicity of the text and privileges the experiences of its audience. Nonetheless, in view of the multiple and interlocking vulnerabilities of Muslim women with respect to HIV and AIDS, Islamic feminism appears inadequate in its narrow focus on gender equality as gender justice. As seen above, gender inequality meets with poverty to amplify women's risk of infection. Thus, for Islamic feminism to meet the challenge of HIV and AIDS today, it needs to embrace a more holistic understanding of gender justice as constituting multiple strands of structural violence, such as poverty, which multiplies and complicates women's oppression under patriarchy.

BIBLIOGRAPHY

Abd El-Hadi, Amal 1996. "Islamic Politics in Beijing: Change of Tactics But Not Substance." *Reproductive Health Matters*, 4(8), 47–54.

Abu-Lughod, Lila 2002. "Do Muslim women really need saving? Anthropological reflections on cultural relativism and its others." *American Anthropologist*,104(3), 783–790.

Ahmed, Leila 1992. *Women and Gender in Islam: Historical Roots of a Modern Debate*. New Haven, Yale University Press.

Al-Ali, Nadje 2005. "Reconstructing Gender: Iraqi Women between Dictatorship, War, Sanctions and Occupation." *Third World Quarterly*, 26(4–5), 739–758.

—— 2007. "Historical Perspectives on Iraqi Women & Gender Relations." Presentation, Boston Consortium for Gender, Security and Human Rights, Boston, MA, April 16, 2007.

Ali, Kecia 2006. *Sexual Ethics & Islam: Feminist Reflections on Qur'an, Hadith, and Jurisprudence*. Oxford, Oneworld Publications.

Badran, Margot 2006. "Islamic Feminism Revisited." *Al-Ahram*, February 9–15, 2006, issue 781. At http://weekly.ahram.org.eg/2006/781/cu4.htm (accessed May 9, 2007).

Barlas, Asma 2002. "Believing Women." In *Islam: Unreading Patriarchal Interpretations of the Qur'an*. Austin, University of Texas Press.

Barnett, Tony, and Alan Whiteside 2002. *AIDS in the Twenty-First Century: Disease and Globalization*. Houndmills, Basingstoke, Hampshire; New York, Palgrave Macmillan.

Cockburn, Cynthia 1998. *The Space Between Us: Negotiating Gender and National Identities in Conflict*. London and New York, Zed Books; distributed in the USA by St Martin's Press.

Cooke, Miriam 2001. *Women Claim Islam: Creating Islamic Feminism Through Literature*. New York, Routledge.

Engineer, Asghar Ali 2001. "Islam, Women, and Gender Justice." In *What Men Owe to Women: Men's Voices from World Religions*, ed. John C. Raines and Daniel C. McGuire. Albany, NY, State University of New York Press, 109–129.

Farmer, Paul 2000. "Women, Poverty, and AIDS." In *Women, Poverty, and AIDS: Sex, Drugs, and Structural Violence*, ed. Paul Farmer, Margaret Conners, and Janie Simmons. Moroe, ME, Common Courage Press, 3–38.

Francesca, Ersilia 2002. "AIDS in Contemporary Islamic Ethical Literature." *Medicine and Law*, 21, 381–394.

George, A., and S. Jaswal 1995. *Understanding Sexuality: An Ethnographic Study of Poor Women in Bombay*. Washington, DC, International Center for Research on Women.

Gupta, Rao 2000. "Gender, Sexuality, and HIV/AIDS: The What, the Why, and the How." Plenary Address, XIIIth International AIDS Conference, Durban, South Africa, July 12, 2000.

—— 2002. "How Men's Power Over Women Fuels the HIV Epidemic." *British Medical Journal*, 334, 183–184.

——, Ellen Weiss, and Purnima Mane 1996. "Talking About Sex: A Prerequisite for AIDS Prevention." In *Women's Experiences with HIV/AIDS: An International Perspective*, ed. Lynellyn D. Long and E. Maxine Ankrah. New York, Columbia University Press, 333–350.

Imam, Ayesha 2000. "The Muslim Religious Right ('Fundamentalists') and Sexuality." In *Women and Sexuality in Muslim Societies*, ed. Pinar Ilkkaracan. Istanbul, Women for Women's Human Rights (WWHR), 121–138.

Kirmani, Mubina Hassanali, and Dorothy Munyakho 1996. "The Impact of Structural Adjustment Programs on Women and AIDS." In *Women's Experiences with HIV/AIDS: An International Perspective*, ed. Lynellyn D. Long and E. Maxine Ankrah. New York, Columbia University Press, 160–178.

Maman, S., J. K. Mbwambo, N. M. Hogan, G. P. Kilonzo, J. C. Campbell, E. Weiss, and M. D. Sweat 2002. "HIV-Positive Women Report More Lifetime Partner Violence: Findings From a Voluntary Counseling and Testing Clinic in Dar es Salaam, Tanzania." *American Journal of Public Health*, 8, 1331–1337.

Mir-Hosseini, Ziba 1999. *Islam and Gender: The Religious Debate in Contemporary Iran*. Princeton, NJ, Princeton University Press.

Moghadam, Valerie M. 2002. "Islamic Feminism and Its Discontents: Towards a Resolution of the Debate." In *Gender, Politics, and Islam*, ed. Therese Saliba et al. Chicago, University of Chicago Press, 15–51.

Moosa, Ebrahim 2003. "The Debts and Burdens of Critical Islam." In *Progressive Muslims: On Justice, Gender, and Pluralism*, ed. Omid Safi. Oxford, Oneworld Publications, 111–127.

Obermeyer, Carla Makhlouf 2006. "HIV in the Middle East." *British Medical Journal*, 333, 851–854.

Shaikh, Sa'diyya 2003. "Transforming Feminism: Islam Women and Gender Justice." In *Progressive Muslims: On Justice, Gender, and Pluralism*, ed. Omid Safi. Oxford, Oneworld Publications, 147–162.

Türmen, T. 2003. "Gender and HIV/AIDS." *International Journal of Gynecology and Obstetrics*, 82, 411–418.

UNAIDS 2004. *UNAIDS at Country Level: Progress Report*. Geneva, Switzerland. At http://data.unaids.org/Publications/IRC-pub06/jc1048-countrylevel_en.pdf.

UNAIDS 2006. *Report on the Global AIDS Epidemic.* Geneva, Switzerland. At www.unaids.org/en/KnowledgeCentre/HIVData/ Global Report/2006/default.asp.

Wadud, Amina 1999. *Qur'an and Woman: Rereading the Sacred Text from a Woman's Perspective.* New York, Oxford University Press.

Wamala, Sarah, and Ichiro Kawachi 2007. "Globalization and Women's Health." In *Globalization and Health*, ed. Ichiro Kawachi and Sarah Wamala. Oxford and New York, Oxford University Press, 171–184.

Zine, Jasmin 2006. "Between Orientalism and Fundamentalism." In "Post-September 11th Developments in Human Rights in the Muslim World," ed. Shadi Mokhtari. Special issue, *Muslim World Journal of Human Rights*, 3(1).

7

FATAL CONFLUENCES? ISLAM, GENDER, AND AIDS IN MALAYSIA

Marina Mahathir

INTRODUCTION

For more than a decade, I have sought to draw the attention of the public and governments to the very real but hidden threat of the AIDS pandemic. In particular, I have advocated immediate action to avoid the disastrous impact of the pandemic in my country, Malaysia, and its surrounding region. My struggle, however, has been an uphill battle. In Malaysia, the number of people with HIV continues to rise. In 1993, when I began my work, more than 6,000 cases were reported. This number rose to over 70,000 by the end of 2005[1] when I stepped down as President of the Malaysian AIDS Council. These statistics are but the tip of the iceberg, as many people simply do not figure in these numbers.

In the course of my activism, I have come to believe that nothing illuminates the failures of a society more powerfully than an AIDS epidemic. Like a dye that is injected into one's body before a scan, AIDS exposes the gaps, malfunctions, inequalities, and corruption in a society. AIDS also reveals the prejudices and willful blindness of governments and societies to what is happening in their midst. In this paper, I will address the intersection of gender inequality and women's vulnerability to HIV infection – one of the many fractures that the red dye of AIDS has highlighted. Specifically, I will explore gender relations in Muslim societies and their impact on women's vulnerability to HIV, as well as make recommendations for better protecting women from infection. In particular, my discussion will focus on Malaysia; my interest and investment in this work comes from my own life as a Muslim woman, living in a Muslim majority country that is facing an AIDS epidemic.

ISLAM AND GENDER

Let me begin with some qualifications in relation to my position and the topic of Islam and gender. First, I would like to emphasize that I am not an expert on Islam. Instead, I take the position of an AIDS activist, seeking both an explanation for the particular vulnerability of women in specific societies and a way of empowering those women to protect themselves. Nonetheless, in my criticism of particular Islamic laws that I believe are discriminatory toward women (for example, the recent amendments to Malaysia's Islamic Family Laws[2]), I still consider the Qur'an as the source of guidance for Muslim life. I cannot, however, hold Islamic jurisprudence – the basis for the personal laws in various Muslim countries – in the same esteem. Not only does Islamic jurisprudence come from diverse sources which sometimes contradict one another, it is also dependent on the imperfections of human interpretation of the Qur'an. Chief among those imperfections is the patriarchy that characterized the historical and geographical milieu of the most prominent jurists, and inevitably shaped the way they saw the world.

Secondly, I would like to highlight that when people talk about Islam, they are often collapsing many different "Islams" into one. While there is only one Qur'an, interpretations vary according to time, place, and person. Besides the Qur'an and the hadith (the sayings of the Prophet Muhammad), there are the various Sunni and Shi'ite schools of interpretation, and the laws that are implemented in different Muslim countries. In Malaysia alone there are, in fact, fourteen different Muslim legal schools. Under our federal system, a legacy of British colonialism, each state controls its own Islamic religious laws. Each set of laws differs slightly from others, although there are now slow moves to standardize them.[3] Therefore the assertion "Islam says this", or "In Islam, a thing is allowed or disallowed," is contingent upon different contexts within Muslim societies.

Thirdly, although I focus on gender relations within Muslim societies, I do not claim that Islam is unique in its impact upon women's vulnerability to HIV. While the link between religion and gender roles pertains to many countries, religions, and cultures, I will focus on Islamic societies, given my interest in the situation of my own country.

Through my work, it is clear that understanding the influence religion has over gender roles is key to elucidating women's vulnerability to HIV. First, in many developing countries where AIDS is hitting hard or is beginning to hit hard, religion plays an important role in people's daily lives. In countries like Cambodia, India, Indonesia, Malaysia, and Thailand, people do not confine religion to weekly rituals but live it on a daily basis. Religion governs the very ways people behave, their relationships with one another, and the ways men and women treat each other. Furthermore, religious leaders have a lot of influence in these countries. Their statements can elicit stigma and discrimination toward the disease or alleviate those sentiments. No country concerned with AIDS can afford to ignore religious leaders in its national response.

Women's vulnerability to HIV is at least partly determined by the gender roles assigned to them by society. These roles are often determined by religion, or what are thought to be religious precepts. Women's sexuality, in particular, is often controlled on religious grounds. Religious rules determine when a woman can marry, whether she should have children, whether she has any right to sexual pleasure, and whether she can divorce her husband.

In order to learn how Islam, as it is practiced today, enhances or reduces women's vulnerability to HIV infection, I have sought to understand sexuality within Islam. Sexuality, mirroring power relations between men and women, is central to devising ways of preventing sexual transmission of HIV. In my efforts, I am inspired by the work of Kecia Ali on the source of the Islamic marriage contract and its impact on sexuality, which I briefly discuss below. In this paper, I will offer some thoughts about the way religious laws, as implemented in Muslim countries, heighten women's vulnerability to HIV. Primarily, I will discuss the circumstances within Malaysia because it is the country I know best. Moreover, I am concerned that recent changes in the Muslim family laws there may impact the spread of AIDS, especially to women.

THE AIDS EPIDEMIC IN MUSLIM COUNTRIES

The global AIDS pandemic has affected the lives of more than sixty million people around the world, of whom forty million are currently alive, mostly in developing countries in sub-Saharan Africa and, increasingly, in Asia. While countries are not classified by religion, some parties have made it a point to categorize the impact of AIDS according to religious affiliation. AIDS in the Muslim world is considered particularly worthy of inspection. The 2005 report entitled "Behind the Veil of a Public Health Crisis: HIV/AIDS in the Muslim World" (Kelley and Eberstadt), produced by the National Bureau of Asian Research (NBR), based in the United States, is an example of such an inquiry.

While many controversial assertions and generalizations abound in this report, I will only underscore two points: first, no other disease apart from AIDS has ever merited reports based on the religion of a country. There are no "Avian Flu in Muslim Countries" or "SARS in Muslim Countries" reports. Secondly, while there seems to be a need to have reports on AIDS in Muslim countries, there are none on AIDS in Buddhist, Hindu, or Christian countries. I would suggest that the constant need to define AIDS through religion only serves to underscore the subtle implication that AIDS is always linked to morality. Moreover, the constant need to report on AIDS in Muslim countries, mostly negatively, is, I believe, yet another attempt in certain quarters to disparage whole populations and their governments because of their religion. AIDS is unfortunately, to my mind, another pawn in the so-called "clash of civilizations."

Despite this attention, HIV prevalence rates in Muslim countries are generally low. According to UNAIDS, prevalence rates in countries with large Muslim populations range from under one percent in Malaysia to four percent in Senegal (UNAIDS, 2005). However, several factors must be taken into account. One is that surveillance in many Muslim countries is generally poor, even in those with the finances to do it. This reluctance may stem from a lack of desire to know the true situation for fear of what it would say about their societies; it may also be attributable to a denial of certain social conditions such as drug use, sex work, and same-sex relations, which contribute to the spread of HIV. Also, as pointed out in many reports, including the NBR one, a low national prevalence rate may mask high local prevalence rates. For example, very high prevalence rates of HIV may exist among drug users or sex workers, but when averaged out with other local statistics may result in low national rates. Having said this, low prevalence rates, whether accurate or erroneous, are no reason for complacency. As the history of the global AIDS pandemic has shown, countries begin with low numbers. These numbers will grow either quickly or slowly, depending on how countries respond.

In essence, I disagree with reports that suggest that Muslim majority countries are particularly vulnerable to AIDS epidemics. Global AIDS statistics clearly indicate that poverty, denial, and social inequalities – not religion per se – are conditions within countries that make them vulnerable to HIV. While religion may have varying impacts upon social relations that enhance HIV transmission, religion cannot be taken as a simple marker of vulnerability. In addition, how any country responds to AIDS is crucial, no matter what level of development it enjoys or suffers from. Poor countries can deflect the worst impacts of AIDS if they recognize its dangers early and respond quickly, as has been seen in Senegal. On the other hand, rich countries can become complacent and witness a resurgence in infections, as we are seeing in parts of Australia.

GENDER AND HIV/AIDS

While biological factors make women more susceptible to infection, gender bias in research and society contributes even more significantly to women's increased vulnerability to HIV. When AIDS first drew the attention of the world, there was a prevailing belief that men were far more affected by the disease. The first high-profile cases came from the West among homosexual men and male injecting drug users. Thus AIDS research focused solely on male sexuality, and AIDS among injecting drug users was compartmentalized as simply affecting injecting behavior and not sexual behavior. As a result, female partners of drug users were ignored. It was only when babies were found to be born HIV-positive that the connection was made. Even so, the first response was antenatal testing for the purpose of administering antiretroviral drugs, such as Zidovudine or Nevirapine, to reduce mother-to-child transmission. However, the mothers of these babies soon died for lack of treatment, leaving the children orphans. Evidently, it took a long while before women were recognized as being not just equally vulnerable, but differently vulnerable and impacted by HIV.

Women are more vulnerable to HIV infection because of their low status in their societies. It is no coincidence that the countries in which women are most vulnerable to HIV are also the countries where women are able to make few decisions in their lives, have little opportunity for education or jobs, bear the brunt of conflict, and suffer violent abuse. In keeping with my focus on the impact of Islamic religious laws on gender and HIV vulnerability, I will discuss some aspects of Muslim views on marriage and sexuality that are particularly relevant to the vulnerability of women. These views concern marriage and the concept of *nushuz*, polygamy, and divorce. I will also touch on Muslim views on abstinence since it is receiving great currency these days.

Marriage in Islam and women's vulnerability to HIV

Surah 30, verse 21 of the Holy Al-Qur'an says:

> And of His [God's] signs is this: He created for you partners from yourselves that ye might find rest in them, and He ordained between you love and mercy. Lo! herein indeed are portents for folk who reflect.

Marriage in the Qur'an is viewed as a "most solemn pledge or covenant" (4:21), a contract based on mutual agreement between two spouses. The Qur'an emphasizes love and tenderness and consorting "in kindness" (4:19), and men and women are "each other's garments" (2:187), meant for mutual support, mutual comfort, and mutual protection, fitting into each other as a garment fits the body. Yet, how have these words translated into Islamic jurisprudence?

Marriage is indeed a contract by mutual agreement between two spouses, who have both rights and responsibilities to each other. As such, many scholars have argued that Islam provides more rights to women than any other religion. But, as Kecia Ali demonstrates in her essay, "Progressive Muslims and Islamic Jurisprudence: The Necessity for Critical Engagement with Marriage and Divorce Law" (2003, 165), the overall framework of the marriage contract is predicated on a type of ownership (*milk*) granted to the husband over the wife in exchange for dower payment, which makes sexual intercourse between them lawful. Further, the major spousal right established by the contract is the wife's sexual availability in exchange for which she is supported by the husband.

Although not controversial during the time it was originally conceived, Ali admits that this view of marriage, as primarily an exchange of money for sexual access, would be unthinkable today, even by the most conservative of thinkers. Nonetheless, I have observed that some of the thinking behind it still exists in modern Muslim marriages. This mindset has a tremendous impact on women's ability to protect themselves from HIV infection: if women marry and then are obliged always to make themselves available to their husbands for sexual intercourse, how can they refuse a husband whom they suspect or know is HIV-positive?

In Malaysia, I have encountered numerous such cases where women who suspect their husband is HIV-positive run to their mothers for help, only to be advised to return to their husbands. They are told that it is a woman's "duty" to not withhold sex from their husbands. (Undoubtedly, no mother educated enough about HIV would consciously send her daughter off to be infected, but at the very least such a mother would be conflicted about what advice to give her daughter.) To refuse sex or to leave the marital home to evade such a demand can lead Muslim women to be guilty of *nushuz*, a term translated as "disobedience," "recalcitrance," or "rebelliousness." According to the Shafi'i school of jurisprudence, a woman guilty of *nushuz* loses her right to financial support for as long as she remains sexually unavailable to her husband. This agreement forms the very basis of the marriage contract.

This thinking explains why many Muslims refuse to accept the notion of marital rape. It is assumed that women entering into marriage are obliged to be sexually available at all times, and therefore marital rape is considered a contradiction in terms. The view of the Hanafi school of jurisprudence elucidates this position: "if she is in his house but she withholds herself from him is maintenance due to her from him? Is it lawful for the husband to have sex with her against her will . . .? It is lawful, because she is a wrongdoer (*zalima*)" (Al-Khassaf; cited in Ali, 2003, 170–171).

This state of affairs diverges from Qur'anic injunctions that provide for love and mercy within marriage. The challenge therefore is one of translating these provisions into reality through a re-emphasis of men's responsibility to care for their wives in mutual love and tenderness, and to avoid transmitting an illness that would bring much pain and suffering to their wives and children. The practical application of this responsibility is the use of condoms. Thus far, however, most responses to women's vulnerability to HIV have been of the punitive kind, where mandatory premarital HIV testing is touted as the best way to protect women from irresponsible men.[4] However, such testing does little to protect women from husbands who may become infected later on in life; it certainly does not empower women. Instead, this programme reinforces patriarchal notions of women needing protection, and, while complicating women's entry into marriage, leaves unchallenged women's difficulty in getting out of it. Thus, while the inadequacies of premarital testing can also be fatal for men, women whose husbands contract HIV after marriage are locked into lifelong consequences even if they evade infection; they will share the brunt of stigma and discrimination along with their infected spouses and will have to provide an enormous burden of care.

Muslim women, therefore, have little recourse in law to protect themselves from HIV infection from their own husbands. Certainly, HIV-positive men also suffer from stigma and discrimination, but it is women, often already invisible in society, who are rendered further invisible within the epidemic, particularly when they have no means to fight injustice.

Polygamy and women's vulnerability to HIV

Although today Islam is the religion most frequently associated with polygamy, it is neither its originator nor the only religion practicing this custom. Polygamy has existed in many parts of the world from pre-Islamic times up until the present: both polygyny and polyandry were practiced in the ancient period among certain sections of Hindu society; writings in the Hebrew Bible mention the existence of polygamy, albeit not approvingly; and in 1650 the parliament at Nürnberg decreed that men could marry up to ten women because so many men were killed in the Thirty Years' War.

Within Islam, there are different views about polygamy. Surah 4, verse 3 in the Qur'an states:

> If ye fear that ye shall not be able to deal justly with the orphans, marry women of your choice, two or three or four; but if ye fear that ye shall not be able to deal justly (with them), then only one, or (a captive) that your right hands possess, that will be more suitable, to prevent you from doing injustice.

One interpretation of this Surah is that the permission for a man to marry up to four wives was a limitation, not an encouragement, at a time when men were used to taking limitless numbers of wives. As such, the *ayah* that puts forward a condition – that if justice cannot be done with many wives, then only one is suitable – is understood as a recommendation for monogamy, which is considered more just. More conservative interpretations, however, regard this Surah as not so much emphasizing monogamy as allowing polygamy, as long as the husband is fair to all his wives, in every way. Nonetheless, it should be remembered that not all Muslim men practice polygamy. In some countries, it is a practice that is dying out, such as in Morocco. In other countries it is even banned, such as in Tunisia. In Malaysia and Indonesia, polygamy remains an issue of frequent debate between conservative and progressive Muslims, particularly feminists.

Within the context of HIV and AIDS, polygamy raises important questions. In many countries, including Muslim ones, AIDS prevention messages have focused on equating promiscuity (casual and indiscriminate sex with multiple partners) with the risk of HIV infection. Prevention campaigns in Malaysia have, in particular, associated promiscuity with any form of illicit sex – sex not sanctioned by marriage, *haram* versus *halal* sex. With an emphasis on the high risk of *haram* sex, prevention campaigns fail to address the potential risk within polygamous marriage, which involves legal, multiple-partner sex. Premarital and extramarital sex, on the other hand, are stigmatized and linked to the risk of infection, regardless of how few partners these relations entail.

Let me illustrate this point with the situation in the state of Kelantan in North-East Malaysia. Kelantan, ruled by the opposition Islamic Party for most of the past thirty years, is known for its religious conservatism. Yet the state has many social problems, including drug use and HIV and AIDS. Between January and June 2004,

Kelantan reported the highest number of HIV cases per state in Malaysia, much of it, like the rest of the country, attributed to inject-ing drug use (Malaysia Ministry of Health, 2005). Over the past two years, nurse-counselors at the General Hospital in the capital city of Kota Baru have noticed a growing number of women diagnosed with HIV, with some eight to nine new cases per month. A new orga-nization, Prihatin, was set up in 2004 to support these women and currently has 105 HIV-positive women as members (Hussin, 2005).

An analysis of the background of these women revealed how potentially easy it would be for many more women to become infected. Many of these women had married young to men who were drug users, who later became infected and then died. These young HIV-positive widows with children had limited means of earning income, and some wished to remarry to ensure their security. In Kelantan state, uniquely, there is no stigma against women marrying several times. Therefore these women would remarry into polyga-mous relationships, becoming second, third, or fourth wives, often without informing their husbands of their status. As such, the pos-sibility of the virus transferring from these women to their husbands and then onwards to other wives is a very real one indeed.

In January 2006, the Kelantan state religious department began a mandatory premarital testing programme for Muslim couples. This programme has met with the approval of women who wished to know whether their potential husbands were already infected. However, it has also deterred HIV-positive women, such as the ones I have described, from remarrying because to do so would mean revealing their status. Barred from remarriage, and without the sup-port of the government and others, these women may resort to sex work for economic survival, thereby leading to further transmission of the virus. Prihatin is trying to avoid such circumstances by pro-viding training and small loans for these women to start their own businesses.

With the current relaxation of regulations governing polygamy in Malaysia, through amendments to the Islamic Family Laws, the spread of infection in areas of high incidence of HIV is a tangible possibility. Prior to these amendments, a husband could only take an additional wife with the knowledge and written approval of his wife/wives. Now, this is no longer necessary, making it easier for men to take additional wives who may be HIV-positive. I am not pinning the fault on the HIV-positive woman who marries for social and economic reasons; the possibility of a polygamous man becoming infected at any point in his life, through either injecting drug use or unsafe sex, always remains. In either case, it is women who are not protected.

To remedy this in the short term would require vast amounts of public education, including the active promotion of condoms for married couples. It would also require programmes raising women's awareness of their right to health and empowering them to insist that their husbands use condoms. As with the majority of places in the world, however, this goal is not easy to achieve when marriages are weighted heavily against women in the first place.

Divorce in Islam and women's vulnerability

It is often said that divorce in Islam is easy, with the man having to only pronounce the *talaq* three times. In many Muslim countries, this simplicity has been tempered by rules and regulations to protect the interests of wives, including, for example, the necessity to pronounce the *talaq* in court before a judge for a divorce to be valid. This practice does not mean that Islam condones easy divorce. As Fathi Uthman explains, "Islam teaches that marriage should be maintained as long as the essential requirement of a peaceful family life and mutual care and respect are there, even if emotions and romance may not be as strong as they were before" (Uthman, 1996, 15). Thus men are exhorted to "consort with them in kindness, for if ye hate them it may happen that ye hate a thing wherein Allah hath placed much good" (Q. 4:19). In the event of marital discord, the Qur'an provides several steps for dealing with the problem, beginning with discussion, the suspension of sexual relations, some "light physical correction," and then arbitration by others.[5] If all these steps fail, then divorce is allowed.

These recommendations do not always translate into practice. In Malaysia, recent amendments to divorce procedures have only served to make divorce easier, to the detriment of women. Given this ease of divorce, HIV-positive women are vulnerable to abandonment should their condition be discovered. With antenatal testing programmes available, women are often tested before their husbands. If diagnosed positive, they face the risk of being divorced without any compensation. They can be accused of *zina* or adultery if their husbands accuse them of acquiring the infection elsewhere. Or they may be accused of bringing shame upon their husbands and families, and face the possibility of being regarded as a *nashizah* (guilty of marital disobedience). Already, in the states of Kelantan and Terengganu, where *hudud* laws based on very strict interpretations of the Shari'ah are imposed, pregnancy can be used as evidence of fornication and adultery against women, even if it is a result of rape. How big a step would it take for HIV infection to be used in the same way?

As it is men who have the power to pronounce divorce, subject to the courts, women who are HIV-positive are left with little recourse in the law and with no means of support. Treatment for AIDS-related illnesses is expensive even with government subsidies in Malaysia. Kindness, therefore, is not a factor that comes into play in these circumstances. Cases of women being thrown out of their own homes, along with their children, have been known to happen, and shelter homes for such women have become a necessity.

My recommendation would be to impose measures preventing men from divorcing their wives too easily. For instance, such measures could include investigations into why men are pursuing divorce. These inquiries may reveal that the "fault," if any, is not on the women's side. If, indeed, the women had been infected by their own husbands, and if the divorce still takes place, they should be awarded just compensation, preferably an amount that would enable them to obtain the treatment they need. Similarly, if a woman wishes to divorce her husband because he has infected her, then she should be allowed the divorce along with the requisite compensations. In every case, however, the protection of all parties, especially children, from stigma and discrimination must be paramount.

Abstinence and Muslim societies

I have often been asked about the role of abstinence as a means of HIV prevention, a concept that is currently regarded as the most effective way of prevention.[6] While I do accept that one sure way of not contracting HIV is by never having sex, I often wonder whom the proponents of abstinence had in mind when they promote this message so tenaciously. I would assume that the architects of abstinence campaigns are mostly talking about unmarried people, people who would be having illicit sex. However, as is evident in reports in every country, the virus does not care about the legal status of sex. In fact, marriage is no protection, particularly for women. Married women are less able to negotiate for safer sex or to refuse sex with their husbands than unmarried women with their partners. Thus abstinence messages ignore the vulnerabilities of married women and are completely ineffective in preventing HIV infection among them.

CONCLUSION

In this essay, I have raised some questions about how we can best protect women in Muslim societies from HIV infection. I believe that if men and women lived their lives as the Qur'an recommends, then we would have very little to worry about. If men truly treated their wives with love and mercy, and if women enjoyed all the respect and rights God, through the Qur'an, says they should, then we would not need to look at ways to empower women in order to protect them.

The reality on the ground, however, is far different. For various reasons, whether poverty, lack of education, or gender norms, men and women do not and are not always able to behave in the ways that the Qur'an prescribes. People take drugs, for instance, even in Muslim countries such as Malaysia and Indonesia. They have illicit sex, they subject women to sexual violence and abuse. In this way, Muslim societies do not differ from any other society in harboring the conditions that make the spread of HIV within them possible.

But as with countries that have been successful in managing their AIDS epidemics, only a sea change in the way things are done can make a difference. Policies, laws, cultures, and traditions that help to spread the virus need to be changed, with the backing of strong political will. Most of all, social inequalities that marginalize certain sectors of society need to be addressed in order to ensure equal access to prevention, treatment, care, and support. As the increasing feminization of the global AIDS epidemic indicates, gender inequality is one of the most important forms of discrimination to be addressed. Gender inequality not only enhances the vulnerability of women, it continues to impact women infected by HIV through inequalities in treatment, care, and support.

Gender inequality often has its roots in religious precepts. In Islam, in particular, while the Qur'an emphasizes the equality of men and women, many Muslim women are often discriminated against through interpretations that are patriarchal and unjust. It is not enough, therefore, simply to educate women about their rights, if the interpretations of these Qur'anic rights are already colored by patriarchy and weighted against them. What is needed is a reinterpretation of the Qur'an within a framework of equality and justice, and the promotion of this new interpretation among both men and women. Only then do we stand a chance of averting the spread of HIV.

BIBLIOGRAPHY

Ali, Kecia 2003. "Progressive Muslims and Islamic jurisprudence: the necessity for critical engagement with marriage and divorce law." In *Progressive Muslims: On Justice, Gender, and Pluralism*, ed. Omid Safi. Oxford, Oneworld Publications, 163–189.

Hussin, Zaimah 2005. "HIV Infections in Women in Kelantan." Conference paper, National Ministry of Health Malaysia Conference on HIV/AIDS, Kota Bharu, Kelantan, Malaysia, December 2005.

Joint United Nations Programme on HIV/AIDS and World Health Organization. *AIDS Epidemic Update: December 2005*. At http://www.unaids.org/epi/2005/doc/report_pdf.asp (accessed March 28, 2006).

Kelly, Laura M. and Nicholas Eberstadt 2005. "Behind the Veil of a Public Health Crisis: HIV/AIDS in the Muslim World." National Bureau of Asian Research Special Report, June 2005.

Uthman, Fathi 1996. *Muslim Women in the Family and the Society*. Kuala Lumpur, Malaysia, SIS Forum (Malaysia) Berhad.

8

THE MUSLIM MAN AND AIDS: NEGOTIATING SPACES FOR NEW CONCEPTUALIZATIONS OF MASCULINITY

Trad Godsey

Yes, I am crying, although I am a man.
But has not a man eyes?
Has not a man hands, limbs, heart, thoughts and passions?
Does he not live by the same food,
is he not wounded by the same weapons,
warmed and cooled by the same summer and winter as a
    woman?
If you prick us do we not bleed?
If you tickle us do we not laugh?
If you poison us, do we not die?
Why should a man be forbidden to
Complain, or a soldier to weep?
Because it is unmanly?
Why is it unmanly?

August Strindberg, The Father (1887)

INTRODUCTION

AIDS is a gendered pandemic.[1] Increasingly we see how women are being disproportionately affected by it and virtually all of the material that addresses questions of gender in relation to AIDS deals with women and their particular vulnerability.[2] It is all too common that a woman is at the mercy of a man when it comes to negotiating sex, socio-economic agency, care, and support for children. Whether or not she contracts HIV is also subject to this gender imbalance. Yet HIV is also very much an issue tied to masculine gender roles in at least two ways. First, men trapped in particular modes of being – patriarchy – also suffer when they cannot be fully human, cannot access the full spectrum of human emotions because of their gender: cannot cry, cannot be seen as weak, cannot embrace their own vulnerability, and cannot ask for help. Men are prevented from being fully alive when they exist in relationships of domination. How do I as a man experience life in its fullness when so much of my energy goes into remaining in control of the woman in my life? Secondly, gender oppression and its implications for AIDS – addressed elsewhere in this volume with regards to women – are problems for men in the same way that race and racism are issues that involve white people. While women are usually the victims of gender violence, they can also be the agents of their own liberation. Yet if men are not incorporated into the dialogue and problem solving surrounding the AIDS pandemic, then much of this effort will really be tantamount to fire-fighting while all the forces which spark fires continue unchecked. We may win a series of minor battles in a never ending war. Thus work towards gender justice not only requires attention to women's situations but to those of men as well – their self-perceptions, their interaction with women, men as individuals, as fathers, and in the context of the family unit.[3]

Men are themselves the product of culture, social institutions, and norms. They fulfill, more or less consciously, expectations from elders, mates, and themselves. In certain situations and under certain conditions their behavior can be harmful, especially for the women who depend on them. We see this particularly in relation to AIDS.[4] Often these situations have the character of crisis or insecurity for the men themselves. Men will surely benefit from improved equality and partnership with women, in both social and family life. As women gain agency with the support of men, they become partners and thus better equipped to battle the many horrors associated with HIV. Whether it be in terms of allowing men to be more open and honest, of healing emotional wounds caused by AIDS, or of making a united front to stop its spread, an improved partnership between men and women offers hope in the face of a seemingly unstoppable force.

This essay is an attempt to start a dialogue in which we address some of the issues relating to Muslim men and constructions of masculinity in relation to AIDS. Within the Islamic tradition itself, there are a wide variety of starting points from which to begin such a reflection. The AIDS pandemic, a tragedy of the present, spans many Islamic contexts and each one is distinct and unique. Because of the numerous influences and realities that make up maleness and men's lives today, reflections on Islam, Muslims, and masculinities will inevitably be incomplete; this becomes a problem when it is not acknowledged, or when an author does not try to account for the multiplicity of identities and factors which frame individual experiences. There is no one "Muslim masculinity" that we can approach. However, the paucity of material on the subject necessitates beginning *somewhere* and that presents the most challenging aspect of this topic.

Religious authority for Muslims is located in the Qur'an and the *Sunnah* (the prophetic precedent), the latter documented in hadith literature. These sources emerged from, and are always approached in, specific social and historical contexts. In this review of the problems of masculinity brought to the forefront by the AIDS pandemic, I will reflect on ideas of masculinity in a) the Qur'an, b) the *Sunnah*, and c) some contemporary Muslim approaches. I will then make the case for the need to foreground these ideas in light of the enormous destruction of human life and suffering in the wake of the AIDS pandemic – particularly for those who are disproportionately affected: women. Though the pandemic provides an urgency to revisit these issues, it will become evident that many of them need to be re-thought regardless of public health concerns. Since masculinity as a problem has typically been addressed in terms of patriarchy as simply the domination of women by men, I hope to show that Islamic masculinities have their own distinctly male pleas for a serious re-evaluation. Patriarchy and gender domination are only one piece of a complex and highly problematic puzzle of constructed masculinity.

As mentioned above, in Islam there is no single, monolithic "masculinity" that may be addressed by a single set of questions and answers. Islamic "masculinities" vary largely due to the diversity of contexts in which Islam is practiced and interpreted. We must first define what we mean by Islamic masculinity. Are we talking about masculine traits of Muslim men? If so, which men and where? Are we talking about traits of masculinity that we can label as exclusively Islamic? Secondly, the masculinities that we address are not only the products of various interpretations of Islamic lifestyles, but also the products of external factors that may or may not have any relation to Islam (whatever else Islam may be, it is also a local historical phenomenon). In the case of female genital cutting in Egypt, for example, Noor Kassamali notes that "Muslim groups that practice this custom often cite religious justifications . . . [y]et religion is not a determining factor" (Kassamali, 1998, 42). In other words, we cannot make assumptions about Islam as a proponent of a particular masculine trait nor can we draw simple causal connections between religion and cultural practices that enforce gender inequity. Instead, we must consider masculinity as a conglomeration of many traits, both religious and otherwise. Indeed, the lines between the sacred and the profane are not always as clear as one often imagines. It is difficult to know which traits of masculinity have been merely justified by Islam (through the Qur'an, hadith, local traditions, etc.), which traits have been inspired by Islam, and which – if any – have nothing to do with the religion. Often religion simultaneously inspires and justifies existing inclinations.[5] Nonetheless, it is helpful to begin reflecting on conceptualizations of the "Muslim man" and some Muslim approaches to manhood by looking at the traditions and texts of Islam.

THE QUR'AN AND *SUNNAH* – PRIMARY ISLAMIC SOURCES

The immediate context for the Qur'an and the *Sunnah* was sixth-century Arabia. A key term, fundamental to an understanding of the ideal man, is the term "*muruwwah*." *Muruwwah* is translated as "manliness" and, according to Toshihiko Izutsu, this translation is (for all practical purposes) apt for understanding this Bedouin virtue (2002, 27). In *The Encyclopedia of Islam and the Muslim World* the term is described as "combining moral notions of integrity, fidelity, valor, chastity, and honor" (Hermansen, 2004, 436). Izutsu, however, elaborates on the word, explaining that connected to the "honor" aspect of *muruwwah* is a "persistence in seeking revenge" which is manifested through the custom of blood vengeance (2002, 68). *Muruwwah* is a combination of these characteristics that constitute "manliness" for the pre- and post-Islamic Bedouin.

In the contemporary world, such a definition of manliness will not suffice because there is no single "masculinity" for Muslims across a plethora of nations and communities. Nonetheless, there is both an essential text and an essential man in the religious imagination of most Muslims. The Qur'an as a text is at the center of religious life and devotion for Muslims, and the Prophet Muhammad was God's chosen vessel through which God's word entered the world. This event took place during a time and in a place where a common understanding of *muruwwah* existed.

Despite the location of the Qur'an in history and its role in affirming or reforming notions of *muruwwah*, the text itself plays varying degrees in affirming and reforming modern notions of masculinity. However, it is curious that certain interpretations seem to be more often privileged above others. For example, where in male discourses does the notion that "humankind was created weak" (Q. 4:28) fit in? This is a very important verse in the Qur'an, as it legitimizes the weaknesses that all of humankind have, and furthermore attributes these weaknesses to the divine will of God. In male social groups where strength is valorized, where the ideal man is strongest among "strong," where is an acknowledgement of this "weakness"? It seems that, in many cases, modern masculinities are working against the Qur'anic understanding of the state of humanity. If we use the *ayah* above to interpret what *muruwwah* meant in the early Islamic period, we see that the terms "honor, fidelity, and integrity" can be upheld in a Muslim masculinity ideal while incorporating an understanding of the natural "weak" nature of man. Here we see that male identity can be complex and sometimes contradictory. Indeed, this is perhaps a more accurate or humane understanding of human nature.

MASCULINITY AND *KUFR*

The concept of *kufr*, associated with disbelief and non-Muslims, is a recurring theme in Islamic literature. Though *kufr* is often translated as "disbelief," the meaning of the root *K-F-R* is "to cover." Toshihiko Izutsu points out that this was most often used in contexts concerned with bestowing and receiving gifts. Therefore the word came to mean "to cover" or "to ignore knowingly the benefits which one has received" and thence, "to be unthankful"(Izutsu, 2002, 160). Thinking of *kufr* in this way closely associates it with notions of arrogance and pride, both of which are heavily critiqued in the Qur'an: "For God loveth not any arrogant boaster" (Q. 31:18); "For men and women who humble themselves [. . .] for them has God prepared forgiveness and great reward" (Q. 33:35). Izutsu makes this same connection: "*kufr*, as man's denial of the Creator, manifests itself most characteristically in various acts of insolence, haughtiness and presumptuousness." Understanding *kufr* as "one who does not humble himself" or "one who is insolent or haughty" encourages the Muslim man to abandon his erroneous understanding that the *kafir* is "the other" or merely the "unbeliever." Instead, he should look into his own life for elements of *kufr*, elements which are manifested in his own insolence and presumptuousness towards both God and other people.

Other examples of this understanding of *kufr* can be found in men's relationships with others, particularly women. For example, when a man feels the need to compete with other men to see who can have the most sex, this compulsion often produces an insolent attitude toward women, using them as a means to affirm his manhood among his peers. When men seek to affirm their manhood through women in this way, it is often at the expense of the woman's needs and feelings toward sex. In this manner, women become a mere vehicle, a means to an end, and not people assessed in light of human needs. Ironically, this attitude is in clear contradiction to hadith that encourage men to approach their spouses romantically with love and compassion.

MUHAMMAD AS THE IDEAL MAN

Though the Qur'an is the *Kalam Allah*, or word of God, the word "*Qur'an*" literally means "recitation." This recitation was first revealed to the Prophet Muhammad during the month of Ramadan by the angel Gabriel as Muhammad sat meditating in a cave on Mount Hira. The first night of his encounter with Gabriel was a turning point in history, and Muhammad was profoundly changed from that night on. Upon descending Mount Hira, where he had received the divine visitation, Muhammad returned to his wife Khadija with a quaking heart saying, "Cover me! Cover me!" (Lings, 1983, 44). Khadija quickly brought a cloak and covered him, in her efforts to comfort him during his time of weakness and fear (ibid.). If the Prophet was capable of being vulnerable before his wife, as the story indicates, then why does this image seem antithetical to the constructed masculinities of today?

Many Muslims look to the Prophet Muhammad as the ideal man, yet he was also the archetype of humanity, displaying emotions that are universal regardless of time and place. The Prophet's vulner-ability after descending from Mount Hira reveals that even in his greatness there was weakness; this weakness did not detract from his greatness. Muhammad is not thought of as "less of a man" because he was vulnerable and needed the comfort of his wife. Still, his reac-tion has not been taken up in the construction of masculinities in the Muslim world today.

The redefining and reformation of masculinity in the Muslim world to allow manliness to be expressed as weakness and vulner-ability has both a Qur'anic and Prophetic precedent. While the AIDS pandemic creates an urgency for change, the Qur'an and the *Sunnah* have always contained tools to reconstruct manhood in a way that achieves greater gender equity for men and women alike.

SOME MUSLIM PERSPECTIVES ON MASCULINITY

Abdal Hakim Murad, one of the few contemporary Muslim scholars who deal with masculinity, raises interesting questions in his article "Boys will be Boys." He takes a serious look at maleness, engag-ing biological and scientific studies from an Islamic perspective, and suggests that the gendered roles and differences found in his understanding of the Qur'an are supported by scientific discover-ies about the biological attributes of male and female (www.masud. co.uk). Working from the assumption that Islam does not promote oppressive hierarchies of male over female, Murad argues against egalitarian views of men and women on the basis of genetic differ-ences. Using scientific data to argue that males are genetically prone to certain behaviors (such as competition) while females are prone to other complementary behaviors (such as nurturing), he concludes that "men and women are neither equal nor unequal" but that there is a "categorical difference" between them (ibid.). Murad is careful to explain that "the biological advantages of the male, . . . unless one day a massive reconstructive surgery and hormonal reprogramming is carried out on every one of us, do not for us [men] denote superiority, as they must for the secular mind when it follows its own arguments through" (ibid.).

Murad's comments on the genetic inclinations of men and women in reproduction are pertinent to the spread of HIV. According to Murad, competition and aggression in males is due to their ability to "improve their reproductive success through having numerous partners in a way that members of the other sex cannot" (ibid.). If males are genetically prone to this behavior, it can be inferred that this inclination will exist even if reproduction is not consciously desirable in modern society. According to Murad, though polygamy has become more or less unaccepted in the modern world, men are still biologically inclined to have multiple sexual partners. Therefore, men are confronted with the tension between their biological instincts and the "new" rules of society that prohibit multiple sexual partners (ibid.). Using Murad's data regarding gender and biology, one can deduce that men have greater inclinations toward sexual promiscuity than women. However, it is unclear what the connection is between these biological "facts" about men and women and the role Islam plays in dealing with these biological inclinations. Is this an elaborate defense of polygamy as a means to deal with male biology and its will to procreate with multiple partners? Is this a critique of Islamic sexual norms? Or is it a critique of modernity and its ironic take on both sexual promiscuity and monogamy in marriage?

We know that infidelity and promiscuous sex put both men and women at risk of contracting HIV. Regardless of whether or not men are biologically inclined to such behavior, two problems still exist. First, in many cases sexual promiscuity and infidelity have become a part of male identity, often reified by friends and parental examples. Biology cannot be the scapegoat for constructions of masculinity that include such behavior. Secondly, if we are to take seriously a man's biological need/tendency to maintain multiple sexual relationships, it becomes the responsibility of the religious establishment to provide options to curtail this problem or promote sexual health and well-being. The simple declaration that it is *haram*, or forbidden, to engage in such behavior would, according to the data presented by Murad, contradict man's natural tendency. There is no doubt that promiscuity and unfaithfulness are a problem for men and women today regarding AIDS. Religious authorities must move beyond merely preaching abstinence, and innovative approaches must be formulated and endorsed by religious authorities who address the problems surrounding men and sexual habits.

Malik Badri expounds on similar ideas in his pamphlet *AIDS Prevention – Failure in the North and Catastrophe in the South: A Solution*. Badri, assuming that men are naturally more promiscuous, suggests that polygamy might be a better option for men than the alternative of seeking out prostitutes or other sexually risky partners. Badri explains that in places like Nigeria and Tanzania, where polygamy is "the norm," men ridicule advice to "keep to one partner." In such communities it is actually safer to allow men to have a number of faithful wives, claims Badri (2000, 10). This promotes safe sex and, by extension, better public health.

While the subject of polygamy in Islam is outside the scope of this paper, it is important to note that many Islamic thinkers and teachers consider polygamy when addressing scientific approaches to masculinity. I do not see how such scientific approaches can be appropriated for the reform of Islamic norms in the Muslim world, particularly those associated with ideals of masculinity. It seems problematic to use science as a tool for validating Islamic traditions and practices, but not to critique those same traditions and practices through a similar use of science.

One example that is directly related to AIDS involves circumcision and condom usage. Many Islamic teachers and *ulama* have been proud of recent studies that prove that circumcision may actually reduce one's chance of contracting HIV. This is because male circumcision is an almost universal practice in the Muslim world. However, studies also show that condom usage is the most effective way to prevent the acquisition of HIV during intercourse. The *ulama*, however, are reluctant to promote *this* information to largely uneducated masses on the subject of HIV transmission. This double standard when it comes to religion and public health can have dangerous consequences.

In 2004 Positive Muslims, a South African organization working to support Muslims living with HIV and AIDS and to increase awareness about the disease, released a publication entitled *HIV,*

AIDS & Islam: Reflections based on Compassion, Responsibility & Justice. Though the publication's primary concern is not the role of men or masculinity in the pandemic, it does make a few assertions about the responsibilities of men in light of the AIDS epidemic. This publication is particularly important because it is a scholarly work dealing with issues in praxis. Positive Muslims, as a religious organization working to help those living with AIDS and to prevent its spread, has a unique vantage point of working from the Islamic tradition in the contemporary crisis of the AIDS pandemic. According to their publication, AIDS and HIV necessitate new understandings of marriage, challenging what is often "simply . . . a public procedure where a man buys the right to sexual intercourse with a woman" (Esack, 2004, 36) through payment of a *mahr*, or dowry that the husband pays to the wife as part of the Muslim marriage contract. The reasoning behind this is clear: often a wife is infected by the virus from her husband, who contracted it from previous or contemporaneous sexual partners (to whom he may or may not have been married). Because this is the reality, despite whatever ideals may exist about sex outside of marriage, it is insufficient – at least from the perspective of the wife – to confine preaching on gender and sexuality simply to stating that sex outside marriage is wrong, or to offer a "scientific" explanation for a man's natural tendency to have multiple sexual partners. In light of present realities, it is important to reformulate and reassess notions of sexuality and gender roles both inside and outside of the institution of marriage.

In keeping with the argument that old institutions (such as the sexual availability of the wife) need to be challenged, Positive Muslims rightly points out that challenging old institutions is neither new nor innovative in the Islamic tradition. For example, in the case of slavery, the Qur'an clearly condones the institution of slavery and sexual relations by men with their slaves. Despite this fact, slavery and concubinage have not persisted in Muslim societies. Many contemporary Islamic thinkers insist that slavery is a social institution that must be put into a "historical context"; similarly Positive Muslims makes the case that HIV and AIDS have occasioned a new context for Muslims living in Africa. As such, the need has arisen to question and challenge the accepted power dynamics of male domination. Positive Muslims declares it necessary to examine the motivations from which, and by whom, these old institutions are "placed in their historical context," and questions the power politics of theology while seeking to create a space for more nuanced religious interpretations. The publication explains:

> The question is not whether changes occur in religious thinking or not; about that there is no doubt. Rather, what are the impulses that propel these changes? Does religious thinking continuously reinvent itself as a new orthodoxy in order to hold on to its power whereby men act as the agents of Allah over women? Are we merely acting as unwilling agents in response to inevitable social changes? For us, the challenge is to shift our thinking in terms of a deeper understanding of justice and compassion. (Esack, 2004, 40)

It is out of a commitment to justice and compassion that Positive Muslims has been able to participate in the shaping of tradition, seeking to assert certain, sometimes marginalized, aspects of the Islamic tradition. Just as scholars and theologians have been able to reinterpret the Qur'an and tradition in the case of gender equality and the reshaping of feminine identity, it is time to make a similar effort to respond to the problems with masculine identities.

THE REAL MUSLIM MAN

While academic study of ideal masculinities is extremely valuable, the works of Abdal Hakim Murad or even those of feminists such as Kecia Ali on gender and identity do not speak to the lived existences of the majority of Muslim men and women living with HIV and AIDS. While this is often also true of instructional literature published by Imams or local Islamic organizations, this frequently has greater currency with the majority of Muslims who span a wide variety of educational backgrounds and experiences.

One such publication, entitled *Az-Zaujus Salih: The Pious Husband*, by the Majlisul-Ulama (Council of Religious Scholars) of South Africa offers a perspective on masculinity that has a sizable audience, despite the fact that it differs from works produced in academic circles. *The Pious Husband* is a pamphlet that very explicitly defines the role of the husband, and by extension enforces a normative vision of masculinity in the marriage relationship. It states: "In the Muslim home the husband/father is the ruler. For the proper and successful *tarbiyat* (spiritual and moral training) of his family it is essential that he remains the ruler. If an inversion of roles should overtake the home, the consequence will be disorder, matrimonial breakdown and failure of the process of *tarbiyat*" (1993, 21). The instruction in this passage to husbands is accompanied by expected consequences should their roles not be carried out dutifully: if a man cannot fulfill the role of ruler, he should expect his home to be chaotic and his marriage to unravel. The corollary is that the wife must submit if her husband is to be the ruler of the home; she risks inviting chaos if she tries to assume authority in the home.

In this paradigm, the husband is expected to be the possessor of power and authority in the home. This role is contrasted with that of a servant, or one who is weak and vulnerable. The above model of a "pious husband" therefore places an enormous weight on the man to be the authoritarian figure in the family. In fact, if he cannot bear the responsibilities entrusted to him, he still cannot ask his wife to share those responsibilities (even if she is willing to do so) because of the disastrous consequences that follow a shift in power and authority in the home. Inevitably, this modus operandi emotionally, and sometimes physically, isolates the husband with the responsibilities he must bear. In this context, it should come as no surprise that men encounter problems with being vulnerable; the "pious husband" has no one in the family to be weak around. Such a paradigm conflates masculine normative ideals with power, authority, and responsibility, while maintaining a spousal dichotomy that purposely seeks to disempower the wife.

Such an isolation narrative is furthered by instructions given to the husband about the nature of women. The pamphlet lists seven things that every man should know about his wife. The most interesting for our study of men and vulnerability is the fourth one, which states: "If a man comes down on her harshly, seeking to remedy her natural crookedness and defective thinking, he will break her. This, according to *Rasulullah* (*Sallallahu Alayhi Wasallam*) means Talaaq. The marriage will break down irretrievably" (ibid., 19). This understanding of women further polarizes the characteristics that both men and women are supposed to embody. Women are thought to be weak, with the corollary that men are thought to be strong. This suggests that a man who explores emotions of weakness or vulnerability risks losing his manhood.

VULNERABILITY

If we are to understand that the *"pious husband"* can also be inter-preted as "the pious man," the notion that men are not supposed to be vulnerable is reinstated in gender norms that cast women as the weaker sex and men as authoritarian rulers of the home. In such cases we see religious affirmation of one's refusal to be vulnerable. As a result, a man may not only feel stripped of his manhood when contracting HIV and needing to depend on others and be weak in their presence, but may also perceive himself to be less pious.

Furthermore, we must ask: to whom can a Muslim man turn for guidance or help in a time of weakness? *The Pious Husband* has a very clear message in response to this kind of question. Marriage is not to be viewed as an institution of "love, comfort, mutual understanding and bliss" (20). Such a view is belittled: "Such fantasies are highlighted by the stupid conceptions of love propounded by Westernism which has overwhelmed the minds and lives of so many Muslims" (ibid.). Therefore, it is not in his wife that a husband should find "comfort" and "mutual understand-ing." This leaves the Muslim man further isolated from a com-fortable space where he could be free to express all his emotions, including fear, anguish, and pain. This portrait of Islamic house-hold codes presented by this South African religious instructional material is starkly different from the story presented above detail-ing the Prophet Muhammad's need to be comforted by his beloved wife, Khadijah, when he was distraught. Men schooled in this rote understanding of masculinity who then contract HIV struggle to confront the reality of their vulnerability, leading to a host of unhealthy coping mechanisms such as denial or addictions to drugs or alcohol.

In Khaled El-Rouayheb's book, *Before Homosexuality in the Arab-Islamic World: 1500–1800*, references are given to same-sex sexual activity at a time when a distinctly homosexual identity had not yet emerged in the way in which we understand homosexu-ality today. El-Rouayheb's work shows a clear distinction between the attitudes of those who were penetrated during anal intercourse and those who did the penetrating. During this time period, the receiver was ridiculed for his role, because this was regarded as the role of a woman. The penetrator, however, was perceived in a different light because he retained his "masculine" role during intercourse. El-Rouayheb's work shows that homosexuality as an identity in the Arabo-Islamic world did not exist before the nineteenth century.

The prevailing issue in his work is not one of homosexuality, but rather that of vulnerability as demonstrated through attitudes towards sex. The contemptible manner in which society viewed the "penetrated" person casts light upon conceptualizations and idealizations of manhood. "Real men" were those in positions of power, control, and authority. The one who is vulnerable is detested; the one who is dominating is praised. El-Rouayheb also cites the work of a Damascene scholar, Abd al-Ghani al Nablusi, explaining, "to dream that one is sexually penetrating a rival or enemy forebodes that one will get the better of him in real life, whereas being penetrated by him is ominous, signifying the reverse" (El-Rouayheb, 2005, 14). This reveals more about attitudes towards masculinity than it does about sexual mores. It highlights the fact that sexual acts are not always merely about sexual pleasure; but rather can often be an issue of male control and domination. One would hardly call al-Nablusi's work "sexual" in a romantic or erotic sense. Nonetheless, a sexual act, namely penetration, is a manifestation of control over another. The inverse is also true: to be under the control of another, to be dominated by another, or to be vulnerable was antithetical to male identity in the Arab-Islamic world. This is certainly not restricted to homosexuality. El-Rouayheb's work shows a clear connection between male identity and the need for control, and though El-Rouayheb's study is historical, the same issues are present today.

In the modern context, with respect to the spread of HIV, we see some of the mutually damaging consequences of ideal masculine traits surrounding sex. Though sex is a taboo subject in many societies, one cannot overlook the importance of "control" in sexual relationships and the manner in which it informs one's sense of what it means to be masculine. Addressing masculinities and problematizing masculine identity will inevitably affect sexual ethics. The rapid rate at which HIV is spreading attests to the fact that these sexual ethics themselves need to be re-evaluated and reformed.

MASCULINITY AND AIDS: NEGOTIATION OF SEX

Kä Mana, a Christian theologian originally from the Democratic Republic of Congo, delivered a speech in 2004 on the topic of African masculinity, HIV/AIDS, and sex. He said:

> This male has made of sexuality the confirmation of his power, the place to manifest his masculinity as an indomitable energy. In his illusion, he doesn't think of disposing of the prerogative of his male power. To propose to him fidelity as a way of life is to diminish his power. To impose abstinence on him is to harm his manly powers. To advise him to use condoms equals to take from him his masculinity. He can therefore, not submit – in spite of all the campaigns of awareness building and information – to the principles of and means for the struggle against HIV/AIDS.[6]

Examining sex as the "confirmation" of the male's power sheds light on the mechanics at work in the negotiation of sex. Most married Muslims assume that the wife is sexually available for her husband as he pleases. Though this attitude is often seen in many religious traditions and cultures, Muslim men have the added authority of religious teachers affirming this assumption (cf. Q. 2:223) "Even if she happens to be involved in cooking or any other work, her husband's call has priority," commands *The Pious Woman*, the female equivalent of *The Pious Husband* (1992, 15). It is this "truism" that wives must be sexually available to their husbands, combined with conceptions of sex as an extension of one's masculinity (as noted by Kä Mana and endorsed by *The Pious Husband*) that is literally fatal. Consider a survey from southern Africa in which 12.8% of men admitted to having relations with a sex-worker in the last year.[7] What defense does the wife have against contracting HIV when she is taught to have sex at her husband's whim, and the need to sexually dominate his partner is a major part of masculine identity for the Muslim man? Kä Mana elaborates on the African male's attitude toward sex vis-à-vis power, and concludes that negotiating the terms of sex involves relinquishing some power and, by extension, relinquishing some masculinity. According to Kä Mana, this explains why many campaigns fighting the spread of HIV are unsuccessful in changing male behaviors which contribute to transmission. "These campaigns are directed to a type of man whose ears do not understand the message and whose behavior complies with the logic that he knows, a logic that is contrary to the logic of fidelity, abstinence and the condom."[8] It therefore becomes imperative that masculinity should be deconstructed in such a way that these behaviors and practices are no longer threatening to the Muslim man's constructed ideal of masculinity.

What approach can be taken to achieve this? One strategy is to convince men that negotiating sex is not a threat to their power and does not involve relinquishing their authority. In addressing the immediate crisis at hand – the spread of HIV – this seems like a prudent approach as it is directly related to the means of HIV transmission. However, if a man is stripped of this method of demonstrating his power/authority/control, yet these qualities are still presented to him as essential elements of his masculinity, he will look for other ways to demonstrate these qualities. This merely shifts the problem into a different sphere.

The only sensible, effective, and comprehensive approach to the AIDS problem (including all of the aforementioned problems surrounding it) is the eradication of the need for power and control as masculine qualities. We must create new but viable constructs of masculinity which serve to empower both men and women without reinforcing gender inequity or hierarchies of power.

HIV COUNSELING AND THE MUSLIM MAN

The amusing stereotype of a man refusing to ask directions and losing his way because of his pride retains its humor because it is true. This resistance to asking for help is less funny, however, when it manifests itself in HIV positive men's reluctance to get counseling and help. The pride that prevents a man from being vulnerable is the same pride that makes him reluctant to seek counseling, perhaps at times even too arrogant to see the importance of counseling. The story of the Prophet descending Mount Hira into his wife's arms not only shows the Prophet's ability to be vulnerable when he became afraid in the angel's presence, but sets an example for all Muslims who have been afraid, whose hearts have quivered with fear and trepidation. Just as the Prophet insisted that Khadijah cover him, so too should the Muslim man that finds himself infected with the HIV virus and is faced with the fear of his own death insist that there be counseling available. Where such services exist, he should take advantage of them. There is a need for Khadijah-figures to help those who are faced with the reality of HIV and AIDS; there is also a need for Muslim men to shake their arrogance and walk the humble path of the Prophet to accept comfort and aid. Following Toshihiko Izutsu's reworked definition of *kufr*, pride and arrogance that takes the form of an unwillingness to be vulnerable, honest, and receptive to help can also be understood as an act of *kufr*.

CONCLUSION

I have argued that the AIDS pandemic necessitates an immediate reconsideration of what it means to be both masculine and Muslim. The gendered nature of AIDS makes this plea an obvious and relevant one. Though the subject of masculinities is admittedly complex, similar complexity has not stopped many feminists in their commitment to take up the issue of femininity – an equally complex task – in an effort to respond to the call for equality in male-dominated societies. The realities which are shaped by HIV and AIDS also demand a call for compassion and justice. Responding to constructions of masculinity can be a major tool in the struggle to combat the spread of HIV.

I hope to have shown that Islam already has these tools within its tradition, not only in the Qur'an and the *Sunnah*, but also through a tradition marked by creative and passionate struggles for new interpretations, new understandings, and reformation. As Islamic modes of masculinities are re-examined it is imperative that we look to compassion and justice as guiding ethico-moral principles to ensure that attempts at deconstructing masculinities do not fall victim to replacing one form of oppression with another.

BIBLIOGRAPHY

Ali, 'Abdullah Yusuf 1989. *The Holy Qur'an: Text, Translation, and Commentary*. Revised edition. Brentwood, MD, Amana Corporation.

Ali, Kecia 2006. *Sexual Ethics & Islam.* Oxford, Oneworld Publications.

Badri, Malik 2000. *AIDS Prevention – Failure in the North and Catastrophe in the South: A Solution.* Durban, Islamic Medical Association of South Africa.

Center for Disease Control (www.cdc.gov) on the transmission of HIV/ AIDS, http://www.cdc.gov/hiv/resources/factsheets/transmission.htm (accessed September 1, 2007).

El-Rouayheb, Khaled 2005. *Before Homosexuality in the Arab-Islamic World, 1500–1800.* Chicago, Chicago University Press.

Esack, Farid 2004. *HIV, AIDS, & Islam: Reflections based on Compassion, Responsibility & Justice,* Observatory (South Africa), Positive Muslims.

Hermansen, Marcia 2004. "Masculinities," entry in Richard Martin (ed.), *Encyclopedia of Islam and the Muslim World.* New York, Macmillan.

Izutsu, Toshihiko 2002. *Ethico-Religious Concepts in the Qur'an.* Montreal, McGill-Queens University Press.

Kä Mana. "African Masculinity and HIV/AIDS." At http://www.uu.nl/ content/tbvSAGA18–01–2005tekstkamana.doc (accessed December 1, 2007).

Kassamali, Noor J. 1998. "When Modernity Confronts Traditional Practices: Female Genital Cutting in Northeast Africa." In *Women in Muslim Societies: Diversity within Unity.* Ed. Herbert L. Bodman and Nayereh Tohidi. Boulder, CO, Lynne Rienner Publishers, 39–61.

Khan, Sharful Islam, et al., "Safer Sex or Pleasurable Sex? Rethinking Condom Use in the AIDS." At http://www.publish.csiro.au/?act=view_ file&file_id=SH04009.pdf (accessed December 1, 2007).

Latief, Muhammad Faadil and Omar Faried Pandie 1997. *Towards Understanding Sexual Courtesy in Islam.* Cape Town, Islamic Centre for Research and Activity.

Lings, Martin 1983. *Muhammad: His Life Based on the Earliest Sources.* Cambridge, George Allen & Unwin.

Mujlisul-Ulama 1993. *Az-Zaujus Salih: The Pious Husband.* Benoni, Young Men's Muslim Association.

Mujlisul-Ulama 1992. *Al-Mar'atus – Salihah: The Pious Woman.* Port Elizabeth, Young Men's Muslim Association.

Murad, Abdal-Hakim, "Boys Will be Boys: Gender Identity Issues." At http://www.masud.co.uk/ISLAM/ahm/boys.htm (accessed December 1, 2007).

UNAIDS (www.unaids.org) on "Stigma and Discrimination." At http:// www.unaids.org/en/Issues/Prevention_treatment/stigma.asp (accessed December 1, 2007).

9

AIDS, MUSLIMS, AND HOMOSEXUALITY

Scott Siraj al-Haqq Kugle and Sarah Chiddy

INTRODUCTION

At the end of November 2007, approximately 200 people from over fifty countries came together in Johannesburg, South Africa, to consult on a wide range of issues affecting Muslims living with HIV. Present at the Islamic Relief International gathering were (mostly Muslim) people living with HIV, Islamic scholars, senior Muslim and non-Muslim HIV and AIDS activists, doctors, and representatives of Muslim donor agencies. They spent five days struggling to develop "religiously acceptable approaches to the HIV pandemic that would help governments and organizations" by examining a range of issues from mandatory testing to overcoming stigma and discrimination (http://www.islamandhivaids.org/consult_bkgnd.aspx).

In the midst of this gathering, Suhail Abu al-Sameed took a brave and difficult step. The previous day, a number of the *'ulama* at the gathering had denounced homosexuality, calling it un-Islamic and evil. Shaking inside, Abu al-Sameed stood in the midst of this conference and spoke to those gathered there, "As a gay Muslim, I feel unsafe, unloved and unrespected in this space. Were I to become HIV-positive, the first thing I would lose is my Muslim community. I couldn't come to you guys for support." Amidst shocked silence, he continued, "I wish you did not refer to gays with the (Arabic) words '*shaz*' and '*luti*' – perverts and rapists – because we are not" (PlusNews, March 12, 2007).[1]

To talk about homosexuality and Islam is to venture into difficult territory. Abu al-Sameed – a Jordanian man now living in Canada – was speaking to Muslims from around the world, many of whom come from countries where expression of same-sex sexuality is a punishable offence. Iran, Mauritania, Saudi Arabia, United Arab Emirates, Yemen, and the twelve northern states of Nigeria all invoke Shari'ah law to make consenting acts of homosexuality a crime punishable by death. And yet Jaffer Inamdar, the HIV-positive founder and program manager of the India-based "Positive Lives Foundation," welcomed Abu al-Sameed's comments, saying "There are many gays in my group. Islam says it's a sin and we have to follow Islamic rulings, but we are all human and deserve respect" (PlusNews, March 12, 2007). Both because of the truth Abu al-Sameed spoke, and because of the fact that HIV's association with homosexuality and the West has contributed to difficulties in mounting a serious Islamic response to the HIV pandemic, there is a real need to revisit what "Islam" and Islamic rulings have to say about homosexuality and re-evaluate what that means in a time of AIDS.

It is our goal in this paper to advance this difficult conversation in a way that affords all its participants the human dignity and respect that Inamdar speaks of, to lay out the terrain of Islam and homosexuality in a way that will allow the reader to tease out some of the complexities inherent in the subject. What follows is best understood as a modest attempt to untangle some of the threads that have brought us to the point where Abu al-Sameed was terrified to stand in front of his fellow Muslims and "come out" as a gay man, yet felt he had to. We begin by briefly examining the historical development of sexual identity to give context to the current historical moment. We follow this with a discussion of the different ways that Islam's sacred sources and rulings address homosexuality. Crucial to that endeavor is realizing how all interpreters are socially located and influenced by the prejudices of their time. Because of the content of the texts and their almost obsessive focus on anal sex between men, this paper primarily addresses male homosexuality. Finally, we foreground the stories of gay Muslims, some of whom are HIV positive.

THE HISTORY OF HOMOSEXUALITY

One of the most fiercely contested questions about homosexuality is whether it is a genetic predisposition or a "lifestyle choice." One can see vestiges of this debate any time a religious group explains its opposition to homosexuality; however, most religious groups take a somewhat confused position. An example of this is found in Malik Badri's work elsewhere in this volume. Badri advises psychologists treating gay Muslim patients not to accept the "Western" argument of "biological rationalism." His argument for this is not, however, that there is no such thing as a gay sexual *orientation*, something that is inherently part of gay people, but rather that such an argument is unhelpful and in fact "psychologically damaging to the guilt-laden gay Muslim patient who wants to get rid of his culturally and religiously shameful habit" (see chapter 2). Many gay people are also deeply invested in this question. Often when facing persecution and stigma – from any corner – a gay person will turn to or advance the argument that they were "born this way," no more able to change their sexual orientation than another person might be able to change their eye or skin color. An important and difficult thing to realize, however, is that this way of talking about sexual orientation – homosexual *or* heterosexual – is a relatively recent phenomenon.

To understand how the Qur'an, the *Sunnah*, and Islamic law originally spoke about "homosexuality," one needs to acknowledge that the way we talk about homosexuality today – as an orientation – is a relatively new historical phenomenon. This does not mean it is not real, or that it does not shape people's real experiences in the world. It also does not mean that people in earlier times did not have sexual orientations. It does, however, mean realizing that when Islamic laws were codified, making homosexuality "a sin," there was nothing in the jurists' world that they understood as and called a "sexual orientation"; consequently, they were speaking simply about sexual *acts*.

In the past thirty years, a historical discipline (the history of sexuality) has been developed to try and trace how our understanding of sexuality has changed through time. Historian John Boswell advanced the thesis that homosexuality has existed for as long as human history and that the tightening of social mores against this version of human sexuality is a relatively recent event in human history (Boswell, 1981). This book was published three years after Michel Foucault's first volume of his *History of Sexuality*, in which he advanced a thesis of the social construction of homosexuality (Foucault, 1979). These two authors represent the two major positions when it comes to the history of homosexuality. In this matrix, David Halperin and others have argued vigorously that the only language we use to accurately describe sexuality over time is the language of sexual acts. In this argument, homosexuality as we understand it today is an extremely new phenomenon, dating from the late nineteenth-century medical profession's attempts to classify and codify human sexual behavior. Indeed, the terms "homosexual" and "heterosexual" did not exist before then (Chauncey, 1999, 199); neither did a widely accepted understanding of human beings as people with sexual *orientations*.

A clarification point is in order. The social constructivists do not suggest there were no people who participated in same-sex sexual acts before Victorian medicine's obsession with cataloging and naming sexual "pathologies." Such acts have been taking place for all time; even those who maintain the innate sinfulness of these acts generally do not dispute this. They only suggest that the people in power, the ones writing books and making legal decisions, would not have the same understanding of what it meant to participate in these marginalized same-sex sexual acts as we do today. How is this relevant to the current question? In brief, if this is true, it raises the radical possibility that neither Islam, nor any of the other major world religions, have anything in their foundational texts to say about sexual orientation – the concept that today is accepted and lived as reality by both homosexuals and those who forbid and condemn homosexuality.

In this paper, we propose a slightly more complicated interpretation. We suggest that innate sexual orientation did exist in the time of the Prophet Muhammad (peace be upon him), that the Prophet recognized these tendencies in people, and that the Qur'an speaks positively about diversity in all forms; we also suggest, however, that the injunctions against same-sex behavior that can be found in Islamic texts and rulings base themselves on an understanding of sexual acts, not orientation.

With this understanding, we can now turn to examining both the social context of the Qur'an and *Sunnah*'s early interpreters, and what the actual Islamic texts might say about sexual orientations or particular sexual acts.

Diversity and sexuality in the Qur'an

As Imam 'Ali (d. 661) reminds us, religious texts only acquire a voice through living people. He tells us clearly that the Qur'an "does not speak with a tongue; it needs interpreters and interpreters are people" (Al-Razi, 1979, 249). Although all Muslims revere the Qur'an as the word of Allah, and the Prophet Muhammad as a living example of that, statements about these sources of divine guidance are always interpretations of them expressed by people.

The general picture that emerges from the traditions preserved about the Prophet Muhammad's teachings is that sexual activity is an important form of worshipful pleasure. Beyond its procreative function, sexual play was valued for establishing effective and emotional bonds of caring between partners. The Qur'an addresses the question of non-procreative sexual acts directly and affirms their goodness (Q. 2:223). This openness to sexual play is within established relationships, in which partners acknowledge their relationship through some kind of contract. Such relationships were not limited to formally matrimonial relationships (*nikah*), but included sexual relations through time-bounded contract (*mut'a*), ownership in slavery (*milk*), and other less formally legalized relationships.[2]

In assessing how Muslim theologians in the past have treated sexuality and considering how Islamic theology might address it now,[3] we must start with the Qur'an, which asserts that human beings are created in variety and assesses this variation positively. A verse in the Qur'an declares that "everyone acts according to his or her own disposition" (Q. 17:84). Disposition or *shakilah* is the inward sense of personality that develops within each individual. This suggests that human nature has been created diverse, not just in language, ethnicity, and appearance, but also in inward disposition and personality. This disposition includes many dimensions of the personality, one of which is sexuality and sexual orientation.

The Prophet Muhammad knew of men in his era who belonged to this category of "men who are not attracted to women." The Qur'an calls such men *ghayr uli'l-irba min al-rijal* (Q. 24:31) in a verse which notes their existence and exempts them from normal rules of gender segregation without implying any negative judgment upon their persons. In Arab society at the time there were "effeminate men" (*mukhannathun*) who lived outside the patriarchal heteronormal sexual economy, as described in the detailed study of Everett

Rowson (1997). The evidence presented by Rowson from early Islamic literature shows that the Prophet accepted these men-who-acted-like-women as members in Medina, as long as they did not transgress certain ethical rules. They attracted the criticism of the Prophet only when they helped arrange clandestine affairs between men and women.[4]

After the Prophet Muhammad's death, his community gradually reverted to overtly patriarchal norms of social organization, adopted from pre-Islamic Arab custom and from the Persian and Byzantine cultures which were conquered and absorbed. In the prevailing patriarchal environment, Muslims began to formulate Islamic law, and some same-sex acts were censured as an affront to morality and a sin against God. Contemporary Muslim communities in general maintain the attitude of condemnation formulated by Muslim jurists in the classical and medieval periods, a condemnation based more on patriarchal culture than a literal reading of scripture.

The Qur'an and same-sex sexual acts

The Qur'an contains no word that means "homosexuality" (as an abstract idea denoting a sexuality of men who desire pleasure with other men or a sexuality of women who desire pleasure with other women). The terms that became popular in Arabic in later times (*liwat* for acts associated with same-sex relations between men, and *luti* for men associated with these acts) are not found in the Qur'an at all. The Qur'an does not explicitly specify any punishment for sexual acts between same-sex couples whether male or female.[5] The closest it comes to directly addressing people of a homosexual orientation is the phrase "men who are not in need of women (or have no sexual guile before women)", a phrase descriptively presented in neutral tone.[6] To such people, the Qur'an does not explicitly address its discourse.

The Qur'an does, however, have words for certain acts. Many jurists sought to draw equivalence between adultery between a man and woman (*zina*) and other sexual acts between two men or between two women. However, this equivalence is based on analogy (*qiyas*) utilizing a legal fiction and is not based on the explicit wording of the Qur'an. The Qur'an does specify an abstraction for the underlying moral attitude that gives rise to behaviors and actions that are deemed *fahishah* or transgression; it calls this attitude *fisq* or *fusuq*, which is usually translated as "corruption." As an action, *fusuq* means to break out of the bounds of moral restraint. As an attitude or spiritual condition that causes such action, *fusuq* means not being bound by obedience to the ethical demands of God and is synonymous with the worship of idols (Kugle, 2003, 216–218).

The story of the Prophet Lut (peace be upon him) is the constant reference for most Muslims' understanding of same-sex relationships, and underscores the association between homosexuality and anal sex between men. This story is found in several *suras* (Q. 7:80–84, 11:69–83, and 26:159–175). While the story bears many resemblances to the parallel Biblical story, it is another telling, emphasizing different aspects, adding and leaving out different details. Briefly, the story involves two visitors – angels from Allah – coming with a message for the Prophet Ibrahim (peace be upon him) and with judgment for the people of the Prophet Lut. Lut's people are wicked, and try to attack these guests with a view to raping them; when Lut offers his daughters as replacement, they ignore him. Accordingly, Lut's people are destroyed in a pre-ordained punishment from Allah.

Word-for-word replacement in classical commentaries has given rise to the equation of the Divine punishment of Lut's people with a condemnation of a homosexual orientation and legally enforceable punishment for same-sex acts. This is a conclusion that looks less inevitable (and less intelligible) when one pursues different techniques of interpretation, such as the semantic or thematic interpretation presented elsewhere by Kugle or Amreen Jamal.[7] Suffice to say that while it is clear that some of Lut's people's crimes were sinful and that they were destroyed by Divine punishment, it is not obvious that all the Qur'anic terms describing their wickedness and destruction are ones that specify same-sex relationships.[8] Jamal notes that the terms that the Qur'an uses to denounce Lut's people are not unique to Lut's people; some imply sexual activity but are not limited to sexual activity.

We suggest that the overall condemnation of Lut's people was not about their sex practices in general, but rather the sexual acts of specific persons in the community. Lut's people were destroyed after some of their men "threatened to assault his male guests sexually." Why did these men threaten to assault them? What was the social, political, and moral context of this assault? Should readers of the Qur'an understand this "sexual assault" as an expression of sexuality (let alone homosexuality) or rather as an exercise of coercive power through rape?

The hospitality, generosity, and care for the poor, strangers, and travelers that were exhibited by the Prophets Ibrahim and Lut elsewhere in the story contrast vividly with the "practices of the people of Lut." They do not host strangers; they chase them away. They do not feed travelers; they rob them. They do not take care of guests and the needy; they rape them as a demonstration of power over them. Clearly the sexual acts of the people of Sodom are only one expression of their overall ethical corruption. Their acts are not important as expressions of sexuality, but rather as expressions of their disregard for ethical care of others and their rejection of the prophethood of Lut.

The Sunnah

We find no evidence in hadith reports, accounts of the traditions of the Prophet Muhammad, that he ever punished any men for anal sex or punished any women for same-sex behaviors. There are, however, some hadith where the Prophet is reported to curse men who engage in sodomy, people who act in transgender ways, and some hadith which stipulate death as the punishment for sodomy. The question is whether these reports are authentic and truly relate the Prophet Muhammad's actual words, or whether they represent the prejudice of Muslim communities in the period after the Prophet's death which are attributed posthumously to the Prophet himself. Below, we argue that the hadith reports which punish men for having anal sex were retroactively attributed to the Prophet Muhammad.

The hadith commanding the death penalty is not linked to any specific case or event in the Prophet's life. This is in marked contrast to the ones that address the issue of adultery between a man and woman, which are linked to very detailed cases that preserve the names of the men and women involved during the Prophet's lifetime. A review of hadiths from the two most reliable collections (*Sahih Muslim* and *Sahih al-Bukhari*) reveals no evidence that the Prophet asserted, in word or deed, that homosexual relations were a *hadd* crime, or were to be equated with adultery, or that he ever punished any actual persons for "crimes" relating to homosexuality.[9] Nor do these collections contain hadith in which the Prophet Muhammad discusses the Prophet Lut in relation to sexual acts or relationships. The suspicion that hadith reports commanding the death penalty are not actually authentic is supported by the fact that the earliest Muslim jurists argued for the death penalty for sodomy through analogy (rather than in reference to any Qur'anic verse or hadith report), or through relying on incidents after the Prophet's death, where followers of his punished a man accused of sodomy with death.

Could it be that the Prophet never addressed the issue because he did not see it as an issue of crime and punishment, but rather as one variety of indiscretion? The Prophet certainly did encounter people in his Arab society in Mecca and Medina who had uncommon sexual identities and practices that contradicted the heterosexual norm.[10] Yet he is not known to have censured any of them for sexual acts or sexuality.

Islamic law

Using the Qur'an as God's word, the hadith reports as the Prophet's guidance, and their own analogical reasoning, Muslim jurists debated and formulated a code of conduct for Muslims, a process known as *fiqh*, or "understanding" God's will. Based upon the same divine sources, different schools of jurists had different methods of reasoning and came to different conclusions on specific issues. However, Muslims tend to downplay the diversity of legal decisions and refer to the whole body of rulings with a single abstract term – the Shari'ah or "way of behavior" that conforms to God's will. Shari'ah refers collectively to the whole body of jurists' decisions, methods of arriving at them, and principles from which they are derived.

After the Prophet Muhammad's death, the community gradually reverted to overtly patriarchal norms of social organization, and in this environment, Muslims began to formulate Islamic law. Same-sex acts among men were regarded as an affront to morality, and jurists viewed male-male anal intercourse as a punishable crime. Many jurists, though not all, stipulated corporal punishment for sodomy (on condition that the act was publicly witnessed).[11] Other male-male sex acts that did not clearly involve penis penetration were legally ambiguous, and led to varied decisions. In general, patriarchal male jurists created legal norms which encouraged men to marry women and to keep their sexual acts within the bounds of their contractual relationships with wives or slaves whom they owned. Sexual acts outside these bounds were judged by how acutely they threatened the patriarchal order. Sex acts that were judged to involve a man in womanly postures (sodomy, called *liwat*) were most severely censured because such acts were seen as a serious threat to gender roles. Most jurists did not see other forms of intimacy (such as kissing, embracing, caressing, genital stimulation with the hand or other object) as punishable, though they might be deemed shameful.

Two points need to be highlighted here: first, not all Muslim jurists evaluated these acts in the same way. Secondly, Muslim jurists addressed the issue of sexual acts rather than sexual orientation. What Muslims jurists decided in the medieval period has been handed down collectively to us Muslims today as "Islamic Law." This legal code does not solve the problem of sexual ethics, as pointed out insightfully by Kecia Ali (2006). Ethics is wider than law, and takes into account issues of principle, psychology, and justice that are truncated by law. This means that as contemporary Muslims debate the status of homosexual persons and homosexuality in Islam, they cannot refer back only to the medieval body of legal norms, as if obeying the Shari'ah alone can solve the challenges raised, as if we are living in the same historical moment as when they were written.

Now that we have examined, however briefly, what the sources have to say about Islam and sexual acts and orientation, we can turn to the current moment. We have spoken a little about how people with non-heterosexual orientations were described at the time of the Prophet; what do they look like now?

ARE THERE GAY MUSLIMS?

Oftentimes, homosexuality is construed as a "Western" phenomenon, foreign to Muslim societies. Many do not think it unreasonable to ask whether there is such a thing as a "gay Muslim." Giving prominence to the lives of gay Muslims who are brave enough to tell their stories, as well as examining the little sociological research that has been done, makes questions of whether these people exist obsolete. Suhail Abu al-Sameed, the man who "came out" at the Islamic Relief Worldwide conference, and Nabil Fawzi – a young man from Palestine whose story is discussed later in this essay – are real human beings, both gay and Muslim. While it is certainly true that the "gay liberation movement" in the West has no equivalent in the "Islamic world," it is simply untrue that there are not people who grew up in Muslim homes, in Muslim communities, who identify as Muslim, and who also identify themselves as having a homosexual orientation.

That being said, the obstacles facing someone who is both gay and Muslim are considerable, and it should not be surprising that few choose to be open about it. In an unusual and important study, British sociologist Andrew Yip interviewed forty-two self-identified and selected Muslims of South Asian ethnicity living in England who are "non-heterosexual."[12] Studies such as this provide important insight into the struggles of this group to reconcile apparently conflicting parts of their identities. The emergence of groups on-line from Egypt to England also provides important personal testimony from people whose voices would otherwise not be heard, and allows connections to be made where otherwise individuals would be isolated.

Stigma's devastating effects

A 2003 documentary, *I Exist*, gives voice to a number of gay Arabs living in the USA (Barbosa, Peter, and Lenoir, 2003). All of them were either recent immigrants to the USA or are first generation Arab-Americans. All of them speak of fear and suffering before telling their families about their sexual orientation; almost all who did tell experienced rejection, anger, or violence, or were kicked out of their homes. Several of the interviewees in *I Exist* recounted physical attacks by family members, discussed considering suicide, and explained how they had been emotionally, physically, and financially cut off from their families and communities. Muslims who publicly acknowledge their sexuality often risk ostracism, loss of income linked to community standing, and other forms of informal punishment which arise from stigmatization. Another recent documentary film, *Jihad for Love* (Sharma, 2007), takes a wider frame of reference not limited to Arab ethnicity and USA residency; it interviews gay and lesbian Muslims from countries as widespread as Indonesia, India, Turkey, South Africa, and the USA.

These films show that gay Muslims exist in all Muslim communities, but that their opportunities for flourishing with integrity vary greatly, depending upon their personal courage, family background, economic position, and religious environment. For most, it is a difficult and painful struggle to articulate an identity as both gay and Muslim, and to do so often places them at risk of vigilante justice from their own community. Threats of murder (or actual attempts) are common, often from within their own family. If they avoid actual violence, the symbolic violence of ostracism is very common as they are rejected by family and community. If they do live independently from family, they often face the internal challenges of depression or self-loathing, which are exacerbated by family rejection or the feeling that they are betraying their religious tradition.

COMPOUNDED SHAME: HIV AND HOMOSEXUALITY

How does all of this relate to the global HIV pandemic? It has been clear from the early days of the crisis that AIDS disproportionately affected gay men because of the fact that anal sex is a particularly "high risk" sexual activity for HIV transmission;[13] as a result, AIDS has devastated and continues to devastate many individual lives and communities.

The depth of the personal suffering that gay Muslims with HIV endure is captured in the story of "Nabil." Nabil was a young Muslim man who reportedly contracted the HI virus in Syria. He found out about his status from a mandatory HIV test order by an American employer. As a teenager in Syria, Nabil reportedly knew little about HIV and AIDS. Like many growing up in an Arab or Islamic environment, he assumed it was not something that could affect him personally; like many, he accepted the myth that Muslims do not get AIDS. When the doctor informed him he was HIV-positive, Nabil was shocked.

When Nabil turned for support to his family, they rejected him. His father declared him dead; when he tried to talk with his sisters they would tell him to pray and read the Qur'an. Nabil felt he had ruined the lives of his three younger sisters as well – "I felt no one would propose to my sisters if they knew their older brother had AIDS." Nabil moved to the USA where he slowly came to terms with his HIV infection and the shame he felt about it. Nabil eventually volunteered as an HIV-educator at a New York organization MENTORS

(Middle Eastern Natives Test, Orientation, and Referral Service). He was quick to point out that "Some fellow Arabs and Muslims treated me well and accepted me the way I am. They accepted my humanity." The effect this acceptance had on Nabil was profound: "this reversed my view of life."

As Nabil's conditioned worsened, MENTORS' founder, Wahba Ghaly, called Nabil's family to let them know that Nabil was very ill and might soon die. When Nabil's sister heard, she said, "Please let him read the Qur'an so that he doesn't die like this, away from religion." Ghaly was furious, arguing that "If anyone was close to religion and the Qur'an, it was Nabil. He was very much a Muslim." When he went to ask the imam of Nabil's local mosque to offer a prayer for him in the following Friday's service, Ghaly refrained from mentioning how Nabil died for fear that he would be refused.

Before his death, Nabil agreed to share his story for a MENTORS educational video. While in the video he claims to have contracted HIV from injecting drugs in Syria in his youth, Ghaly told journalist Mubarak Dahir that Nabil had altered his story to make it more palatable for the video. "Nabil" was actually a Palestinian Muslim man named Fawzi, and had in fact contracted the virus through sex with a man. Ghaly explained how Fawzi was run out of his hometown in Palestine because of his homosexuality, and had been shunned by his family until the end. Fawzi had agreed to talk about his life as a person with HIV on the condition that his name was changed and his homosexuality concealed. "He desperately wanted to talk about what it was like as an Arab and a Muslim, to have AIDS . . . but he was afraid the message about HIV would get lost in the scandal of admitting he was gay." That Fawzi could speak passionately about being HIV positive and Muslim but would not admit publicly that he was gay underscores the power of homophobic stigma (Dahir, 2002).

There are many ways that stigma can affect a person. Self-loathing and depression can lead to seeking consolation in fleeting sexual encounters which lack intimacy and care, and in which some indulge in unsafe sexual practices and fall into high risk of contracting sexually-transmitted diseases such as HIV. Some flee both family and religious tradition, and seek solace in a "secular" gay subculture; however, as with Fawzi, some react against this and see it as hedonistic, antithetical to their religious tradition, lacking a real sense of community, or impeding their spiritual growth. Some then turn back to Islam as a religious tradition, and seek to reconcile their gay identity with their Muslim religious beliefs (Kugle, 2005, 14–15).

Who cares? Some additional practical considerations

If the stories and suffering of men like Fawzi are not enough to convince readers of the importance of revisiting a conversation about homosexuality and Islam, there are a few additional practical reasons for just thinkers to (re)consider these issues in a time of AIDS. As can be seen throughout this volume, AIDS' association with homosexuality and immorality in much Muslim literature often prevents information about HIV and how to prevent its spread from circulating widely. This is still true some thirty years after the AIDS crisis hit, when the vast majority of people infected with HIV are certainly not gay men. The equation of the pandemic with a stigmatized sexual orientation hampers the global effort to fight the AIDS pandemic; because of this, untangling the threads that link a homosexual orientation with AIDS and therefore with something that does not happen to "good Muslims" is in the interests of anyone hoping to win the battle against the HI virus.

In addition, despite the stigma against gay Muslims, many of the organizations in predominantly Muslim societies that have emerged to tackle the issue of HIV and AIDS alongside people actually living with HIV are linked to organizations that advocate the rights of gay, lesbian, and transgendered people. In East Java in Indonesia, an organization known as Gaya Nusantara, which was founded in 1998, "focuses specifically on health issue of the transgendered, running a free health clinic that provides HIV and AIDS counseling and free condoms to transsexual sex workers" (Ireland, 2006). In Malaysia, Pink Triangle is a registered AIDS-prevention and counseling organization founded by a number of gay men, which provides information in fifteen Indian, Malay, and Chinese languages (Murray, 1997, 297). Another example of this is the Naz Project, based in London and New Delhi, which provides HIV and AIDS awareness, transmission information, and support to those living with the virus (ibid., 299). While AIDS can no longer accurately be called a "gay disease," it remains a fact that many in the vanguard of the fight against the virus are gay, lesbian, or transgendered themselves.

An Islamic approach that hopes to address the AIDS pandemic honestly and justly must acknowledge and take into consideration the existence of gay Muslims. It must move beyond moralizing to a discourse that takes seriously the lived experience of people living with HIV, their allies, and the full complexity of the issues which include homosexuality.

CONCLUSION – ISLAM AND SEXUAL ETHICS IN A WORLD WITH HIV

We began this paper by telling the story of Suhail Abu al-Sameed's courageous decision to "come out" at the Islamic Relief Worldwide consultations on HIV in Johannesburg. But what happened next?

Abu al-Sameed says that after the session where he spoke, "veiled women, bearded men, the most religious types, came to me and apologized if they had said something offensive, if they had made me feel unloved and unsafe." Though he was terrified when he first started speaking – a reaction prompted by memories of physical violence – Abu al-Sameed was relieved and reassured by the responses of his co-religonists: "This is us: our culture is intimate, warm, based on relationships" (IRIN/PlusNews, 1). The next day brought more surprises. The *'ulama* (religious scholars) attending the conference stood up and presented a document they had prepared and signed. A collective statement was read, "saying that although Islam does not accept homosexuality, Islamic leaders would try to help create an environment in which gay people could approach social workers and find help against AIDS without feeling unsafe" (IRIN/PlusNews, 1). Sheikh Abul Kalam Azad, chairman of the Mosque Council for Community Advancement in Bangladesh expressed support for such a groundbreaking action, saying that "Homosexuality is a sin but we should not be cruel. They [gay people] suffer a lot in the Muslim world" (IRIN/PlusNews, 1). These reactions, while a far cry from accepting and supporting gay Muslims, are an incredibly important and positive step. They demonstrate the fact that, as Abu al-Sameed said, Islamic culture has the potential to be "intimate, warm, based on relationships"; in such an environment, and with such humility, particularly in a time of AIDS, entering into the difficult theological terrain of rethinking Islam and homosexuality might not only be necessary, but possible. It is our hope that this paper, through loosening the knot of homosexuality, AIDS, and Islam, provides the reader with some more tools for understanding both the history of homosexuality in Islam, and what is at stake in this debate.

And what of the people of Lut? As Scott Kugle argues elsewhere, the deeper message of Qur'anic verses about Lut is about the need for a prophetic ethic of care, to highlight the urgent need for the rich and those in power in any society to care for those who are vulnerable and marginal (Kugle, 2003). Those who are obsessed with anal sex between men, an obsession with roots in patriarchal culture and not Islamic scripture, miss the point of the Prophet Lut's story. Perhaps there are more ethical principles that the Muslim community can deduce from the story of Lut, once the story is freed from a narrow attention to sex acts. Lut was exemplary in revealing the challenge of hospitality, generosity, and protection of the vulnerable. He struggled with his community to get them to support the needy, the poor, and those who appeared as strangers. He challenged their arrogance, their inhuman exertion of power over vulnerable people, and their creation of a coercive system out of trade and economic relations. Is this not a more compelling reading of the story of the Prophet Lut in a time of AIDS?

BIBLIOGRAPHY

Al-Din Munajjad, Salah 1975. "Sexual Life among the Arabs from Pre-Islamic Age to the Fourth Century Hijri." In *Al-Hayat al-Jinsiyyah 'and al-'Arab min al-Jahiliyya ila Awakhir al-Qarn al-Rabi'a al-Hijri*. Beirut, Dar al-Kutub al-Jadid.

Al-Razi, Fakhr al-Din 1979. *Tafsir al-Fakhr al-Razi*. 32 vols. Mecca, al-Maktabah al-Tijariyyah.

Al-Shami, Salih Ahmad (ed.) 1995. *al-Jami' bayn al-Sahihayn*. Damascus, Dar al-Qalam, 3:505–520.

Ali, Kecia 2006. *Sexual Ethics and Islam: Feminist Reflections on the Qur'an, Hadith, and Jurisprudence*. Oxford, Oneworld Publications.

Barbosa, Peter and Garret Lenoir 2003. *I Exist: Voices from the Lesbian and Gay Middle Eastern Community in the U.S.* Arab Film Distribution Studio.

Bertozi Stefano, Nancy S. Padian, Jeny Wegbreit, Lisa M. DeMaria, Becca Feldman, Helene Gayle, Julian Gold, Robert Grant, and Michael T. Isbell 2006. "Disease Control Priorities in Developing Countries." At http://files.dcp2.org/pdf/DCP/DCP18.pdf (accessed April 21, 2008).

Boswell, John 1981. *Christianity, social tolerance, and homosexuality: gay people in Western Europe from the beginning of the Christian era to the fourteenth century*. Chicago: University of Chicago Press.

Chauncey, George 1999. "The Invention of Heterosexuality." *Sexuality*. Ed. Robert A. Nye. Oxford, Oxford University Press, 198–204.

Dahir, Mubarak. "Unveiled." May 2002. At http://www.poz.com/articles/177_832.shtml (accessed April 21, 2008).

Foucault, Michel 1979–1988. *The History of Sexuality*. London: Allen Lane.

Ireland, Doug 2006. "Indonesia: Gays fight Sharia laws." *Znet*, October 18, 2006. At www.zmag.org/znet/viewArticle/2944.

IRIN/PlusNews: Global HIV/AIDS news and analysis. "Global: Doors of tolerance begin to open for gay Muslims." December 3, 2007. At http://www.plusnews.org/Report.aspx?ReportId=75660 (accessed April 24, 2008).

Islam and HIV/AIDS – Compassion & Action 2008. "The Consultations: Background." At http://www.islamandhivaids.org/consult_bkgnd.aspx (accessed April 24, 2008).

Jamal, A. 2001. "The Story of Lot and the Qur'an's perception of the morality of same-sex sexuality." *Journal of Homosexuality*, 41(1): 1–88.

Kugle, Scott Siraj al-Haqq 2003. "Sexuality, diversity and ethics in the agenda of progressive Muslims." *Progressive Muslims: On Justice, Gender, and Pluralism*. Oxford, Oneworld Publications.

—— 2005. "Living Islam the Lesbian, Gay and Transgendered Way: a view of the Queer Jihad from Cape Town, South Africa." In *ISIM Review* (Autumn 2005),14–15.

—— 2007. "Sexual Diversity in Islam." In Vincent Cornell, Gray Henry and Omid Safi (eds), *Voices of Islam*, vol. 5. New York, Praeger Press.

Levy, Jay 2007. *HIV and the Pathogenesis of AIDS*. Washington, D.C., ASM Press.

Murray, Stephen and Will Roscoe (eds) 1997. *Islamic Homosexualities: Culture, History and Literature*. New York, New York University Press.

Rowson, Everett and J.W. Wright (eds) 1997. *Homoeroticism in Classical Arabic Literature*. New York, Columbia Univesity Press.

Schmitt, Arno 2001. "Liwat im Fiqh: Männliche Homosexualität?" *Journal of Arabic and Islamic Studies*, 4, 49–110.

Yip, Andrew K. T. 2004. "Embracing Allah and sexuality? South Asian non-heterosexual Muslims in Britain." *South Asians in the Diaspora*. Leiden and Boston, Brill, 294–310.

10

ON SEX, SIN, AND SILENCE: AN ISLAMIC THEOLOGY OF STORYTELLING FOR AIDS AWARENESS

Kate Henley Long

When Madenieja Adams of Mitchell's Plain [South Africa] was diagnosed HIV positive 10 years ago, the first thought that crossed her mind was that she was going to die immediately. Madenieja found out about her HIV status when she took ill in 1993 while pregnant with her youngest son. The stigma and rejection she initially faced from family and friends was unbearable. It even cost her her marriage as her husband couldn't accept the fact that she was HIV-positive. "He started to beat me and would sometimes rape me accusing me of being the original carrier of the virus. After enduring abuse from him for several years I decided to end the marriage. I come from a very strict and private Muslim family who didn't let me talk about my status publicly. I lost my family and best friends who became hostile and indifferent towards me. They separated the eating utensils and would clean every chair I sat on," she said. (Maposa, 2003, para. 1–5)

INTRODUCTION

While Madanieja's story is unique, it reflects the trauma and stigmatization that Muslim PLWHIVs often face when "discovered" – a reaction not limited to Muslim communities. This stigmatization caused Madenieja to lose her sense of physical safety, her economic well-being, the emotional support of her family and friends, and her dignity, as she was treated as sub-human by the people she expected to love her unconditionally. The stigma surrounding HIV in Muslim societies is directly linked to the many cultural and religious taboos that exist around issues of sex and sexuality. Because of these taboos, talking openly about HIV and AIDS is considered inappropriate and is avoided. Many Muslims argue that such taboos are necessary because when the realities of sexual behavior are spoken about openly they are tacitly or explicitly condoned; still others naïvely believe that sexual promiscuity is a Western problem that has no corollary in Muslim countries. Still others disagree, suggesting that focusing exclusively on confining sexual activity to marriage is impractical and simply will not work.

Because of the strong cultural taboos, many of the current awareness-raising strategies may not reach a wide enough audience. In this paper, I argue that by looking at the issue of silence and speech from a theological perspective, we can develop additional strategies that acknowledge the tensions. Performative local storytelling techniques that address the complex intersections of HIV and AIDS with other social, political, and religious issues are uniquely well-suited to be used for such purposes. However, it is important to understand first the role that silence and taboo play in some Muslim cultures and their impact on responses to the AIDS pandemic.[1] It is to this preliminary discussion that we will now turn.

ON SILENCE, MODESTY, AND PROPER MUSLIM BEHAVIOR

There is a loose consensus among health professionals and activists that in order to offer prevention, treatment, and care in the face of the pandemic, there must be open and honest dialogue about HIV and AIDS. This involves open discussion about sex, including forms of sexuality considered illicit or taboo by many Muslims: sex outside of marriage, same-sex sexual activity, anal and oral sex, and commercial sex. Many Muslims view simply speaking about the reality of illicit sex as condoning it, and it is therefore not seen as a viable option for an Islamic response to the pandemic. This presents an enormous dilemma for those wishing to confront the pandemic. Simply demanding that these taboos be broken is unrealistic, so for those who are serious about confronting the pandemic it is important to understand why the silence around sex exists and what purpose it serves. "Our culture is to be discreet," says Serigne Theirno Lo, a village chief in Niomré, Senegal (cited in Quist-Arcton, 2001b). But why is discretion so highly prized in Muslim societies?

First, it is because of the tendency of many Muslims, like many traditionally religious people, to place great emphasis on religious ideals even when such ideals do not directly correspond with the reality of modern life. "[D]espite the evidence of an advancing epidemic, the typical response from the policy makers in Muslim countries is to propagate Muslim ideals, mainly abstention from illicit drug and sexual practices, for protection against HIV infection . . . there is a denial by most governments in Muslim countries that they are facing an increasing HIV/AIDS threat" (Hasnain, 2005). Though the spread of AIDS indicates that there are those in the Muslim world whose behaviors do not align with religious ideals, such reactions indicate that the focus is still on the ideal at the expense of acknowledging reality. Many feel that any open acknowledgement of this failure both betrays those ideals and facilitates further betrayals which will ultimately destroy society. This underlines a tension between the ideals of living of a devout life and the realities of an invariably flawed human existence.[2]

Because HIV and AIDS are linked with "sinful" sexual conduct, the focus is on the ideal of sex confined to marriage rather than the reality of it occurring outside marriage. To complicate matters further, drawing attention to the reality of sinfulness is considered a double sin, for implicating others in the sinful act. Mark Sedgwick explains that in Islamic societies "the only thing worse than doing wrong is to *advertise* doing wrong. To drink alcohol is wrong; to drink alcohol in public is doubly wrong. To tell everyone that someone else is drinking alcohol is also wrong, since, in a different way, this too is advertising the drinking of alcohol" (Sedgwick, 2006, 162–163). It is better to keep one's sin to oneself rather than implicate the entire community in it. This approach is problematic when the sinful act already does implicate the whole community; by not speaking about it, the perception of the sin is minimized and therefore it is made to seem like less of a problem than it really is. As Sedgwick notes,

> in many Muslim societies there is a deep reluctance to discuss general social problems. Evils that everyone knows exist are publicly denied, not only to outsiders but also within Muslim societies. In

many countries, everyone will assert – quite against the facts – that there is no problem of AIDS or prostitution. This not only skews perceptions, but also often means that action is not taken to address problems. Unless it is admitted that a problem exists, there is no need to do anything about it. (ibid., 163–164)

Avoiding speaking about sex or AIDS becomes another way to avoid implicating the entire community in what is perceived to be the sins of a handful of isolated individuals. Even if this were true, the inter-related taboos of contraction, prevention, and disease demonstrate that silence allows HIV to spread and affect more people, thereby implicating much of the community anyway.

A third factor contributes to the silence around sex: avoiding condoning illicit behavior. Many fear that speaking openly about illicit sex and acknowledging its widespread existence will send the message that such behavior is acceptable. As a result, the behavior could become even more widespread since people will no longer feel guilty about it. This same logic fuels opposition to condom use and clean needle distribution.

SEX, SIN, AND SILENCE

Regardless of the logic behind such silence, these taboos are deeply entwined with how people contract the virus and whether they are able to get proper treatment and care. There are several distinct taboos whose combined effect imposes silence about the virus in many Muslim communities. One may conveniently group them into three distinct, interrelated areas: a) contraction, b) prevention and c) disease. Taboos of contraction include taboos around "licit" (marital) as well as "illicit" (extra-marital) sexual activity. This allows the conviction that illicit sexual activity does not happen in Muslim communities and underscores the belief that "good Muslims" do not contract HIV. Chief Lo summed up this sentiment to a reporter when he stated that "The truth is, if everyone just stayed where they were meant to be, as they should be doing, then AIDS simply couldn't spread" (cited in Quist-Arcton, 2001b). This belief contributes to the taboo around getting tested for HIV. As AIDS educator Amina Bashair of Kenya points out, "Many Muslims refuse testing; many believe that you are working as a commercial sex worker [if you go for testing]" (IOL HIV-AIDS, 2006, para. 5).

The refusal or inability openly to acknowledge sexual activities that can facilitate the spread of HIV also affects prevention. If one cannot acknowledge many forms of illicit sexual activity, it is impossible to discuss adequate protection during these activities. Furthermore, discussion on protection during "appropriate" sexual activity may also be unacceptable since it implies that one or more parties in the marriage is at risk of HIV exposure, presumably from "illicit" sexual activity. Of course, this can increase a person's likelihood of contracting HIV since he or she may not take proactive steps towards preventing transmission. General education in condom usage sometimes falls under the taboo of prevention. Mabeye, a Senegalese man who is HIV-positive, explained why he did not protect himself while having sex outside of marriage when he said, "You know, condoms are for those guys whose sexual behaviour demands it, profligates and serial adulterers. But I'm not that sort of man. I don't frequent that sort of company. That's perhaps the reason I don't use condoms. The thought of AIDS couldn't have been further from my mind" (Quist-Arcton, 2001a, para. 14).

The stigma surrounding sexually transmitted diseases means that many who test positive refuse to disclose their status, even at the expense of treatment. Many fear loss of crucial emotional and financial support from their families and friends, physical violence, and general ostracization. "I lost my family and best friends," says Madenieja Adams, "who became hostile and indifferent towards me" (Maposa, 2003, para. 5). Some Muslims even fear how medical professionals will respond to their status. Shukria Gul, a Pakistani woman, recalls that when she was diagnosed as HIV-positive, "The doctors treated me as if I had an illness you get from just touching people. In my neighbourhood people started pointing at me, saying 'she's the one with AIDS'" (cited in Anderson, 2004, para. 15).

There is tremendous tension in Muslim societies between the desire to preserve modesty and standards of sexual ethics and the need to address the pandemic in a just way. This is exacerbated by the fact that both silence and breaking it can be justified as "proper" Muslim responses, and equally that both can be presented as "un-Islamic." It is understandable, then, that there is anxiety among many that either course of action involves surrendering important aspects of Muslim religious and cultural ideals. One possible response to this dilemma is to suggest that in the interest of justice we must speak openly about taboo topics such as sex, thereby giving precedence to the justice/ethics argument over the sexual ethics/modesty argument. I argue that by looking at the issue of silence and speech from a theological perspective, one can develop additional strategies that honor and acknowledge this tension and may also reach a wider audience.

TENSION AND CREATIVITY – INTEGRAL PARTS OF MODERN RELIGIOUS LIFE

This tension that exists about how to deal with HIV and AIDS is not an isolated occurrence in Muslim societies. In fact, it is common both in modern religious life and in the religious history of Islam. Human life is ever changing because it is imperfect: this is complicated by globalization, the lingering effects of colonialism, and unjust worldwide distribution of wealth and resources. Arguably there exists an even greater tension today between being human and the requirements of a life in obedience to the will of God.

Marsden points out that it:

> is often assumed because Islam is a religion of submission that whilst the relationship between the intellect (*'aql*) and faith (*iman*) is important for Muslims there is little place for the expression of individual creativity in the living of a Muslim life, and that morality in Muslim societies is a ready-made and uncontested category simply deriving from a single set of scriptural codes. (Marsden, 2005, 8)

This assumption is incorrect. "[L]iving a Muslim life . . . involves the active experience of intellectual creativity, and the making of decisions and voicing of opinions about contentious issues in fraught social settings" (ibid., 26). Muslims are constantly confronted with high-tension social and political issues, and therefore it is necessary in their daily lives to deal creatively with issues for which there is no clear "Muslim" response.

The need actively and creatively to live one's faith, though heightened in the modern world, is not new to Islam. The early struggles of the Muslim community in the generations after the Prophet Muhammad illustrate how Islam, since it depends on the Qur'an for guidance about issues that the text may not refer to directly, necessitates a level of dynamic creativity on the part of believers. Fazlur Rahman (d. 1988) calls this process the "comparative and interpretive procedure for a fresh application of the Qur'an to any given new situation" (Rahman, 1979, 69) and reminds us that this process is necessary because, in the Qur'an, "the emphasis is on faith-in-action" (ibid., 85). Since it is a lived religion, not a simple set of dogmatic decrees, Muslims are faced daily with the tensions inherent in living their faith in an increasingly complex modern world while honoring the Qur'an and tradition. Muslims are certainly not alone in facing such tensions – Jews and Christians, as "People of the Book" who hold God's Word as a central aspect of their faith, are faced with similar tension. As the conditions we face in the modern world move further and further away, historically, from the moment in which the text was revealed, the process of applying the text to new situations becomes increasingly challenging. In fact, an important aspect of modern religious life may be the ability to address this tension creatively without forcing its resolution, when we are presented with situations, such as HIV and AIDS, for which one "Islamic answer" may be completely unclear.

The creative process for dealing with tension also unfolds in the realm of Islamic theology which, like every other aspect of the faith, occurred in, was shaped by, and continues to develop in its context. Examining how this process dealt with tension and complexity can be useful in determining creative ways to deal with parallel tension in the modern context of the AIDS pandemic. This could also assist us in understanding what role, if any, theology can play in addressing the AIDS pandemic.

Early Islamic theology developed largely as a result of the interplay between tradition, as embodied in the Qur'an and Hadith, and the world and context in which theologians lived. As new situations brought about new questions, early Muslims turned to the texts to seek out answers. It was in the tension that existed between these questions and texts which did not address the specific questions and context of the early Muslims, as well as the effort to resolve this tension, that the Muslim religious act was located. This process is described by the Muslim–Christian Research Group in *The Challenge of Scriptures*: "The religious act is . . . always both a faithfulness to a tradition, a re-statement and a rupture, a novelty in relation to a personal history. The act of believing is a decision that finds real meaning, based on a tradition and a drawing away from it with a view to re-creation" (Muslim–Christian Research Group, 1989, 43). Living a Muslim life, then, involves both a faithful reference to tradition and the creative act of applying tradition to the context at hand. It is the work of theology to place these two forces in conversation with each other and limit the tension they present.

Tradition and modernity are thus two forces inherently in tension which through the work of theology may become harmonious. Such harmony does not come easily, though. In his examination of the development of Islamic theology, Fazlur Rahman elaborates on this theme of theology as dynamic process of struggle. He describes the work of the first generations of Muslims after the Prophet as heavily marked not by the following of clearly defined dogma but by the asking of questions. One of the first questions the community faced was what actions defined a person as Muslim, especially in relation to sin (Rahman, 1979, 86). It is important to realize that in grappling with the question of what we do in order to be Muslim, the early Muslim theologians were in fact being Muslim: the very action required of Muslims was to grapple with such questions. As these early Muslims demonstrated, it was in the struggle, not in the answers, that the religious journey was found.

The way early Islamic theology developed demonstrates how theology is a creative process, one which necessitates grappling with factors both internal and external to the Islamic religious system. Rahman himself acknowledges the importance of theology as process even when the theological assertions resulting from that inquiry are deemed incorrect or unorthodox. It is useful, in the context of complex modern situations such as the AIDS pandemic, to keep this example in mind since it reminds us that even "incorrect" theology can, and does, play a positive role within religious systems because it can offer new ways of grappling with difficult questions. The role of theology in modern religious life is thus twofold. First, theology is doctrine articulated by past scholars whom we revere as possessing some level of authority. This is a reference point when seeking answers to contemporary questions. Second, theology is a creative and dynamic process by which we can think about religious issues as they relate to multiple and nuanced contemporary concerns, a process firmly grounded in Islamic theological tradition. In this capacity theology claims not to provide all of the answers to our modern issues, but rather provides a way of approaching such issues that honors both the wisdom present in the theological tradition of Islam and the new and often uncharted territory that modern life presents.

THEOLOGY AS PROCESS – THE CASE OF SILENCE AND SPEECH

Considering the task of compiling hadith literature is very useful when thinking about theology as process. The early hadith scholars used "a fairly broad-minded exercise of their 'orthodox' insight" to determine what material was authoritative and fell "within the scope of the acceptable Hadith" (Rahman, 1979, 91). They premised their work on a particular basic understanding of orthodoxy and applied that understanding to the particular situation of deciding which hadith were authoritative. They let the process guide them rather than allowing a rigid orthodoxy to dictate their thinking, and so from their work emerged "latitude and integration of points of view and opinions that could not be fitted into one mold" (ibid., 91). Using this creative process allowed a broader and more integrated result than would have been achieved otherwise. Furthermore, this case demonstrates that tradition and the above process may each offer different perspectives. Therefore, not only is it entirely appropriate to rely on either approach, but theologians are encouraged to consider both in approaching the same problem.

This approach is useful for our purposes since it both opens up space for a creative response to HIV and AIDS that takes into account the complexities of the pandemic and is also central to the survival of any religious system in a complex and changing world. Rahman describes the contribution of theologian and mystic Abu Hamid al-Ghazālī (d. 1111) as indicative of the potential that this process has for sustaining religious systems. Ghazālī "brought the formal, dogmatic formulation of the orthodox *kalām* into contact with the living religion, thereby revitalizing them and infusing into them the original spirit of the Revelation" (Rahman, 1979, 95). The creative process not only revitalizes lived religious experience, but infuses orthodox dogma with new and continued relevance. This intersection of dogma and lived religion is what keeps Islam dynamic.

Islamic tradition places great emphasis on the spoken word, the medium through which God's guidance has been revealed to humankind. The weight given to the spoken word is something that carries over into other aspects of Muslim life, and "[M]uslims are not only required to communicate the Word of God, but also to live it" (Ansari 1977, 443). This implies that in word and deed, Muslims must communicate the Word of God. Does this mean, however, that one must *only* communicate the Word of God? Does it mean that all speech must be imbued with a level of truthfulness and sanctity? It may be a relief to realize that humans need not fear that the words we speak carry the same power and weight as the revealed Word of God. It is helpful to remember that while the Word of God was revealed through speech-acts, this very Word is held in Islamic theology to be inimitable. The fact that the Qur'an was revealed through spoken words attests to the creative and powerful nature of speech. While this does imply that what gets spoken about requires extra care, it also means that the spoken word can be a valuable tool in creatively confronting HIV and AIDS from an authentically Muslim perspective.

There is significance in the Qur'anic text beyond simply the words and concepts that it states. There is something about the poetic nature of the language that allows it to express beauty and emotion that are not inherent simply in the definitions of the words themselves. The Qur'an uses language to express what language alone cannot, demonstrating in exemplary form the aspiration of all poetic speech. The combined effect of its message with its eloquent literary style is what makes the Qur'an so beautiful and compelling. This effect is amplified when the Qur'an is recited. The Qur'an reaches its height of meaning when it is recited aloud as it was when it was first revealed by the Prophet. It is clear that beyond what the Qur'an teaches Muslims with the actual words of the text, what the Qur'an teaches Muslims about the *use* of words is equally important. From this conclusion we can begin to think about the possibility of using words in this way as a "theology of storytelling" to address the issues surrounding HIV/AIDS.

A THEOLOGY OF STORYTELLING: MUSLIMS IN CHITRAL

Magnus Marsden, author of *Living Islam: Muslim Religious Experience in Pakistan's North-West Frontier*, discusses the creative tensions between doctrine and modern life among Muslims in the Chitral region of Pakistan. He shows how storytelling as a Muslim practice assists a community in dealing creatively with "sensitive" issues. The people of Chitral whom Marsden introduces are dealing with a tense political situation created largely by their geographical proximity to the Afghan border and the resultant influence of the Taliban movement. Here we encounter a religio-political attempt to "Islamize" the area by enforcing uniformity of lived religious practice competing with a desire to nurture local indigenous religious expressions. Like many Muslims for whom the AIDS pandemic causes great anxiety about the influence of Western customs and sexual norms on their Islamic practices, the Muslims in Chitral deal with the anxiety of outside forces impinging on their religious experiences.

Marsden's work focuses on the intersection between this highly charged political situation and the "important role that music, poetry and travel played in the living of a Muslim life in Chitral" (Marsden, 2005, 4). These media serve as creative outlets through which Chitral Muslims can recognize and confront the ever-present political tension in their society. Not only does this creativity allow them to address their differing political views, it lets them do so in a way that largely avoids friction and encourages the interaction and cooperation of those with vastly differing perspectives. His focus on creativity is particularly useful to us in developing a creative theological response to the AIDS pandemic. The level of anxiety which emanates from the tension between what is hidden and what is open in their lives is also strikingly reminiscent of the experience of people whose sexual practices are "illicit" (ibid., 7).

The approach to this tension and anxiety that Marsden documents involves musical and dramatic performance which exists as "an emerging and contested site where Chitral Muslims debate the relationship between local and global visions of a world made perfect by Islam" (ibid., 123). In the musical performances by the Nobles this tension is acknowledged and its causes confronted. The Nobles are a local music group who perform for free at private and semi-private house parties throughout the Chitral region. Their status as locals lends them credibility with their audience; humor, parody and self-parody, rhetorical devices common to local poetry, local music, and impersonations are all literary and performative devices that the group employs to diffuse the tension that is part of the daily lives of their audience members (ibid., 130).

The group uses these devices to contest and resist homogenizing impulses from within and outside their community and to subvert trends towards unquestioning traditionalization. Despite this overall agenda, the Nobles are not themselves a homogenous, like-minded group. Every aspect of their act, from the make-up of the group to the skits and songs they perform, is designed specifically to address the tension that Chitral Muslims experience. Incorporating social criticism into these performances, they expose their audience and themselves give voice to a variety of ideas about Muslim identity not usually publicly discussed (ibid., 144).

The impact of these performances is extraordinary. Marsden notes,

> The men present were not only rejoicing because they were participating in these daring displays of creative individuality. They were also laughing because they realized the world they lived in and experienced outside the room . . . is one of intense anxiety, and, for a few moments at least, [the performer] had prised off the lid and the pressure had been released. (ibid., 144)

Marsden further explains that the pressure release was even more notable because the subject of the performer's parody was not an innocuous subject, but a known religious figure who played an integral role in the very anxiety that the performance was releasing. It was in addressing the topic that caused the audience anxiety in a way that both acknowledged this anxiety and offered humor that the performer was able to diffuse it for the audience. Since the moment was a temporary one, it was less threatening for the audience, who need not fear that their temporary freedom would have long term consequences, as, for example, writing a response could have.

The approach the Nobles take to address their high-tension and anxiety ridden subject is unique because it allows both performers and audience to exchange, reflect upon, and seriously consider ideas that differ from their own in a safe and non-threatening environment. Through these performances, all participants are invited to entertain alternate viewpoints and to understand an issue in all its complexity. Furthermore, they are invited to respond not only in an intellectual way, but more importantly, in an emotional way to issues that may not have an easily resolved intellectual answer; this highlights, as Marsden puts it, "the richness and complexity of the interaction between emotional and intellectual activity" (ibid., 239).

STORYTELLING AND AIDS

The example of the Nobles reveals several benefits to storytelling (including poetry, musical performance, etc.) as a technique for addressing tension-laden subjects such as HIV and AIDS within Muslim communities. First, the literary devices used in the spoken word can imbue it with a deeper meaning beyond the literal. Secondly, performative speech has the advantage of drawing on the traditions of the local community, allowing it to feel and be organic, avoiding the sense of an external imposition. As it deals with a specific local audience, this approach is also helpful because it can be easily tailored to address the needs of a specific community, avoiding generalizations about HIV and AIDS that might miss the mark with any given audience. Thirdly, storytelling and performative speech are useful in that they can acknowledge, and perhaps even directly address, the tension between the creative power of the spoken word and the potential for speech to be violating. Marsden notes the profound impact of the potentially violent nature of speech:

> A key dimension of violence as experienced by Rowshan people, then, is the violence of the word, and this is seen as being even more damaging than physical violations of the body. While there have been no major incidents of sectarian violence in Rowshan itself, the violence of the word, whose wounds, unlike those of the sword, never heal, is a source of deep anxiety for Rowshan people. (Marsden, 2005, 249)

That speech has the power to violate is particularly evident from the stories of those living with HIV in Muslim communities who fear their status being made public: if someone were to disclose their status against their will they could suffer physical or verbal violence. By performing stories which exemplify the power of speech both to create and to destroy, this tension too can be unearthed. Storytelling also allows for a level of complexity and for personal touches that avoid the pitfalls of a "just the facts" approach to HIV and AIDS. This is not, of course, to say that educating people about the facts of

HIV prevention and treatment should be eschewed; rather, simply giving people facts is an insufficient approach. Adding compelling stories of real people to "the facts" increases a presentation's appeal and taps into natural human feelings of empathy. Finally, storytelling as performance has a further advantage over written storytelling in that it is by nature impermanent. It is true that now, in the age of the internet, anything written down has the potential to be distributed to untold numbers of readers. In the case of storytelling around HIV and AIDS, the fear may be less about leading readers astray and more that subtleties and circumstances intended for a local audience may not have the intended meaning or effect on global audiences. What performative storytelling can provide that the printed word may not be able to offer is the potential for truly addressing localized audiences. Its strength lies in the fact that it actually may *not* have global appeal.

Performative storytelling work is currently happening at an even more localized level in many communities, including communities with significant Muslim populations. Louise M. Bourgault notes that in many African communities a technique called Theatre for Development is currently being used as a tool to spread awareness about and acknowledge anxiety surrounding AIDS (Bourgault, 2003, 219). Theatre for Development is a grassroots movement that uses theatre exercises and productions in local communities to address political and social issues relevant to that community. In Mali, several predominantly Muslim theatre groups use this technique specifically to deal with issues surrounding HIV and AIDS. Techniques such as humor, farce, double-entendre, and the use of jester-like characters are common in these productions, and plays are often used to "poke fun at those in power, especially older heads of household" who "conduct themselves as mature heads of families, serious Muslims, role models for the community" (ibid., 234–235, 237). These productions have great potential to disseminate information within these communities, Bourgault notes, because they use humor both to attract audience members and to hold their attention as they deal with a tension-ridden subject.

When tailored for a specific audience, performed by local community members in a way that is culturally authentic and appropriate in language to transcend literal meaning and convey a deeper message, storytelling may prove to be a tool that is more successful in acknowledging the anxiety that the pandemic causes for so many Muslims. This may be effective in dealing with HIV, AIDS, and Islam, when picking a side in the modesty/justice debate simply does not suffice.

BIBLIOGRAPHY

Anderson, Paul 2004. "Battle to beat Pakistan's Aids taboo." 1 December 2004. At http://news.bbc.co.uk/2/hi/south_asia/4054937.stm (accessed April 21, 2007).

Ansari, Zafar Ishaq 1977. "Some Reflections on Islamic Bases for Dialogue with Jews and Christians." *Journal of Ecumenical Studies*, 3 December, 433–447.

Bourgault, Louise M. 2003. *Playing for Life: Performance in Africa in the Age of AIDS*. Durham, NC, Carolina Academic Press.

Hasnain, Memoona 2005. "Cultural Approach to HIV/AIDS Harm Reduction in Muslim Countries." *Harm Reduction Journal*, 23 February. At www.harmreductionjournal.com/content/2/1/23 (accessed April 21, 2007).

IOL HIV-AIDS 2006. "Muslim women defy custom to fight Aids." 9 November. At www.iolhivaids.co.za/index.php?fSetId=582&fSectionI d=1591&fArticleId=3529236.

Maposa, Sipokazi 2003. "Stigmatisation now the biggest obstacle." 2 December. At www.iolhivaids.co.za/index.php?fSetId=609&fSectionI d=1592&fArticleId=2912001.

Marsden, Magnus 2005. *Living Islam: Muslim Religious Experience in Pakistan's North-West Frontier.* Cambridge: Cambridge University Press.

Muslim-Christian Research Group 1989. *The Challenge of Scriptures*. Trans. Stuart E. Brown. Maryknoll, NY, Orbis Books.

Quist-Arcton, Ofeibea 2001a. "Living with AIDS – Mabeye's Story." 27 June. At http://allafrica.com/stories/200106270171.html.

Quist-Arcton, Ofeibea 2001b. "Women – Vulnerable but Vital Campaigners against AIDS." 2 July. At http://allafrica.com/stories/200107020491. html.

Rahman, Fazlur 1979. *Islam*. 2nd edn. Chicago, University of Chicago Press.

Sedgwick, Mark J. 2006. *Islam & Muslims – A Guide to Diverse Experience in a Modern World*. Boston, Intercultural Press.

11

THE QUR'AN, POVERTY, AND AIDS

Caitlin Yoshiko Buysse

INTRODUCTION

As AIDS disproportionately claims the lives of the world's poor, it becomes imperative to discuss economic justice as a factor in the AIDS pandemic. The Qur'an speaks profusely about poverty and economic justice, offering an alternative ethical framework through which to understand an epidemic such as AIDS which is driven by the conditions of poverty and injustice.

Poverty (*faqr*) in the context of the Qur'an takes on two distinct meanings: a spiritual condition connected to the quest for closeness to God and an unjust physical condition imposed by some human beings on others. Spiritual poverty is the desired state of the believer in relation to God; in this state the believer is in need of no one and nothing else but God. An unjust poverty, however, puts the human being in need of something other than God Himself, imposing an idolatrous hierarchy in which the individual is forced to submit to one other than God. It is only to God that humans should be poor and in need; anything else is oppression. God's call to all of humanity to be maintainers of justice is an imperative not only to secure a just order on earth, but also, most importantly, to ensure that all humans are able to worship only God – to be only His servants – and to be free from any persons, structures, or circumstances that force an individual to be in need of anything other than God. It is to combat this form of unjust physical poverty that the Qur'anic principles of economic justice are intended. This paper will outline Qur'anic principles of economic justice to develop a theological and ethical framework for Muslim Persons Living with HIV to interpret the pandemic. I will reflect on Qur'anic principles of economic justice and charity, examine the relationship between poverty and AIDS, and consider how these Qur'anic principles can inform responses to the AIDS pandemic.

SOCIO-ECONOMIC JUSTICE AND THE QUR'AN

Justice is a central theme of the Qur'an. In particular, a major current throughout the text is the importance of justice towards the poor (*fuqara*) and needy (*masakin*). The Qur'an outlines the components of economic justice towards the poor, which broadly consist of two ideas: an equitable economic system, and charity. While an equitable economic system is the foundation upon which charity is offered, both factors work together and neither can be separated from the other. Although the Qur'an speaks most profusely about charity when dealing with economic justice, charity needs to be understood as intrinsically connected to an ethos of systemic economic equity. This section will first address the major themes in the Qur'an's discourse on an equitable economic system: the relationship between the theological unity of God (*tawhid*) and socio-economic justice; distributive justice; the right of the poor to the wealth of the rich; and the prohibition on usury. Secondly, this section will address charity in the Qur'an: its meaning; its relationship to piety and prayer; who is deserving; and the way charity ought to be given.

Tawhid *and economic justice*

The monotheism espoused by the Qur'an challenged both the polytheism and socio-economic order of seventh-century Arabia. Mecca, the birthplace of the Prophet Muhammad and the site of the first revelations, was both the religious and commercial center for the pre-Islamic inhabitants of the Arabian Peninsula. The Ka'bah in particular was both a shrine to many gods in the pre-Islamic pantheon and a commercial hub for the newly mercantile Meccan society. This society was an economic order that advocated individualism, the neglect or oppression of the weak, and the elevation of wealth as the ultimate form of power, security, and meaning (Watt, 1961, 50–51). Polytheism and economic injustice were consequently viewed as parallel structures: polytheism was the theological representation of a fragmented society that bred socio-economic inequalities. The Qur'an harshly critiqued both and offered the solution of monotheism, the only theology that could unify humanity and secure justice within it (Rahman, 1994, 38). The Qur'an's assertion of monotheism, therefore, was inextricably tied to the establishment of a just socio-economic order. Fazlur Rahman (d. 1988), the renowned Islamic reformer, argued that "the two [socio-economic justice and monotheism] must be regarded as expressions of the same experience" (1994, 12). *Surah al-Ma'un* succinctly conveys this relationship:

> Have you observed the one who belies *al-din* [the Faith]? That is the one who is unkind to the orphan and urges not the feeding of the needy. So, woe to the praying ones, who are unmindful of their prayer, they do good to be seen, and refrain from acts of kindness. (Q. 107:1–7)

The right of the poor to wealth

A second aspect of Qur'anic economic justice is the poor's right to the wealth of the rich. Wealth does not belong exclusively to the individual who has earned it; rather, a portion of this wealth belongs to the poor members of society. Giving to the poor should not be thought of merely as an act of kindness but as an obligation to return to the poor their due right.

> In their wealth there is a definite right of the indigent and the deprived. (Q. 70:25)

> Indeed the righteous will be amid gardens and springs, receiving what their Lord has given them, for they had been virtuous aforetime. They used to sleep a little during the night, and at dawns they would plead for forgiveness, and there was a share in their wealth for the beggar and the deprived. (Q. 51:15–19)

Distributive justice

Distributive justice is a third aspect of economic justice advocated by the Qur'an. Distributive justice entails free circulation of wealth amongst all members and classes of society, and prohibition of accumulation amongst the rich. Wealth should not remain amongst the rich, but should be perpetually distributed from the rich to the poor:

> The spoils that Allah gave to His Apostle from the people of the townships, are for Allah and the Apostle, the relatives and the orphans, the needy and the traveler, so that they do not circulate among the rich among you. (Q. 59:7)

This *ayah* was revealed in the context of the distribution of war spoils between poor Meccan immigrants and wealthy Medinese. Despite this specificity, the *ayah* points to the broader principle of distributive justice, which may be applied well beyond its historical circumstance (Rahman, 1994, 41). It is important to note that this *ayah* speaks to economic systems in society; it is not hoarding individuals that are critiqued, but the absence of a process of just distribution. It would therefore seem that any economic system or policy that contains wealth amongst the rich is in violation of the principle of distributive justice; likewise, a system of distributive justice entails not only rich individuals offering their money to the poor, but an economic order that ensures the free circulation of wealth amongst all members of society.

Prohibition of usury

A fourth principle of Qur'anic economic justice is the prohibition on exploitative practices. The Qur'an specifically acknowledges usury, the lending of money at high interest rates, as a form of exploitation that is strictly prohibited:

> That which you give in usury in order that it may increase people's wealth does not increase with Allah. (Q. 30:39)

Usury is prohibited for its exploitative nature: it earns profit at another's expense without effort or risk. But usury is just one aspect of this prohibition, since the Qur'an forbids any inequitable economic activity. Fair trade between parties is imperative:

> Do not eat up your wealth among yourselves unrightfully, but it should be trade by mutual consent. (Q. 4:29)

Asghar Ali Engineer, the contemporary Muslim liberation theologian, interprets these prohibitions in the modern context to include all exploitative practices, "including the profit earned by large scale modern industrial establishments" (1990, 91). Like the notion of distributive justice, this principle addresses economic systems embedded in society, and not simply the individuals who practice them. Indeed, Engineer's application of the prohibition of usury to the "modern industrial economy" accurately depicts the systemic nature of this prohibition. These principles of economic justice constitute the repeated Qur'anic imperative to "spend in the way of Allah." Spending in the way of Allah is a form of worship: it seeks to give the poor their due right, and avoids all exploitation of the weakest members of society. *Surah al-Baqarah* provides an interesting parable on spending in the way of Allah:

> The parable of those who spend their wealth in the way of Allah is that of a grain which grows seven ears, in every ear a hundred grains. Allah enhances severalfold whomever He wishes, and Allah is all-bounteous, all-knowing. (Q. 2:261)

Spending in the way of Allah is therefore productive in its ability to multiply upon itself. Economic justice is not primarily concerned with a single action between two individuals, but in the quality of multiplication, the ability of actions to establish a just economic order on earth. Spending in the way of Allah and economic justice, therefore, are not isolated acts of charity, but constitute deep-seated mechanisms that comprehensively affect society.

CHARITY

While charity is central to Qur'anic economic justice, standing alone it does not constitute economic justice, nor can it be considered the single solution to the problem of poverty. Charity, to be effective and virtuous, must be situated in a foundation of economic justice. Without the most basic systems in society operating in a just manner, charity quickly becomes irrelevant. The Qur'an is not interested in simply "alleviating poverty" to make it bearable; instead, the Qur'an directs humans towards systemic changes to uproot the very existence of poverty. This section will address all three forms of charity in the Qur'an – *zakah, sadaqah,* and *ma'un* – and their relationship with poverty. This discussion will center around several themes of charity: its relationship to piety and prayer, who is deserving of it, and how it ought to be given.

Relationship to piety and prayer

Just as monotheism and socio-economic justice are intimately connected in the Qur'an, so are the worship of the One God and the pursuit of justice: prayer and charity. *Zakah,* from the root *z-k-y* (to be pure), rarely occurs alone in the Qur'an: at least twenty-five times it is paired with *salah* (prayer). This pairing occurs in variations of the phrase "maintain *salah* and *zakah*", usually as an example of what true faith is:

> Indeed those who have faith, do righteous deeds, maintain prayer and give the *zakat*, they shall have their reward near their Lord, and they will have no fear, nor will they grieve. (Q. 2:277)

> But the faithful, men and women, are comrades of one another: they bid what is right and forbid what is wrong and maintain the prayer, give the *zakat*, and obey Allah and His Apostle. (Q. 9:71)

This frequent pairing of *salah* and *zakah* links ritual worship of the One God with an active pursuit of justice; *salah* and *zakah* are complementary aspects of belief that interact and cannot exist without the other (Osman, 1997, 775). Prayer alone does not signify piety; rather, prayer and charity are equally important, complementary aspects of faith.

The word "*ma'un*" occurs only once in the Qur'an, in *Surah al-Ma'un,* and is used in a similar manner as *zakah,* as described above:

> So, woe to the praying ones, who are unmindful of their prayer, they do good to be seen, and refrain from acts of kindness. (Q. 107:1–7)

This *surah* also pairs charity with prayer, but in a different pattern to *zakah,* which paired *salah* and *zakah* as equal aspects of faith. Here, charity – kindness to the orphan and feeding the needy – is considered the true manifestation of faith, even over prayer. Sayyid Qutb

(d. 1966), the Egyptian reformer, explains in his commentary on this *surah* that the fundamental nature of Islam is the benefit of humanity. Therefore, sincere worship of God will result in righteous action in social behavior. Prayer that is done simply to "be seen" is hypocritical; true prayer is that which leads to the caring of society. Qutb also makes the interesting point that this *surah* offers a very untraditional definition of faith that intentionally surprises the listener. This *surah*, in its criticism of superficial prayer without charity, overturns old notions of faith and virtue, and replaces them with this notion that justice is the cornerstone of Islamic faith (Qutb, 1954).

Sadaqah is the third word for charity used in the Qur'an. Unlike *zakah* and *ma'un*, *sadaqah* is not often linked with prayer in the text but rather with fasting and pilgrimage. It is also used in a more technical way to describe how charity ought to be given and its benefits to the giver. Charity in this regard is frequently used as a method of atonement or ritual substitution. Although *sadaqah* is not paired with prayer like the other two forms of charity, its relationship to other integral components of the outward demonstration of faith is significant, as it indicates its importance. Like *zakah* and *ma'un*, the practice of *sadaqah* is intimately connected to the worship of the One God. That *zakah*, *ma'un*, and *sadaqah* are all linked with prayer, fasting, and pilgrimage, and are all used in Qur'anic definitions of faith, is significant. This union of ritual worship of One God and an active pursuit of justice indicates that one cannot be tied to the oppression of others in order freely to worship God.

Who is deserving of charity?

The Qur'an is at times frustratingly vague about the recipients of charity. A verse in *Surah al-Tawbah* states:

> Charities are only for the poor and needy, and those employed to collect them, and those whose hearts are to be reconciled, and for [the freedom of] the slaves and the debtors, and in the way of Allah, and for the traveler. (Q. 9:60)

Although this verse specifies slaves, debtors, and travelers, the "poor and needy" remain vague. The Qur'an does not answer questions about what constitutes poverty, who the poor are, where they are located, what they do, and to which religion they subscribe, thus explicitly avoiding any qualifications alongside the imperative to serve the poor. In this way, the Qur'an implicitly instructs a universal notion of charity in which need is the only quality one must possess to deserve charity. The Qur'an, however, is specific about the duty to provide charity to needy non-Muslims:

> It is not up to you to guide them [the poor]; rather it is Allah who guides whomever He wishes. And whatever wealth you spend, it is for your own benefit, as you do not spend but to seek Allah's pleasure. (Q. 2:272)

This verse, revealed in Medina, reminded the Prophet Muhammad and the Muslims that charity should be given only on the basis of need, and not faith (Osman, 1997, 773). Additionally, the givers of charity should not proselytize the recipients or expect conversion in return. Ibn Kathir, the fourteenth-century Shafi'i scholar from Damascus, commented on this verse by quoting 'Ata al-Khurasani: "You give away charity for the sake of Allah. Therefore, you will not be asked about the deeds [or wickedness] of those who receive it" (2006, 63). Ibn Kathir also quotes a lengthy hadith, narrated by Abu Hurayrah:

> A man said: "Tonight, I will give charity." He went out with his charity and [unknowingly] gave it to an adulteress. The next morning the people said that alms were given to an adulteress. The man said: "O Allah! All the praises are for You. [I gave my alms] to an adulteress. Tonight, I shall give alms again." He went out with his charity and [unknowingly] gave it to a rich person. The next morning [the people] said: "Last night, a wealthy person was given alms." He said: "O Allah! All the praises are for You. [I gave alms] to a wealthy man. Tonight, I shall again give charity." So he went out with his charity and [unknowingly] gave it to a thief. The next morning [the people] said: "Last night, a thief was given alms." He said: "O Allah! All the praises are for You. [I have given alms] to an adulteress, a wealthy man, and a thief." Then, someone came to him and said, "The alms that you gave away were accepted. As for the adulteress, the alms might make her abstain from adultery. As for the wealthy man, it might make him take a lesson and spend his wealth that Allah has given him. As for the thief, it might make him abstain from stealing." (ibid., 64–65)

This hadith not only points to the acceptability of giving charity to the sinful, but the importance of it. Although the man giving charity appears slightly foolish in this hadith, his absence of questioning to the recipients of charity provides an important lesson. The recipients of his charity did not need to answer any questions before obtaining his charity; he offered assistance solely on the basis of perceived need. Only the community around him quarreled about the morality of his recipients, but in the eyes of God it made no difference. Additionally, this hadith highlights an important point that will be discussed in greater detail later, the relationship between poverty and limited choices. The "someone" at the end of the hadith explained to the man that in its restrictions on free will, poverty has the ability to compel moral transgressions. Thus poverty impacted the thief's stealing and the adulteress's promiscuity; the alleviation of poverty, however, would provide options out of these choices.

How charity ought to be given

Finally, the Qur'an is instructive about the social objective of charity, and a common reason why people abstain from it:

> O you who believe! Spend of the good things which you have [legally] earned, and of that which We have produced from the earth for you, and do not aim at that which is bad to spend from it, [though] you would not accept it save if you close your eyes and tolerate therein. And know that Allah is Rich [free of all needs], and worthy of all praise. Shaytan threatens you with poverty and orders you to commit evil deeds whereas Allah promises you forgiveness from Himself and bounty, and Allah is All-Sufficient for His creatures' needs, All-Knower. (Q. 2:267–268)

Ibn Kathir comments on the phrase "Allah is Rich" by quoting Al-Tabari: "Although Allah commanded you to give away the purest of your money in charity, He is far Richer from needing your charity, but the purpose is that the distance between the rich and the poor becomes less" (2006, 56). Ibn Kathir points to the role of charity as uprooting poverty itself, "lessening" the gap between rich and poor. Charity is not a gift or small kindness, but a necessary process of ensuring the equality of humankind. These verses also explain that Satan threatens individuals with the fear of poverty to prevent them from offering charity. Ibn Kathir says that this is a false fear (ibid., 58); indeed, the desire to preserve one's own security over justice for all is a whispering of Satan. Also important in these verses is the first line, which explains that money spent must come from legitimate means. That is, money spent (including that which is given in charity) must not have originated from a corrupt source. This principle again points to the importance of structural justice alongside charity and the imperative to view it in the context – and not in lieu – of the broad-based principles of economic justice.

POVERTY AND AIDS

There is now widespread acknowledgement that poverty is "fundamentally social forces and processes come to be embodied as biological events" (Farmer, 1999, 14), and that the HIV virus spread primarily along international "fault lines" of social inequality and injustice, and that these factors are "central" to the distribution of the virus (ibid., 50, 265). Indeed, the countries with the highest rates of HIV and AIDS also have populations of over twenty-five percent living below the poverty level. In Zimbabwe in 2004, for example, the national adult HIV prevalence rate was estimated to be 24.6%, with about 1.5 million infected adults, 56.5% of whom were women. In addition, 165,000 children below 15 were living with HIV/AIDS, and over 50% of the country's population was receiving food or relief aid (UNAIDS, 2004, 98). At the same time, Zambia had an HIV rate of approximately 21.5%, and 86% living in poverty (UNAIDS, 2004, 97). Of course, not all poor populations have high HIV infection rates, and not all populations with high HIV rates are poor. The relationship, however, is evident.

The vulnerability to AIDS that poverty creates is twofold. First, conditions of poverty limit a person's autonomy. Patricia Siplon and Kristin Novotny explain that in Tanzania widespread unemployment forces young women into imbalanced sexual relationships with older men "as a survival strategy: to pay for school fees or basic needs such as food, clothing, and housing" (Siplon and Novotny, 2007, 94). A UNAIDS publication provides an additional example of poverty frequently encouraging women into "high-risk income-generating activities such as sex work," where they may even consent to "sex without condoms for higher fees" (UNAIDS, 2001, 41). Just as poverty frequently forces individuals to engage in unsafe sexual relationships to survive, poverty also forces women to remain married to abusive or unfaithful husbands because they lack the economic stability to survive divorce. These examples demonstrate that poverty affects moral agency: in dire circumstances, immediate physical survival takes precedence over moral obligations – a point of convergence with the dialogue of the "someone" in the hadith quoted in the previous section.

A second important factor in the relationship between poverty and AIDS is the structural economic imbalance between rich and poor countries. For instance, in 2004 sub-Saharan African countries owed $300 billion to international creditors (Harris and Siplon, 2007, 267). Charity does not counter this debt: "For every dollar received in grant aid, low-income countries pay $2.30 in debt payments" (ibid., 267). This tremendous amount of debt ensures that these poor countries spend more money on their wealthy creditors than on public services like health care. Both poor individuals and poor countries are especially vulnerable to AIDS as a result of unequal economic relationships that inhibit their ability to engage in healthy practices.

THE QUR'AN, POVERTY, AND AIDS

Understanding the AIDS pandemic through the lens of Qur'anic principles of economic justice reveals a particular vision of moral culpability and necessary action. In this view, AIDS emerges, as Sanjay Basu describes, as effectively a "symptom of Empire" (Basu, 2003), and offers a critique of charity organizations that ignore structural concerns; an entirely personalist discourse that stigmatizes Persons Living with HIV (see also Kabir Bavikatte's article in chapter 12 of this volume); and the role of pharmaceutical companies and economic structures of imperialism that grossly violate all Qur'anic principles of economic justice. This final section will consider the Qur'anic principles of economic justice discussed in the previous sections, in an attempt to reflect on ways that the Qur'an could respond to the challenges presented by the AIDS pandemic. This is an attempt to create a theological framework to understand the pandemic, and to challenge the dominant view that AIDS is a deserved consequence of sexual and drug-related transgressions.

Imperative of economic justice

As discussed in previous sections, the pursuit of economic justice is integral to the definition and practice of Muslim faith. In order to worship genuinely the One God, the command of economic justice must be heeded. The pursuit of economic justice is not only critical to one's own worship of God, but to others' ability to worship as well. It is imperative to secure the liberation of all those trapped in unjust poverty so that they are free to be poor only in relation to God, and are not forced to make decisions which may harm their physical and spiritual well-being.

HIV and AIDS discourse

A UNAIDS publication reported that in the year 2007, the number of people living with HIV rose to 33.2 million, from 29.0 million in 2001. In 2007 2.5 million people were newly infected with the virus and 2.1 million people died of AIDS-related illnesses. A shocking two-thirds of those individuals infected with HIV were living in sub-Saharan Africa, the poorest region in the world (UNAIDS, 2007). Considering the severity of the disease and the extent to which it converges with poverty, there should be no confusion that PLWAs constitute many of the weakest members of society. The Qur'an outlines the framework for monetary charity, but in the context of AIDS, with treatments priced at exorbitant rates, monetary charity is the equivalent of medical care and access to drugs. At the most basic level, the Qur'an speaks directly to this in the necessity to support the weakest members of society. As was discussed previously, the Qur'an places the imperative upon humans to support all weak members of society unconditionally, regardless of religious affiliation or "moral behavior." It is clear that an effective response to AIDS has been hindered in part by the stigma and relative powerlessness of many of its victims: sex workers, intravenous drug users, prisoners, migrant workers, gay and bisexual men, women, and people of color (Csete, 2007, 247). The Qur'an, however, instructs its listeners to maintain justice in spite of passions, to "follow not the lusts, lest you may avoid justice" (Q. 4:135). Refusing to allow the "hatred you

have against others [to] lure you into injustice" is an especially pertinent command in the context of AIDS. The intentional vagueness of
the Qur'an with regard to who deserves charity is an implicit stipula-
tion that need is the only qualification for assistance; there is nothing
one must do or be to deserve help. This is indeed a critical point to
be stressed in the AIDS discourse, and a potential mechanism for
eliminating the stigma that is frequently attached to AIDS victims.
Assistance must be given to those living with HIV regardless of any
personal feelings towards the mode of virus transmission.

Charity without justice

As the Qur'an informs its listeners, charity alone is not an adequate
solution to poverty and cannot ensure economic justice. Instead,
charity must exist in the context of structural economic justice.
This insight informs the AIDS situation as well. As Patricia Siplon
argues in her article, a "charity based model cannot solve problems"
because "it leaves unresolved the fundamental problem of power
inequity. In other words, *charity is a means of transferring resources
without altering power relationships*" (Siplon, 2007, 30–31). Along
these lines, William Easterly explains that AIDS charities fail when
they address only the treatment of Persons Living with AIDS, not
broader issues of poverty such as nutrition, clean water, health care,
and other less publicized diseases (Easterly, 2006, 251). Both power
relationships and basic issues of poverty need to be addressed in
addition to AIDS itself. Following the example of the Qur'an, deep-
rooted structural changes must be made alongside charity for it to
be effective. This means working to provide economic stability,
health care, clean water, nutrition, and employment for all those
who need it, instead of simply distributing the necessary anti-
retroviral medications. A clear example of charity without justice is
George W. Bush's promise in 2003 to commit $15 billion to fight
AIDS (ibid., 239). At the same time, the United States was aggres-
sively pursuing policies to prevent poor countries from developing their own generic and affordable drugs, in order to preserve the
profits of the pharmaceutical companies (Russell, 2007, 254).
Similarly, the Bill and Melinda Gates Foundation has donated over
$2 billion to fight AIDS, while in a single year holding $1.5 billion
in the stocks of Abbott Laboratories, a pharmaceutical company that
prices drugs far out of reach of the patients they seek to help (Piller,

Sanders, and Nixon, 2007). Both the United States and the Bill and Melinda Gates Foundation, while offering enormous amounts of charity to combat AIDS, ultimately prove ineffective because they contribute to the same power structures that create poverty and sustain AIDS.

Pharmaceutical industry and empire

In her article, "Trading Life and Death: AIDS and the Global Economy," Asia Russell details the economics of pharmaceutical companies and their distribution of anti-retroviral (ARV) drugs. Central to their economic policies is the use of patents under the Agreement on Trade Related aspects of Intellectual Property Rights (TRIPS), which was undertaken by the World Trade Organization in 1994 to protect pharmaceutical patents. In the case of patent monopolies on pharmaceutical products – which confer exclusive rights over the manufacture, sale, importation, or use of a product for a period of twenty years – TRIPS can restrict access to life-sustaining medicines when patent rights holders use their temporary monopoly to charge prices that are as high as the market will bear (Russell, 2007, 229).

As a result of this monopoly, ARV drugs in the year 2000 cost between $10,000 and $15,000 to residents in the West (Patterson, 2007, 212). Such an exorbitant cost for necessary life-extending medicines clearly demonstrates the power imbalance between those living with HIV/AIDS and those in control of their ability to live. Although prices have changed since the year 2000 as a result of aggressive activism and the emergence of generic drugs, necessary treatment remains prohibitively expensive; in 2006, only one-sixth of individuals living with AIDS had access to necessary treatment (Russell, 2007, 227). Meanwhile, pharmaceutical companies remain one of the world's most profitable industries. While preserving high corporate profits, these prices tightly restrict who is able to purchase the drugs – effectively, who is able to live.

The discourse of economic justice in the Qur'an speaks effectively to these unjust policies. Firstly, the Qur'an advocates a system of distributive justice, in which wealth is not contained within the rich segments of society but is equitably distributed to all (Q. 59:7). The pharmaceutical companies possessing ARV drugs are in clear violation of this principle: their prices prohibit the distribution of important drugs to the poor, and ensure high corporate profits, which effectively contain wealth amongst the already-rich. Secondly, the Qur'an speaks against economic exploitation and trade that is not conducted by mutual consent (Q. 4:29). The public outcry against these prices, the 1997 South African Medicines Act to permit compulsory licensing, and the development of generic drugs in India and Brazil are examples of the discontent over American ARV drug prices and the lack of "mutual consent" in ARV drug commerce. Additionally, the enormous power imbalance between the pharmaceutical companies who hold life-saving drugs and the poor individuals who need them ensures that these are not equal business partners in a mutually consenting business relationship. Consequently, the patents protecting the monopoly and high prices of ARV drugs are examples of economic exploitation: with no alternatives, individuals are forced to pay exorbitant prices to bolster corporate profits or face death. Thirdly, the Qur'an explains that Satan lures individuals away from charity with the threat of poverty, offering the false fear that charity will result in one's own poverty (Q. 2:268). The pharmaceutical companies appear to have completely succumbed to this temptation: they claim that the primary reason for high prices is to sustain the costs of research, i.e., to sustain the wealth of their own companies. The objective of pharmaceuticals is to preserve high profits (Russell, 2007, 213), not to distribute aid to those desperately in need, despite their products' importance in sustaining life. The fear of negotiating prices, even in the face of a medical emergency, demonstrates the extent of this Satanic temptation. Fourthly, and most importantly, is the Qur'anic articulation of the poor's right to the wealth of the rich (Q. 70:25, 50:15–19). The Qur'an is explicit about the principle that a portion of wealth rightfully belongs to the poor, and that the rich have an obligation to return to the poor their due share. In the context of AIDS and the extraordinary price of medical treatment, wealth does not only indicate currency, but medical care and ARV drugs; wealth in the context of AIDS is equivalent to health care. Treatment resides in the hands of the wealthy and powerful, and has been largely denied to the poor. The policies of the pharmaceutical industry reflect an attitude that ARV drugs belong solely to them, that the poor must earn access to life-saving treatment. However, in a Qur'anic context, this wealth absolutely must be shared – it is the right of the poor and the obligation of the rich.

184 *Islam and AIDS*

CONCLUSION

Economic justice in the Qur'an offers Muslims a theological and ethical framework to interpret the AIDS pandemic. This framework asserts the culpability of the unjust economic policies of wealthy nations and pharmaceutical companies that facilitate and exacerbate suffering, offers an avenue to eliminate the stigma connected to those living with HIV, and demands the establishment of economic justice as a means to alleviate the AIDS crisis. Indeed, it is a Qur'anic duty to ensure that all human beings are free from unjust poverty, so they may be spiritually poor and have the freedom to be in need of only God Himself.

BIBLIOGRAPHY

Basu, Sanjay 2003. "AIDS, Empire, and Public Health." *Z-Net* August 2003. At www.globalpolicy.org/socecon/develop/2003/0802public. htm.

Csete, Joanne 2007. "Rhetoric and Reality: HIV/AIDS as a Human Rights Issue." In *The Global Politics of AIDS*. Ed. Paul G. Harris and Patricia D. Siplon. Boulder, CO, Lynne Rienner Publishers.

Easterly, William 2006. *The White Man's Burden: Why the West's Efforts to Aid the Rest Have Done So Much Ill and So Little Good*. New York, Penguin Press.

Engineer, Asghar Ali 1990. *Islam and Liberation Theology: Essays on Liberative Elements in Islam*. New Delhi, Sterling.

Farmer, Paul 1999. *Infections and Inequalities: The Modern Plagues*. Berkeley, CA, University of California Press.

Harris, Paul G. and Patricia D. Siplon 2007. "International Relations and Global Ethics of HIV/AIDS." In Paul G. Harris and Patricia D. Siplon (eds), *The Global Politics of AIDS*; Boulder, CO, Lynne Rienner Publishers.

Ibn Kathir, Isma'il ibn 'Umar 2006. *The Exegesis of the Grand Holy Qur'an*. Trans. Muhammad Mahdi al-Sharif. Beirut, Dar al-Kutub al-'Ilmiyah.

Osman, Fathi 1997. *Concepts of the Qur'an: A Topical Reading*. Los Angeles, CA, MVI Publications.

Patterson, Amy S. 2007. "The UN and the Fight Against HIV/AIDS." In Paul G. Harris and Patricia D. Siplon (eds), *The Global Politics of AIDS*. Boulder, CO, Lynne Rienner Publishers.

Piller, Charles, Edmund Sanders, and Robyn Nixon 2007. "Dark Cloud Over Good Works of Gates Foundation." *Los Angeles Times*, 7 January. At www.latimes.com/news/ nationworld/nation/la-na-gatesx-07jan07,0,6827615.story?coll=la-home-headlines.

Qutb, Sayyid 1954. *In the Shade of the Qur'an*. Trans. islamworld.net. At www.islamworld.net/qutb/shade.html.

Rahman, Fazlur 1979. *Islam*. 2nd edn. Chicago, University of Chicago Press.

―― 1994. *Major Themes of the Qur'an*. Minneapolis, MN, Bibliotheca Islamica.

Russell, Asia 2007. "Trading Life and Death: AIDS and the Global Economy." In Paul G. Harris and Patricia D. Siplon (eds), *The Global Politics of AIDS*. Boulder, CO, Lynne Rienner Publishers.

Siplon, Patricia D. 2007. "Power and the Politics of HIV/AIDS." In Paul G. Harris and Patricia D. Siplon (eds), *The Global Politics of AIDS*. Boulder, CO, Lynne Rienner Publishers.

Siplon, Patricia D. and Kristin M. Novotny 2007. "Overcoming the Contradictions: Women, Autonomy, and AIDS in Tanzania." In Paul G. Harris and Patricia D. Siplon (eds), *The Global Politics of AIDS*. Boulder, CO, Lynne Rienner Publishers.

UNAIDS 2001. *The Report on the Global HIV/AIDS Epidemic*. Geneva, Switzerland. At www.unaids.org.

UNAIDS 2004. *UNAIDS at Country Level: Progress Report*. Geneva, Switzerland. At http://data.unaids.org/Publications/IRC-pub06/jc1048-countrylevel_en.pdf.

UNAIDS 2006. *2006 AIDS Epidemic Update*. Geneva, Switzerland. At www.unaids.org.

UNAIDS 2007. *Key Facts by Region – 2007 AIDS Epidemic Update*. Geneva, Switzerland. At http://data.unaids.org/pub/EPISlides/2007/071118_epi_regional%20factsheet_en.pdf.

Watt, W. Montgomery 1961. *Muhammad: Prophet and Statesman*. London, Oxford University Press.

12

MUSLIMS, AIDS, AND JUSTICE:
BEYOND PERSONAL INDICTMENT

Kabir Sanjay Bavikatte

INTRODUCTION

There are two recurring themes that have permeated orthodox
Islamic discourse on AIDS since the early 1980s: AIDS is a curse
from God to punish those who engage in immoral sexual behavior;
and the only way to deal effectively with the AIDS epidemic is to
return to the moral way of life prescribed in the Qur'an as interpreted
by Islamic orthodoxy. The implicit assumptions of these themes are
that Islam is static and has no need to engage critically with contemporary problems; that this static version of Islam is "pure" and free
from any human interpretation; and that it does not advocate any
prejudices or privilege the interests of the organizations espousing
it. When engagement does occur, it is limited to those discourses
within the sciences that validate the interpretations of the religious
elite of the day. Discoveries and theories from within the sciences
that agree with the dominant religious interpretations are accepted
as having always been known within Islam, while the discoveries
and theories that challenge the interpretative understanding of the
religious elite are dismissed as "un-Islamic" and therefore untrue.
Simply put, this understanding of Islam has little to do with seeking and reflection and more to do with what serves the interests of
the orthodoxy. Both of the aforementioned assumptions stem from
a deep-rooted anxiety about having an honest and serious discussion about HIV and AIDS, and the desperate need to protect the

interpretive hegemony of the religious elite. Arising from the margins, this article critiques the dominant Muslim discourse on HIV and AIDS by exploring factors other than "sexual immorality" that have played a significant role in this disastrous pandemic. In doing so, space will be opened for further theological reflection around this tragedy.

MUSLIM RESPONSES TO HIV/AIDS

At the Thirteenth International AIDS Conference in July 2000, the pandemic was already described in holocaust-like proportions: "nuclear weapons could not damage the continent of Africa more." Approximately twenty-five million have died from AIDS in the less than thirty years since the HIV virus was first recognized, and the majority of these deaths have happened in the developing world (Harris, 2007, 1). Today, 39.5 million people are living with the virus; two-thirds of these reside in sub-Saharan Africa, the poorest region in the world (UNAIDS, 2006). AIDS-related illnesses will kill two-thirds of teenagers in some African countries; thirty million orphans are expected by the year 2010; and life expectancies are dropping from seventy to thirty years in many African countries (ibid.).

Despite the enormity of this crisis, Muslim responses to it have focused almost exclusively on the culpability of infected individuals who have engaged in sexual immorality. An illustration of this is the paper "Islam and AIDS," published by the Lenasia branch of the Jami'atul Ulama, a South African council of Muslim theologians (www.jamiat.org.za). Here AIDS is presented as a homosexual disease that began in the United States. Examples are presented of an HIV-positive girl in Pinetown, South Africa, who had eighty different sexual partners in a month, and the prostitutes of Nairobi of whom two-thirds are HIV-positive. The reader is directed towards the conclusion that freely chosen sexual immorality is the only reason for a disease that has killed twenty-five million individuals. The article is disingenuous, using shock value and a specific deployment of statistics and examples to serve a predetermined conclusion. Such tactics mask the variety of other causes that have resulted in the spread of the disease.

A survey conducted by Ashraf Mohammed of fifty-three mosques in the Western Cape region of South Africa revealed that over two-thirds of religious leaders believe that AIDS is a curse from God. This belief is also reflected on the websites of prominent Muslim organizations. The Muslim Judicial Council, a clerical body in Cape Town, has not officially put forth any theories on the origins of AIDS, but in an online article entitled "AIDS: Stigmatize or Show Mercy?" suggests that AIDS is a curse from God:

> Allah the Almighty has on occasion punished various tribes of people for their wrongful behaviour. "So We sent [plagues] on them: Wholesale Death, Locusts, Lice, Frogs, and Blood: Signs openly self-explained: but they were steeped in arrogance – a people given to sin" (Al-A'raf, 7:133). (Muslim Judicial Council, www.mjc.org.za)

The Muslim AIDS Committee in South Africa explained in their workshop manual, "Is AIDS a Punishment from Allah for the Immorality that is Rampant in Society?" that: "Those stricken by it [AIDS] due to their indulgence in immoral and illicit deeds and who pay no heed to it are most definitely subjected to the punishment and wrath of Allah" (cited in Ahmed, unpublished). The manual then addresses the children and sexually righteous who suffer from HIV/AIDS:

> These people will not be classified as those being punished by Allah, but rather as suffering from the evil prevailing in society due to the wave of immorality and sexual permissiveness engulfing them. This is due to the fact that the consequence of the evil doers is not restricted only to them but affects society as a whole. The innocent are not spared, with the ultimate judgment resting in the hands of Allah. For these innocent people, it is hoped that the disease becomes a means of kaffarrah [atonement] and elevation of their stages in the Aakhirah [afterlife]. (ibid.)

Such explanations view AIDS only in light of sexual immorality and divine reprimand; even the innocent are part of God's larger plan of punishment. The operating equation is that sexual immorality causes punishment and suffering. Although many theological alternatives exist – later this paper will argue that the prevailing Muslim position is theologically dishonest – the dominant religious interests and the argument that God's motives are inscrutable preclude further debate or reflection as un-Islamic and therefore untenable. Unfortunately, AIDS has been used as a Trojan horse to preserve reactionary interpretations of Islam and specific class and patriarchal interests. In real terms, this discourse has had a devastating impact on Muslims living with HIV, who fear revealing their status and subsequent rejection, isolation, or violence.

BEYOND INDIVIDUAL JUDGMENT TO STRUCTURAL INDICTMENT

According to the Muslim religious establishment, the HIV pandemic is caused by sexual misbehavior. Specific forms of sexual misbehavior, such as marital infidelity, pre-marital sex, and homosexuality, are invariably identified as the result of too little religion and Western-inspired promiscuity. The proposed solution is equally simple: no adultery, no pre-marital sex, and no homosexuality. Drug abuse, alcoholism, domestic violence, rape, lack of bodily integration of women, and poverty and its structural causes are rarely identified by Muslims as reasons for the pandemic, and are consequently not flagged as arenas for religious intervention. Instead, the virus is being used as a vehicle to affirm hetero-patriarchal interpretations of the religion, irrespective of their effectiveness in curtailing the spread of the disease.

Although unsafe sex is universally acknowledged as a major factor in the spread of HIV/AIDS, sexual promiscuity alone is not an indicator of one's HIV status. To gain a fuller and more realistic picture of the spread of HIV, we must ask: what are the conditions that make some groups – the poor and especially poor women – particularly vulnerable to HIV infection, while other sexually promiscuous groups remain marginally affected? Put another way: what makes impoverished individuals indulge in high-risk behavior and why is there a lower infection rate amongst the wealthy and promiscuous? The logic of the religious establishment states that sexual promiscuity is freely chosen, and that individual actions have little to do with socio-economic conditions. This logic ignores most of the available data on AIDS prevention initiatives. Though the following examples are of non-Muslims, they may offer some lessons to the Muslim community.

The HIV education program put forward by the Ugandan government has often been hailed as a model of effectiveness. Although their education strategies have succeeded in reducing HIV prevalence in certain populations, reduction has not been uniform between the wealthy urban and poor rural classes. Physicians in wealthy urban clinics observed a decreased prevalence among their patients as a result of education initiatives, while prevalence has not reduced amongst the poor rural populace, who constitute eighty-seven percent of the country's population (Parkhurst, 2002). The limited effectiveness of the Ugandan model is based on several mistaken assumptions. Studies have repeatedly shown that the top epidemiological predictor for HIV infection around the world is not "risk behavior," but low income level. This means that education models that promote sexual abstinence will not significantly benefit those most vulnerable to HIV infection. The problematic assumption here is that people living in poverty possess sufficient agency to control the circumstances of their lives even in the contexts of gender inequality and minimal income opportunities outside commercial sex work (Jewkes, Levin, and Penn-Kekana, 2003). The risk to which the vulnerable expose themselves has little to do with ignorance or heedlessness, but is the outcome of the marginalized situations in which they find themselves. A number of surveys affirm this conclusion: irrespective of the moral presumptions of the religious and political establishments, those most at risk of HIV frequently do understand how the virus is transmitted, and ironically have sex rates lower than wealthy regions in the United States and Japan (Farmer, Connors, and Simmons, 1996). A sex worker from Harare in Zimbabwe sums this up in the following statement: "I can choose to die of starvation now, or of AIDS later." Clearly, in relation to AIDS, sex is not the problem as much as the circumstances surrounding it. The relevant question is evidently why sex among the poor seems to lead to far greater HIV transmission than sex among the wealthy,

Another example is the South African mining sector, where HIV infection rates are relatively high. This example demonstrates what other interviews have shown: that amongst the marginalized, clean water, food, financial independence, and housing are greater concerns than possible infection (Wojcicki, 2002). One miner explained:

> Every time you go underground you have to wear a lamp on your head. Once you take on that lamp you know that you are wearing death. Where you are going you are not sure whether you will come back to the surface alive or dead. It is only with luck if you come to the surface still alive because everyday somebody gets injured or dies. (Campbell, 1997, 276)

Living every day with a forty-two percent injury rate, it is clear that a disease which may kill a man ten years later is a miner's last concern. Instead, alcohol and commercial sex become avenues for relieving the exhaustion from work and the perpetual anxiety stemming from fear of a sudden and violent death. Personalist and psychological approaches will label the problem as essentially one of a certain norm of "masculinity" (expressed through the solicitation of prostitutes) in South African "culture" and classify the miner cited above as a person with low self-esteem. To locate "culture" (and personality) as the problem is to ignore the perspective of miners themselves and their circumstances of poverty (Basu, 2003).

The idea that AIDS is simply the consequence of religious negligence and that the answer is merely to "return to Islam" ignores the role of structural violence, inequality, and lack of resources. When these basic issues are left unaddressed, even the most fervent of Islamic exhortations will be of no avail. Even after Islamic messages with threats of divine wrath are dispensed amongst believers, studies have shown that "providing information about health risks changes the behaviour of, at most, one in four people – generally those who are more affluent and better educated," according to a systematic review of evidence in the *British Medical Journal* (Campbell and Mzaidume, 2002).

In response to evidence that many education initiatives are failing in poor regions (those hit hardest by HIV), and belated but growing awareness of the increase in prevalence among Muslims, there has been a shift towards "culture specific interventions." This shift follows the belief that education models have failed due to their neglect of unique cultural and religious beliefs in each community, and that a return to "tradition" is the solution. This line of argument bears an uneasy resemblance to the calculus of imperialist rhetoric that brands the many social scenes in Islam as one. Here too, the solution for both Muslim men and women, rich and poor, are the same: a return to the faith. These responses aim to solve the AIDS problem simply by Islamizing the secular education intervention without addressing the structural causes of the pandemic.

Also ignored in this discussion is the impact of neoliberalism on the transmission of HIV. Neoliberalism is the context in which the rapid movement of capital is privileged over long-term investment and people's ability to secure their own livelihoods. Although rarely acknowledged, increases in forced migration are strongly

correlated with some of the most significant increases in HIV transmission across Southern Africa, East Asia, Eastern Europe, and Latin
America. As such, migration occurs most frequently when rural
agricultural sectors are destroyed after the liberalization of markets
and the subsequent drop in primary commodity prices, leading predominantly to male laborers leaving their families to find work in
urban centres. In sectors of southern Africa, miners are housed in
all-male barracks for months at a time, worked six days a week, and
given alcohol to "keep them happy" (or to keep them from rebelling)
on the seventh day. The seventh day of intoxication and depression
leads to the solicitation of prostitutes. The men are returned home
only to die, and frequently find that their wives have either left them
or entered prostitution to find other sources of income. Other women,
who awaited their husbands' return, are then infected with HIV. The
"rural women's epidemic" – women in rural zones who have been
infected by their migrant male husbands – is an unsurprising piece
of a larger context of injustice and poverty (Vaughan, 1991, n.12). In
fact, as early as 1992, a UN report stated that for most women, the
greatest risk factor in HIV transmission is not being a sex worker,
but simply being married (cited in Farmer, 1999, 105–106). Instead
of looking simply at sexual acts, the circumstances surrounding sex
need to be examined. This includes the lack of agency that poverty
imposes, and gender inequities, among many other factors.

TREATMENT

UNAIDS estimated that a relatively small amount of annual money
could provide medication for those infected with HIV/AIDS, and
prevent a significant percentage of new infections. In 2002, this
amount was $10 billion per year, with the United States contrib-
uting $1 billion; in the 2006 Political Declaration on HIV/AIDS,
the UN member states recognized that this figure will have climbed
to $20–23 billion per year by 2010. This amount of money seems
daunting, so it should be understood in perspective. The US spent
$60 billion in a special military appropriation shortly after the
World Trade Center was destroyed, and budgeted $556 billion for
military aircraft in 2007. Despite the relatively small size of this
request, only $450 million was pledged and only half of that – $250

million – distributed in 2001. To put this $250 million of actual aid in perspective, sub-Saharan Africa pays $270 million per *week* to its international creditors. During the same year that the US gave just one-quarter of the UN's request, three million people died from AIDS – the equivalent of about 1,000 September 11 attacks – and five million new people were infected with HIV. In 2006/7, UNAIDS received a pledge of $42 million from the USA. Even with this apparent improvement, the total voluntary contributions as released in the UNAIDS "Making the Money Work" report of 2007 was still just over $250 million (UNAIDS, 2007, 60).

The accelerated rate of HIV infection in the developing world and beyond is inextricably tied to two major economic factors. First are the policies of the International Monetary Fund (IMF), the World Bank, and the efforts of the United States and other governments to maximize profits. In the past twenty years, the policies of these organizations have led to the reinforcement of social inequalities, consequently exacerbating the level of suffering and death from AIDS related causes. An example of this occurred in 1995, with the creation of the World Trade Organization (WTO) and the increased protection of intellectual property rights. The birth of the WTO gave rise to the formalized protection of intellectual property in a new agreement called Trade Related Aspects of Intellectual Property Rights (TRIPS). Under TRIPS, developing countries were not permitted to make or buy unlicensed generic copies of the new drugs. Even before the creation of the WTO, the American administration of President Clinton sought to extend patent protections globally. In securing these policies, however, the WTO ensured that drug company profits took precedence over saving lives. Starkly put, new drugs failed to reach the individuals who most needed them.

Secondly, the accelerated rate of HIV infection in the developing world has coincided with, and was exacerbated by, the adoption of neoliberal policies, also known as Structural Adjustment Programs, as the primary method of dealing with debt and poverty in developing countries. For example, in the 1980s African nations experienced a debt crisis and became increasingly dependent on the World Bank and IMF for loans. The conditions attached to these loans required African countries to enact economic changes that favored "free markets," including cutbacks in government spending and the privatization of government industries and services. While these adjustments were purportedly intended to make African economies stronger and more competitive, in fact they made them weaker and more dependent on foreign loans. World Bank and IMF loan conditions reversed progress by making drastic cuts to health care spending; as a result, infant mortality rates rose and life expectancies decreased. According to a report by the Inter-Church Coalition on Africa, spending on health care fell by fifty percent in the forty-two poorest African nations during the 1980s.

CONCLUSION

Merely being Muslim is insufficient security against a pandemic that breeds in conditions of misery and affects the people living therein irrespective of their faith. To be a Muslim who understands something about the Qur'anic imperative to be just and to uphold justice is to appreciate and oppose the structural causes for the present crisis, and to know that all of us are complicit in them. It is easy to blame individuals and thereby shift the blame from ourselves. It is far more convenient to do this than ask "How have I supported these structures of capitalism, racism, and patriarchy that have caused this untold misery?" It is only when we do this that we truly emulate the justice of the Prophet of Allah (peace be upon him). For this we must begin to move away from laying easy blame on the victims, and fight against the very roots of oppression. The Prophet of Allah has told us "the best jihad is to speak a word of truth to an unjust ruler" (Khan, 2008, 9).

BIBLIOGRAPHY

Ahmed, Abdul Kayum. "Islam and AIDS," Chapter 2, unpublished. Available from author.
Basu, Sanjay 2003. "AIDS, Empire, and Public Health." *Z-Net* August 2003. At www.globalpolicy.org/socecon/develop/2003/0802public.htm.
Campbell, C. 1997. "Migrancy, Masculine Identities and AIDS: The Psychosocial Context of HIV Transmission on the South African Gold Mines." *Social Science and Medicine*, 45(2): 273–81.
Campbell, C., and Y. Mzaidume 2002. "How can HIV be prevented in South Africa? A Social Perspective." *British Medical Journal*, 324: 229–232.

Farmer, Paul 1999. *Infections and Inequalities: The Modern Plagues.* Berkeley, CA, University of California Press.

Farmer, Paul, Margaret Connors, and Janie Simmons (eds) 1996. *Women, Poverty and AIDS: Sex, Drugs, and Structural Violence.* Monroe, ME, Common Courage Press.

Freilich, Stuart 2007. "Roaring skyward: military aircraft spending provides the boost to surging aerospace alloy values." *Recycling Today*, 1 January. At www.encyclopedia.com/doc/1G1–158681568. html (accessed March 3, 2008).

Harris, Paul G. 2007. "Local, National, and International Perspectives." In Paul G. Harris and Patricia D. Siplon (eds), *The Global Politics of AIDS.* Boulder, CO, Lynne Rienner Publishers.

Hunter, M. 2002. "The Materiality of Everyday Sex: Thinking Beyond Prostitution." *African Studies* (2002): 99–120.

Jewkes, R. K., J. B. Levin, and L. A. Penn-Kekana 2003. "Gender Inequalities, Intimate Partner Violence and HIV Preventive Practices: Findings of a South African Cross-Sectional Study." *Social Science and Medicine* (2003): 125–134.

Khan, Maulana Wahiduddin 2008. *Non-Violence and Islam.* Goodword Books.

Parkhurst, J. O. 2002. "The Ugandan Success Story? Evidence and claims of HIV-1 Prevention." *The Lancet* (2002): 78–80.

UNAIDS 2001. *The Report on the Global HIV/AIDS Epidemic.* Geneva, Switzerland.

UNAIDS 2006. *2006 AIDS Epidemic Update.* Geneva, Switzerland.

UNAIDS 2007. *UNAIDS Annual Report: Making the Money Work.* Geneva, Switzerland. At http://data.unaids.org/pub/Report/2007/2006_unaids_annual_report_en.pdf.

Vaughan, M. 1991. *Curing Their Ills: Colonial Power and African Illness.* Palo Alto, CA, Stanford University Press.

Wojcicki, J. M. 2002. "She Drank His Money: Survival Sex and the Problem of Violence in Taverns in Gauteng Province, South Africa." *Medical Anthropology Quarterly* (2002): 267–293.

13

INJECTING DRUG USE, HIV, AND AIDS
IN THE MUSLIM WORLD

Chris Byrnes

INTRODUCTION

Shafeeq has a bright smile that warms over his broken teeth. One eye is cloudy and the other clear, and both quickly dart around as his attention wanders. Proudly, he shows me his necklace: a leather cord with a silver-colored scorpion. Shafeeq is forty-two years old and has been living on the streets of Lahore since he was twelve. Popularly known as *Shikra* (eagle), he is a local in the area behind Data Darbar, one of the city's famous Sufi shrines. A medic that he encounters nearly every day in the park is Dr. Hafiz Khair, who is my guide today. Dr. Khair works with injecting drug users (IDUs) and explains that the park behind Data Darbar is one of the most popular places for local drug users. Shafeeq is what you might call the park's chargé d'affaires. Twenty years of drug injecting has given him expertise in doing other users the favor of helping them inject more safely. Shafeeq politely bids Dr. Khair and me "*Khuda hafiz*" (God protect) and goes to tend to another user before taking his high.

Shafeeq and his proximity to Data Darbar are not unique either to Pakistan or to the Muslim world. Similar stories are plentiful in countries like Malaysia, Iran, Bangladesh, and Indonesia, each of which has more than 100,000 injecting drug users (Aceijas et al., 2004). The rates of IDU growth are especially high in and around countries with large opiate drug trafficking operations, such as Afghanistan,

Iran, Pakistan, and the Central Asian Republics. However, when it comes to obtaining indisputable facts and reliable figures about injecting drug users and their lives, social stigma and regional instability greatly hinder efforts to characterize IDU communities over large geographical areas (Hasnain, 2005, 1). The task becomes even more difficult when coupled with the fact that injection drug use is a primary cause of the spread of HIV in much of the Muslim world (UNODC, 2005a, 148).

When we talk about injecting drug use and HIV in the Muslim world, and often in other communities as well, we are essentially talking about the lives of a group of people, frequently from low-income and marginalized communities, living with a condition that often remains seriously misunderstood. IDUs are often located in the midst of a much larger cross-section of society that is shaped by a complex underworld of black-market drug sales and often-dangerous sex work. In much of the Muslim world, where sexuality is seen as a private matter and drug use is socially forbidden, the taboos that surround most people living with HIV lead to serious stigmatization and marginalization (Hasnain, 2005, 1). Stigma often takes the form of oversimplification and dehumanization, as individuals are seen as one-dimensional beings that can be comprehensively and categorically defined as "drug abuser" or "prostitute." Even the more acceptable terms of "injecting drug user" and "sex worker" can be used to these ends. The outcome of these attitudes has been popular intervention and rehabilitation programs that do not deal holistically with the lives and living conditions of the human beings behind the labels.

This paper looks first at the current situation of injecting drug use and its role in the spread of HIV within the Muslim world, and secondly at several responses to IDUs. It draws on examples from Iran, Saudi Arabia, Pakistan, Bangladesh, and Malaysia. The study does not provide a comprehensive or definitive picture of injecting drug use and HIV in the Muslim world, but rather uses the selected countries to exemplify tendencies across an array of social and political contexts. Finally, the paper highlights key components of relatively successful responses that deal directly with problems central to the intersection of injecting drug use and the spread of HIV.

INJECTING DRUG USE AND THE SPREAD OF
HIV AND AIDS

Injecting drug users are faced with two occasionally incompatible health goals: preventing injection-related health problems, and preventing the transmission of HIV. For users who do not know about the dangers of HIV, injection-related health problems are often avoided with the help of expert users. Although injecting with expert users helps to minimize the risk of injection-point infection, abscess, and overdose, it can create a health risk because expert injectors often use the same needle on multiple users without sterilization. When needles are scarce, proficient injectors are known to inject a group of IDUs up to four times per day over a period of two months with the same needle (Razzaghi, 2006). It is for that reason that Dr. Khair described Shafeeq as both a great help and a great hindrance to the IDU community. He is the quintessential long-term IDU. The fact that he knows how to inject others in a way that minimizes their risk of injection-point infection is important because in Lahore most hospitals refuse to treat people like Shafeeq (Khair, 2007). As Dr. Khair treats a client with a severely infected and abscessed injecting point, he notes that without this care the wound may become terribly debilitating and painful.

On the other hand, Shafeeq represents one of the greatest health risks to the IDU community and the whole of Pakistani society. As a long-term IDU who has spent much of his life on the streets, Shafeeq and people like him are great concerns to a region trying desperately to stave off an HIV epidemic. Throughout the Muslim world, sharing syringes is often the most prevalent method of HIV transmission (UNODC, 2005a, 148). The longer one is on the streets spending time in places like the area behind Data Darbar, the greater the risk one will become infected and spread the virus through needle sharing.

Coupled with this risk is a tendency for IDUs to engage in high-risk sexual activity (ibid., 157). Between Data Darbar, a major Pakistani symbol of Sufi and folk Islam, and the Badshahi Masjid, one of the world's largest mosques and symbol of religious orthodoxy, lies Lahore's famous red light district. The organization for which Dr. Khair works, Nai Zindagi (A New Life), has established a drop-in center in the heart of this area, popularly known as Heera Mandi ("diamond market"). This center provides free treatment for sexually transmitted infections and distributes condoms and educational materials about safe sex, HIV, and AIDS. Here the connection between the world of IDUs and the world of sex work can be easily seen. While I was visiting, a number of clients at the drop-in center had come from behind Data Darbar, whereas others had come from a house across the street known for its male and female sex workers. Nearly all of Nai Zindagi's drop-in center clients live in the Heera Mandi area.

In the Muslim world, as elsewhere, the risk of HIV infection was originally thought to be limited only to the sphere of the IDU and sex work community (Hasnain, 2005, 1). However, as illustrated by the fact that a wealthier business-class clientele patronizes Heera Mandi, this perception is faulty. The social fabric of many societies is often woven tighter than many like to believe; anyone engaging in high-risk sexual behavior puts his or her life at risk. In practice, it is mostly men who do this, which puts their spouses at a similar risk, and once a woman contracts HIV there is roughly a thirty percent chance of her passing the virus on to her child during pregnancy and childbirth (Salahuddin, 2001, 55). Thus the reality of HIV in any one part of society is a reality that must be faced by all.

The two primary ways in which injecting drug use contributes to the spread of HIV – needle sharing and high-risk sexual behavior – must be directly addressed in order to deal effectively and constructively with injecting drug use and HIV in the Muslim world. Heera Mandi is but one of many instances where these two behaviors come together. In the following two sections we look more closely at where and how this occurs.

Sharing of drug paraphernalia

Needle sharing is one of the most common methods of HIV transmission. The HI virus cannot naturally survive independent of bodily fluids; thus when we speak of contracting HIV through injecting drug use we are often speaking of contraction through sharing a needle with another user. When IDUs inject, blood remains in the needle and can infect another person. Another mode of transmission is the "cookers" that injecting drug users use to prepare their drug solutions. This is because they are both exposed to many points of contamination during drug preparation, and are often saved and reused multiple times with multiple people without sterilization (Clatts, 1999). The patterns that bring people to begin injecting are important precursors to understanding who shares needles and why.

Shafeeq has a friend named Ahmed whose story embodies themes found in the lives of many IDUs: displacement, economic and family pressure, and unemployment. He is an unmarried twenty-nine-year old who left Faisalabad for Lahore five months prior to our meeting. Ahmed had come for more job opportunities and to escape family pressures. He speaks about his regular heroin smoking breaks during his visits to Data Darbar, a common habit for some people who visit the shrine. After one month of heroin smoking, he began injecting a cheaper, more potent cocktail of pharmaceutical drugs popular with his smoking circle. Within two months he lost his job and had been out of work for over a month when we met. After losing his job, Ahmed began to inject more frequently, often with the help of Shafeeq. In doing so, Ahmed has assumed the risks of injecting with shared needles.

The nodding heads that accompanied Ahmed's story indicate that the constellation of economically motivated displacement, family pressure, and consequent unemployment is endemic to many of the roughly 500,000 chronic heroin users in Pakistan (UNODC, 2007). It is estimated that at least twelve percent of these are injecting drug users who assume the risks that accompany needle sharing (ibid.). Comparable situations are found throughout much of the Muslim world.

In Iran, more than two-thirds of all HIV infections result from injecting drug use. Unsurprisingly, a drug treatment clinic reviewed for a World Health Organization (WHO) study of IDUs and HIV in Iran found that "more than two-thirds of the injected drug users reported sharing syringes at some time, usually in a place other than their home or in prison" (Razzaghi et al., 2006). This report tells of how and where needles are commonly used. The study found that individuals who often inject in public spaces such as parks, gardens, streets, alleys, public bathrooms, or abandoned buildings had a higher incidence of HIV infection through needle sharing. Individuals who inject either at home or in "safe houses" are more likely to purchase new needles from pharmacies and disinfect their needles and spoons by boiling them and exposing them to heat. Although boiling and exposing needles to heat are not as sterile as using new needles, these methods are more effective than other methods like cleaning the syringe with saliva or water and wrapping the syringe in tissue or plastic to keep it clean for the next use (ibid.). A scarcity of needles may also fuel a dangerous black market trade. The WHO report recorded several occurrances of homeless individuals and IDUs collecting used syringes, washing them with plain water, and peddling them to other IDUs (ibid.).

Both the story of Ahmed and the ways in which needles are used in Iran typify patterns and behaviors of IDUs common across the Muslim world and beyond. These examples point to incidents of needle sharing by people on the margins of society, but it would be foolhardy to assume that needle sharing and injecting drug use are limited only to those margins. In Pakistan, for example, there is a growing trend of injecting drug use among female college students, and a Karachi-based study found that 18.1% of students in elite private schools have used heroin (Niaz et al., 2005).

High-risk sexual behavior

High-risk sexual behavior involves having unprotected sex with multiple partners. Several studies have found that frequent drug users, including IDUs, are more likely than non-drug users to have high-risk sex (UNODC, 2005a, 155). This reality links the two most prevalent methods of HIV transmission.

Besides Heera Mandi, there are numerous examples of how IDU and high-risk sexual behavior are woven together in different contexts throughout the Muslim world. In Kuala Lumpur, Malaysia's capital, the worlds of injecting drug use and sex work are melded together on Chow Kit Road. Despite Malaysia's strict drug trafficking policy – those caught trafficking drugs are likely to receive the death penalty – the WHO reported in 2003 that 76.3% of HIV infection was due to injecting drug use (Mazlan et al., 2006). Social stigma is always a huge obstacle obscuring the accuracy of HIV data, but the high incidence of IDU infection and its avenues to spread through Chow Kit Road are likely major reasons why the WHO identifies Malaysia as being in the initial stage of an HIV epidemic (Kuppusamy, 2005).

Iran is facing similar problems, with a high rate of HIV infection from injecting drug use (67.3%) and a growing rate of transmission through sexual intercourse (Razzaghi, 2006). In nearly 85% of reported AIDS cases, the person claimed a history of injecting drugs and had contracted the virus from either intercourse or needle sharing (ibid.). However, unlike Lahore and Kuala Lumpur, the interconnection between drug use and high-risk sex is not found in red light districts, which would have a difficult time surviving under

Iran's strictly enforced religious and social conservatism. Instead it is found in the Iranian prison system (IRIN, 2002). Under Iran's strict anti-drug laws the majority of incarcerated individuals are being held for drug offences (Samii, 2006). This equates to the prisons being filled primarily by drug users who face the usual risks of contracting HIV via needle sharing prior to entering prison and in prison itself (Razzaghi, 2006). Dr. Minoo Mohraz, one of Iran's leading experts on HIV and AIDS, has found that there is high incidence of men who have sex with men within prison (IRIN, 2002). This couples drug use and high-risk sexual behavior within prisons, which then greatly increases the rate of HIV transmission. Many of these incarcerated people will eventually leave prison and return to their families and communities with a much higher likelihood of being HIV positive.

In Bangladesh the interconnection between injecting drug use and high-risk sexual behavior has economic overtones. A 2004 United Nations Office on Drugs and Crime (UNODC) study determined that money spent on drugs exceeded the average per capita income (UNODC, 2005b). In part, this may be explained by wealthy elites spending large sums of money on illegal drugs, but this trend also resonates with what we know about average users and the realities of drug addiction: a lack of income does anything but stifle drug consumption. In Dhaka it was reported that sixteen percent of male IDUs had exchanged sex for cash or drugs, and that IDUs in Central Bangladesh were more likely to have a sex worker as a sex partner (ibid.). It is unlikely that this trend is only found in Bangladesh.

Each of these cases illustrates general ways in which drug use and high-risk sexual behavior are connected in the Muslim world (and outside it). In many instances another, or a combination, of these trends may better characterize this interconnection. Whether it is driven by Chow Kit Road's red light district, Iran's prison system, or basic economics, the relationship between injecting drug use and high-risk sexual behavior has deep and systemic roots.

RESPONSES TO THE IDU COMMUNITY

Most societies, regardless of religion, respond to IDU communities with either compassionate and multifaceted outreach, or indifference. In general IDU communities are relatively small and are largely made up of economically exploited and marginalized people. The communities are often considered social problems and so programs are developed to "deal with the problem" rather than dealing with the larger context that forces these conditions on people. Often the method of HIV transmission is isolated and strategically approached, reducing a human being to how they got infected with HIV (Khair, 2007). "Just say no" campaigns are an example of this atomized approach which imagines all people as entirely autonomous subjects free from socio-economic pressures in decision-making. These programs fail in many IDU communities precisely because they oversimplify the problems facing IDUs. For many drug users it is not an issue of just saying "no" to the drugs, but rather saying "no" to the systemic social problems that have permeated the user's life. Without adequate support and rehabilitation programs that also provide users with job skills, confidence, and a sense of self-worth and hope, "just say no" programs are doomed simply to fall into the cycles of marginalization that users already face. The inability of the user to "just say no" leads to further dehumanization and alienation. Successful responses recognize the complex social, economic, religious, and cultural functions that govern personal responses, and design their programs accordingly.

The theological and Qur'anic basis for Islamic responses to drug addiction and HIV is dealt with elsewhere in this anthology (see McTighe, chapter 14). This section will examine responses to the IDU community in the Muslim world as a *sociological* phenomenon, asking what kinds of programs are being implemented and where. The aim is not to evaluate whether or not certain kinds of responses are "Islamic"; not all of these organizations claim to be theologically grounded in Islamic tradition. The goal is instead to report on responses that have proven to be successful in addressing the multi-faceted issues facing the IDU community, and which have effectively helped to curb the spread of HIV. The section will first examine the difficulties in popular responses, and then look at how successful programs have been structured to deal holistically with IDU communities. It concludes with an overview of the critiques raised against many of these responses.

Difficulties in popular responses

As previously established, the two primary ways in which HIV is spread within the IDU community is through high-risk sexual behavior and needle sharing. Accordingly, any successful response must embody realistic measures to stop these two modes of transmission. While this can be accomplished in a number of ways, the most popular responses include educational programs, condom distribution, and needle exchange programs.

Educational programs encompass a wide corpus of techniques ranging from "just say no," which educates users about the harmful effects that drugs and high-risk sexual behavior have on the body, to multi-faceted rehabilitation programs. Rehabilitation programs often incorporate a curriculum on hygiene, safer sexual practices, and drug addiction, while providing users with psychotherapy, marketable work skills, and confidence building exercises. Educational programs are widely encouraged throughout the Muslim world, although curriculum content may change according to surrounding cultural and theological contexts (Kuppusamy, 2005; Mandani, 2004).

Condom distribution and needle exchange programs, though proven to be highly effective in curtailing the spread of HIV through high-risk sexual behavior and needle sharing, are naturally more contested responses as they directly confront certain moral and theological positions. It is not uncommon to see the legality of these prevention programs depend upon the Islamic values of the government and the contestations for the "real meaning" of these values among various players in Muslim society. For example, needle exchanges are prohibited in Saudi Arabia yet funded by government bodies in Senegal, Iran, Pakistan, Bangladesh, and Malaysia (Kuppusamy, 2005; Madani et al., 2004, 7).

Problems emerge when responses fail to substitute a successful prevention technique for one that is prohibited. In Jeddah, a port city on the coast of the Red Sea in western Saudi Arabia, HIV rates amongst IDUs are currently very low (0.15%; Madani et al., 2004). However, injecting drug use is on the rise and the vast majority of new HIV cases are from growing immigrant populations (ibid.). Without a needle exchange program, how will Saudi Arabia begin to deal with a growing IDU community and growing HIV rates?

Some suggest that the problem may be avoided by strengthening both Islamic and health education. This strategy encourages people to follow and implement the Islamic laws and values that prohibit adultery, homosexuality, and injecting drug use, and to practice safe sex only through legal marriage (ibid.). Increased education and the strengthening of Islamic values may yield positive results, but such strategies must be sure to move beyond a simple "just say no" campaign and face the economic and social realities that drive much regular drug use and addiction. The utility of this strategy is further threatened by the fact that recent immigrants with HIV are less likely to be influenced by educational programs that work with residents over long periods of time. The process of adapting to a new language and culture can create barriers to the effectiveness of Islamic and health education programs (Khair, 2007).

Imams can play a central role in educating people about HIV and AIDS and helping to provide much needed support and guidance for those living with the virus. Unfortunately, miseducation and superficial training characterize many responses. In Bangladesh, although more than five thousand religious leaders have been trained in HIV and AIDS awareness, most imams continue to associate HIV with "sexuality and immorality" (Panos, 2006). These sentiments are not unique to Bangladesh. Training sessions throughout the Muslim world frequently provide essential information about HIV but fail to address fully or challenge the stereotypes maintained by many imams (Esack, 2007). In other instances, responses with well-structured programs run into implementation problems. An organization may be commissioned to operate a needle exchange and distribute condoms, but inadequate funding and understaffing prevent these plans from materializing (Panos, 2006).

Successful responses

Successful responses incorporate programs that are well funded and well managed, and that synthesize educational programs, condom distribution, and needle exchanges into detoxification and rehabilitation programs. Such responses avoid treating the IDU community as a "problem that needs to be dealt with" and instead are informed by an awareness of the individual's suffering and his or her potential to be a clean, fully active member of society.

Nai Zindagi, the organization with a drop-in center in the heart of Heera Mandi, is an example of how successful responses can be implemented when located in a welcoming context. The organization now works with a large array of local and international organizations to secure funding and sustained programmatic support, and most of its staff have been treated by the organization prior to employment. They are therefore deeply aware of the battery of socio-political and economic issues facing their clients, and the kind of suffering experienced by the IDU community.

As is the case with other successful response programs, Nai Zindagi locates itself where injecting drug use and sex work meet, and has established the trust of the clients it treats. Programs work holistically with the IDU community by walking clients from places such as the area behind Data Darbar through comprehensive rehabilitation and psychotherapy to job training and placement. All of this is done free of charge. While on the streets, needle exchange programs provide users with hygienic needles and educate them about safe injection and communicable diseases. Condoms are distributed through a mobile clinic and at the drop-in center. Amidst these other services, classes on health and hygiene appear to be more effective because they can point to contextual examples and are framed by the compassion and care of the program.

Fortunately, Nai Zindagi is only one of many organizations throughout the Muslim world implementing successful responses. In 2006, the Malaysian government inaugurated a harm reduction program that included among other things the distribution of free condoms and a needle exchange in three cities: Kuala Lumpur, Johor, and Penang. The program was later expanded to Kuantan in the state of Pahang, Kota Baru in Kelantan, and Alor Star in Kedah. To date it has reached approximately 130,000 users and sexually active people, providing them with counseling, drug therapy, and information about HIV prevention (Kuppusamy, 2005). Another example is the CARE-SHAKTI intervention in Bangladesh. In 1998 the CARE-Bangladesh HIV Prevention Programme instituted this program, which includes a needle exchange, abscess management, treatment of sexually transmitted infections, education, and condom distribution (Foss et al., 2006).

Multi-faceted and successful responses like those of CARE-SHAKTI, Nai Zindagi, and Malaysia's harm reduction program have not gone without criticism. As alluded to earlier, needle exchanges and condom distribution run counter to certain theological and cultural norms within the Muslim world. The majority of criticism of these programs comes from conservative religious leaders who see them as encouraging sexual promiscuity and rampant drug use. Mahfoz Omar, a leader of the Islamic Party of Malaysia, typifies these sentiments in his argument that the free distribution of condoms and needles only motivates drug users to engage in risky behavior (Esack, 2006). Similar ideas are shared by numerous religious leaders throughout the Muslim world (Esack, 2007). From their perspective, educational programs and the strengthening of Islamic values are the only Islamically appropriate responses. They argue that if one submits to the will of God and follows Shari'ah (Islamic law), one will find the strength to "just say no" (Khair, 2007).

In the examination of popular responses, we considered the difficulties raised by such approaches in Saudi Arabia. These difficulties are derived from a quantitative look at which programs are most effective and efficient in transforming the lives of injecting drug users and curtailing the spread of HIV. Many critics find that this perspective puts the cart before the horse. In his book *The AIDS Crisis: A Natural Product of Modernity's Sexual Revolution*, and elsewhere in this volume (chapter 2), Malik Badri argues that HIV, drug addiction, and high-risk sexual behavior are intrinsic to a Western moral framework (Badri, 1997). Rather than sanction the distribution of needles and condoms, these voices argue, a return to their understanding of Shari'ah is the only way to purge the Muslim world of a virus that emerged from non-Muslim values in the first place.

CONCLUSION

Injecting drug use is a growing problem in much of the Muslim world. Users come from all classes and backgrounds and begin using for a wide range of reasons which include joblessness, family pressure, and economic and social marginalization. From Karachi college students to Iranian prisoners to Shafeeq and Ahmed behind Data Darbar, the IDU community is comprised of a diverse group of individuals that fits no simple description. Patterns do, however, emerge: high-risk sex and needle sharing frequently occur amongst

IDUs. Unfortunately, these two behaviors are the two most prevalent methods for the transmission of HIV.

Like injecting drug use, there is no single group of people to whom HIV is limited. Societies – Muslim and non-Muslim alike – frequently try to push these realities into the fraying edges of our social fabric, which in turn further marginalizes and dehumanizes those already living on those edges. In the Muslim world, responses to the IDU community fall into the same bifurcated tendency witnessed across the globe: compassionate outreach, and indifference. Where there is outreach, successful programs work holistically with users. Multi-faceted and comprehensive rehabilitation programs aim not only to curtail the spread of HIV, but also to help individuals realize their self-worth, and see a way back into the larger social fabric.

However, such responses are not without critiques. At the heart of these critiques is a dispute over what constitutes Islamically sanctioned harm reduction, as well as a deep and more general concern about the influence of Western culture and values on Muslim societies. Other chapters in this anthology address these concerns from an Islamic theological and ethical perspective. Such works are critical to building substantive dialogues where advocates for the responses characterized here and their critics can do more than talk past one another. This can only result in more cooperation and in turn more support for those who need it most: injecting drug users and those living with HIV.

BIBLIOGRAPHY

Aceijas, C. et al. 2004. "Global overview of injecting drug use and HIV infection among injecting drug users." *AIDS*, 18: 2295–2303.

Badri, Malik 1997. *The Aids Crisis: A Natural Product of Modernity's Sexual Revolution*. South Africa: Islamic Medical Association of South Africa.

Clatts, Michael C. 1999. "Risk for Viral Transmission in Injection Paraphernalia: Heating Drug Solutions May Inactivate HIV-1." In Summary of the National Institute on Drug Abuse's Meeting "Drug Abuse and AIDS: Intertwined Epidemics." At www.nida.nih.gov/MeetSum/AIDS.html (accessed April 11, 2008).

Esack, Farid 2006. *HIV, AIDS, and Islam – Reflections Based on Compassion, Responsibility and Justice*. Cape Town, Positive Muslims.

Esack, Farid 2007. Interview on December 1, 2007 by Chris Byrnes. Cambridge, MA, unpublished.

Foss, Anna M. et al. 2006. "Could the CARE-SHAKTI intervention for injecting drug users be maintaining the low HIV prevalence in Dhaka, Bangladesh?" *Addiction*, 102: 114–125.

Hasnain, Memoona 2005. "Cultural Approach to HIV/AIDS Harm Reduction in Muslim Countries." *Harm Reduction Journal*, 2: 23. At www.harmreductionjournal.com/content/2/1/23 (accessed December 16, 2007).

IRIN (Integrated Regional Information Networks) 2002. "Iran: HIV/AIDS and Intravenous Drug Usage." At www.youandaids.org/Features/Iran29thNov.asp (accessed December 16, 2007).

Khair, Hafiza 2007. Interview on June 23, 2007 by Chris Byrnes. Lahore, unpublished.

Kuppusamy, Baradan. 2005. "Gov't Blasted for Bold Steps." *Asiafrica: Features on HIV/AIDS*. At www.aidsasiafrica.net/features/malaysia.html (accessed April 15, 2007).

Madani, T. et al. 2004. "Epidemiology of the human immunodeficiency virus in Saudi Arabia; 18-year surveillance results and prevention from an Islamic perspective." *BMC Infectious Diseases*, 4(25): 1–8. At www.biomedcentral.com.ezp2.harvard.edu/content/pdf/1471-2334-4-25.pdf (accessed April 10, 2008).

Mazlan, Mahmud et al. 2006. "New Challenges and Opportunities in Managing Substance Abuse in Malaysia." *Drug and Alcohol Review*, 25: 473–478. Philadelphia, PA, Taylor and Francis, Ltd.

Niaz, U. et al. 2005. "A Survey of Psychosocial Correlates of Drug Abuse in Young Adults Aged 16–21, in Karachi: Identifying 'High Risk' Population to Target Intervention Strategies." *Pakistan Journal of Medical Sciences Quarterly* 21 (July–September 2005), 3. At www.pjms.com.pk/issues/julsep05/article/article5.html (accessed December 16, 2007).

Panos Global AIDS Programme 2006. "Keeping the Promise? A study of progress made in implementing the UNGASS Declaration of Commitment on HIV/AIDS in Bangladesh." At www.panosaids.org/publications/ungass_ Bangladesh full.pdf (accessed May 7, 2007).

Razzaghi, Emran M. et al. 2006. "A Qualitative Study of Injecting Drug Users in Tehran, Iran." *Harm Reduction Journal*, 3(12). At www.harmreductionjournal.com/content/3/1/12 (accessed December 16, 2007).

Salahuddin, Naseem 2001. *Clinical Management of HIV/AIDS*. Islamabad, Ministry of Health of the Government of Pakistan.

Samii, Bill 2006. "Iran: Drug Control Emphasized as New 'Crack' Gains Popularity." *Radio Free Europe*. At www.rferl.org/featuresarticle/

2006/04/57a99e99-df57-4066–90aa-8a89460a0314.html   (accessed December 16, 2007).

UNODC (United Nations Office on Drugs and Crime) 2005a. *World Drug Report*, Vol. 1. At www.unodc.org/pdf/WDR_2005/volume_1_web.pdf (accessed December 16, 2007).

—— 2005b. "South Asia Regional Profile: Bangladesh." At www.unodc. org/pdf/india/publications/south_Asia_Regional_Profile_Sept_ 2005/08_bangladesh.pdf (accessed May 7, 2007).

—— 2007. "South Asia Regional Profile: Pakistan." At www.unodc.org/ india/country_profiles.html (accessed December 16, 2007).

14

HIV, ADDICTION, AND JUSTICE: TOWARD A QUR'ANIC THEOLOGY OF LIBERATION

Laura McTighe

No One Told Me

No one told me that one day I'd be saving the grains of salt that accumulated in the bottom of a pretzel bag to season my food. No one told me. No one told me I'd be using industrial strength floor wax as nail enamel, applied to my breaking nails with q-tips that I obtained by trading off some other valued necessity. No one told me. No one told me that I'd have crayons soaking in baby oil to use for rouge, lipstick, or eyeliner.

I was never told that instead of good old Elmer's Glue, I'd be using toothpaste as an adhesive. Applied to the back of my precious family photos, the toothpaste made the pictures stick to the corkboard near my bed provided by the county. I was never told that one day I'd be adapting a pair of county panties into a county "sports bra." Removing the crotch, slipping the crotch over my head, inserting my arms through the two orifices designed for my legs. Then I'd pull the inverted waistband down below and under my breast for just the right fit.

I certainly never thought I'd see the day when I'd make a solution of sugar, water, and deodorant to spray on my freshly curled hair; in a feeble attempt to replicate spritz, mousse, or holding spray.

I wasn't given a hint that my Dear Mother would die during my six months incarceration.

Then, when I volunteered to take a free HIV test administered by the prison health system, no one told me that I'd test positive for the virus. No one told me what or what not to do about it. No one told me how or how not to live. In fact, no one told that I could continue to live.

In actuality, I had willed myself to die. But, day after day I kept waking up, ALIVE!

There was no literature provided for me, and no one told me to exercise more, increase my water or even to order extra vitamins on my commissary. I wasn't advised to increase my prayer efforts, meditate, or keep positive thoughts or hope.

No one told me and in return I told no one. It was my very own dark secret and I dared not tell anyone for fear of being shunned, rejected, stigmatized and left alone.

So one day I was compelled to tell myself that living was more important than dying and that if I must live with HIV, then so be it. No one told me, but today I am prepared to tell you, DON'T PANIC! Life is Good. Grasp it. Claim it. Embrace it. Caress it. Salute it. And most of all Assert It.

Waheedah El-Shabazz

ON BUILDING A QUR'ANIC APPROACH TO HIV AND ADDICTION

Waheedah writes of the pain that so many people endure when they are diagnosed with HIV – where fears of dying and fears of rejection intertwine in a grim reality of hopelessness. Where is God in this pain? Where is support? Where is life? Waheedah was diagnosed in a room without curtains in the Philadelphia county jail. She was crying and everyone was walking by. She told me many times that she felt like killing herself. This was still where Waheedah's head was most days when I first met her. She has an undeniable spark, but it often felt as if she was acting, just hoping things would be okay. If you did not know her, you would have thought that things were fine. She had one of the best parole officers in Philadelphia; her health was good; she still had her family's support . . .

I have often wondered what would have happened to Waheedah if she had been diagnosed on the streets, still close to her addiction. Would she have fallen back into using, physically willing herself to die? As it happened, she only had her thoughts. And in the midst of

these thoughts, she met my colleague, John Bell, and found a community of activists. Shortly after her release, Waheedah joined our
TEACH (Treatment Education Activists Combating HIV) Outside
program to learn about living healthily with HIV, accessing the services she needed, and becoming active in local struggles around
prison health care.[1] Over the five-week course, John Bell and I were
able to walk alongside Waheedah as she grappled with her most
distressing moments. We earned not just respect as professionals,
but also trust as friends. Through this closeness, TEACH Outside
became a new beginning for Waheedah. After graduating, she started
doing activist work to fix the health care in the Philadelphia jails.
She found hope in this struggle for justice, and she found her voice
as a Black Muslim woman living with HIV.[2]

Waheedah's story reveals two requirements for working against
addiction in the context of HIV: first, people need to have the genuine support of a community, and, second, people need to believe that
they can create the lives they want to live. It is easy to pass judgment
on people struggling through addiction, asserting that people choose
to use drugs, claiming that such people are without faith and without
concern for the people they could hurt in their addictions. But upon
stepping closer, past this judgment, a different picture emerges. In my
years working alongside people with HIV struggling with addiction,
I have met so many people who are suffering in silence, without the
support of a community. From their vivid memories of loved ones
dying, to their negative experiences with service providers, to their
fruitless attempts at fighting for their needs, to their stories of family and friends abandoning them in the wake of their HIV diagnoses
– every step they have taken to fight back and carve out a different
path for their lives has been crushed. The cumulative impact of these
experiences has left many convinced that things cannot change. For
them, addiction has most often been an anesthetic, a way to cope
with this fact that they are totally distanced and alone. Lifting the
hold that addiction has had on their lives requires more than being
urged not to fall prey to the despair that engulfs them most days.
People need to be able to imagine a life beyond addiction; people
need proof that things can change.

In this paper, I will be locating myself alongside people struggling with HIV and addiction, reflecting on the Qur'an through their
eyes. Theologian Farid Esack presents this orientation as a conscious subjectivity informed by the "divine and prophetic prefer-

ential option for the oppressed." The interpreter consciously places him/herself "among the marginalized and within their struggles," so as to subjectively "interpret the text from the underside of history" (Esack, 2000, 102–103). But this conscious subjectivity extends beyond simply bringing the lives of people struggling with HIV and addiction to the Qur'an. As Esack explains, "the context of a liberation struggle not only has something to say to the text; the text also has something to say to that context" (ibid., 106). Thus, in my interpretation I am concerned not only with voicing the questions of dear friends like Waheedah, but also with listening to what the Qur'an has to say about addiction in the context of their lives. For it is in these answers that people will find the tools they need to make sense of their lives, and to create their futures beyond HIV and addiction.[3]

This paper is divided into four sections: a) a definition of concepts crucial for a Qur'anic theology of liberation; b) an integration of the Qur'an and clinical addiction criteria to outline a personal approach to addiction in the absence of structural oppression; c) a critical look at the forces that marginalize people struggling through HIV and addiction; and d) an exploration of the Qur'anic verses on substance use in the context of this marginalization. While I argue that it is insufficient to interpret the Qur'anic verses on substance use as a prohibition when people with HIV are living through deep socio-economic injustices, I do not claim to provide a definitive Islamic ethic on addiction in the context of HIV. I *am* interested in starting a conversation with the guidance of people like Waheedah, who know best what is at stake if we cannot begin to look to the Qur'an for strategies to transform the realities of HIV and addiction.[4]

KEY CONCEPTS FOR A THEOLOGY OF LIBERATION

Waheedah's story of her incarceration and HIV diagnosis reads as a struggle to maintain dignity in the face of the dehumanization brought on by imprisonment, and to grasp life in the face of the specter of death brought on by HIV. In her witness, Waheedah touches upon a key dynamic in the Qur'an that is critical for understanding addiction in the context of HIV: forgetting and remembering. Her story is both a personal act of remembrance and an act of warning – "no one told me, but today I am prepared to tell you." Throughout the

Qur'an, the responsibility to remember not forget, to create goodness not allow evil, undergirds people's relationships with God and
with each other (Rahman, 1989, p 43).[5] Exploring this responsibility and its bearing on addiction in the context of HIV requires an
understanding of the concepts of *tawhid* (Divine unity), *taqwa* (a
consciousness of God), *al-nas* (humankind), and *mustad'afun* (the
marginalized and oppressed).

Tawhid

While *tawhid* literally means Divine unity (Q. 112:1–4), progressive
Muslim thinkers, including Ali Shari'ati (1986), Asghar Ali Engineer
(1990), Fazlur Rahman (1989, 1996) and Farid Esack (1997), have
identified *tawhid* as a liberatory concept signifying the unity of God,
creation, and humankind. Within this liberatory framework, *tawhid*
is the guide for social action. Since creation has been ordained with
a just order (Q. 45:22) and humankind has been selected to be the
guardian of earthly life (Q. 33:72), humankind's charge is to establish and maintain God's just and ethical social order on earth – to
preserve *tawhid* (Q. 4:135). As such, human life is a constant tension between the injustices that exist in a society and the justice that
people were created to establish. By collaborating with God, however, people are able to work towards establishing and maintaining
a *tawhidi* society (Q. 7:200–201).

Taqwa

People's intentional collaboration with God defines *taqwa*. Often
translated as piety, *taqwa* literally means to be conscious of the
presence of God and to live in awareness of being ultimately accountable to Him. Following the right path is an act of remembrance;
if people forget God, if people abandon *taqwa*, they remove
the meaning and purpose of life (Q. 41:44, 59:19). While *taqwa*
emphasizes people's awareness of and accountability to God,
taqwa should not be understood as encouraging an exaggerated
focus on being ethical that distances people from the socio-political
realities of earth (van Bommel, 1997, 206). This distancing is only
possible if *taqwa* is separated from a holistic appreciation of *tawhid*
and a commitment to the idea of *al-nas*, humankind, as the family
of God. *Taqwa*, therefore, not only enables people to save

themselves from loss, but also requires that they save others from loss. Thus *taqwa* is manifested as a lived concern and compassion for others.

Al-nas

The unity of humanity, or *al-nas* (Q. 114:5–6), is critical for a *tawhidi* society. All human life is a trust from God, and human existence is sacred (Q. 17:70). While people were created individually by God (Q. 32:9) and on the Day of Judgment will be held accountable to God as individuals (Q. 6:94), that for which they are accountable is profoundly social. As Fazlur Rahman notes, "if there were only one person in the world, I don't know what the Qur'an would tell him or her to do or think or how to behave. But the Qur'an is certain that when there is more than one human being, then God is there" (Rahman, 1996, 13). Establishing God's just and ethical order on earth means protecting *al-nas* as the family of God. And it is only in relationships with God and with each other that people can meet this mandate (Q. 23:60).

Mustad'afun

In elaborating on the responsibility to protect *al-nas*, progressive Muslim thinkers have highlighted the Qur'anic concept of the *mustad'afun*, people of an "inferior" social status who are marginalized through socio-economic structures (Shari'ati, 1986, 92; Engineer, 1990, 22–23; Esack, 1997, 98). The Qur'an exhorts people to stand alongside the *mustad'afun* in the face of socio-economic injustice, power imbalances, and arrogance (Q. 4:75), and to struggle actively for the establishment of justice (Q. 5:8). Whenever people fail to take action against these injustices, they are harming themselves: as the Qur'an explains, *all* injustice done to another (whether by commission or omission) is done to oneself (Q. 3:117, 65:1). Failure to work against these injustices cannot be justified by appealing to a person/group's violation of Islamic law or lack of belief. Even when the *mustad'afun* are nonbelievers, God consistently sides with the *mustad'afun* over those with power (Q. 7:136–137, 28:5). But when people are struggling alongside the *mustad'afun* to alleviate these injustices, they are most profoundly linked with God's justice and compassion.

PERSONAL QUR'ANIC APPROACH TO ADDICTION

Islam's prohibition of intoxicants (*khamr*)[6] is often cited as a key example of progressive revelation in the Qur'an, demonstrating a gradual tackling of problems as they arose. A close look at the occasions of revelation for the Qur'anic verses on intoxicants shows that the Qur'an's concern with substance use is grounded in the concepts of *tawhid*, *taqwa*, and *al-nas*. In these verses, the Qur'an responds to the impact of substance use on people's clarity in prayer, remembrance of God, and relationships with other people, ultimately declaring that it is better to avoid intoxicants entirely than to risk people's substance use escalating to a point where it negatively impacts their communities and relationships with God.

A verse revealed in Mecca contains the first reference to the consumption of intoxicants: "And (We give you) the fruits of the palm and the vine from which you derive intoxicants and wholesome food. Surely in this there is a sign for men of understanding" (Q. 16:67). Then in Medina, when a number of Muslims questioned the consumption of intoxicants (Gätje, 1996, 200), a verse acknowledging the harm in drinking, but not calling for an outright prohibition, was revealed: "They ask you about intoxicants and gambling. Say: 'There is great harm in both, although they have some benefit for men; but their harm is far greater than their benefit'" (Q. 2:219). A later verse clearly limited the consumption of intoxicants. The event that occasioned the revelation of this verse was reported to be a party in Medina where a number of people became intoxicated. When one of them led evening prayers, he mispronounced several words from the Qur'an (Gätje, 1996, 200). Following this incident, the next verse, prohibiting people from praying while intoxicated, was revealed: "Believers, do not approach your prayers when you are intoxicated, but wait till you can grasp the meaning of your words" (Q. 4:43). Finally, much later, there was another party where people became intoxicated, which disintegrated into a brawl (Gätje, 1996, 201). Following this event, the final verses, calling for a full prohibition, were revealed:

> Believers, intoxicants and games of chance, idols and divining arrows, are abominations devised by Satan. Avoid them, so that you may prosper. Satan seeks to stir up enmity and hatred among you by means of intoxicants and gambling, and to keep you from the

remembrance of God and from your prayers. Will you not abstain from them? (Q. 5:90–91)[7]

In these final verses, the Qur'an lists intoxicants among the "abominations devised by Satan," marking intoxicants as one way through which Satan tries to thwart people in their charge to establish a *tawhidi* society. In the Qur'an, Satan is depicted as a perpetual and persistent force against humanity. Satan works to confuse people and cloud their inner senses, thereby seducing them away from their path to God (Q. 15:32–40, Q. 17:53). Thus human life is a constant tension between the disorder humans can succumb to and the justice people are entrusted to establish. And because Satan's activities in human life are ceaseless, people always need to be on guard against his coercions (Q. 2:168–169). It is only by collaborating with God that people are able to resist Satan's coercions, and maintain a *tawhidi* society (Q. 7:200–201, Q. 40:9–10). As such, the Qur'an tells people to abstain from intoxicants so that they may pursue lives imbued with *taqwa* and preserve the wholeness of *al-nas*.

This prohibition of substance use represents the Qur'an's standard approach to Satan's coercions: while no one is immune to the lure of intoxicants, all can avoid or just stop using them. However, when addiction is understood as dependence on intoxicants, not just the use of intoxicants, a more comprehensive approach is required. The International Classification of Diseases characterizes "dependence syndrome" by difficulties controlling substance use, persistent use despite harmful consequences, the prioritization of substance use over other obligations, increased tolerance, and physical withdrawal symptoms (World Health Organization).[8] According to these characteristics of dependence syndrome, when use escalates to the level of addiction people are simply unable to stop consuming intoxicants. Their bodies physically need the substance to survive (McLellan et al., 2000, 1689–1695). Thus, in addiction, people's lives become punctuated by cycles of intoxication and withdrawal; personal relationships and relationships with God are at best secondary.

People's powerlessness over addiction is the cornerstone of recovery programs like Alcoholics Anonymous and Narcotics Anonymous. While recovery is marked by participation in a communal project of mutual help, addiction is often referred to as "out there," characterized by total self-abandonment and isolation (Weinberg, 2000, 606–621; Valverde and White-Mair, 1999,

393–410). This characterization of addiction harks back to the Qur'an's warning against Satan's attempts to stir up enmity among people and to prevent remembrance of God. Indeed, as the Qur'an states, when people forget God by fully succumbing to Satan's coercions, God will make them forget their own selves (Q. 59:19). The language of recovery programs proves helpful in clarifying the communal concern of an ideal *tawhidi* society in this state of apparent hopelessness. While individuals may have abandoned *taqwa*, there is no "point of no return"; people can always come back to the faith (Rahman, 1989, 20). It is hardly surprising, then, that community is critical to both narratives. The Qur'an states that people should protect community by avoiding intoxicants; recovery programs assert that a cohesive, therapeutic community is the only hope for escaping addiction. Moreover, the focus of recovery programs on a "God of Your Understanding" easily maps onto the Qur'an's attention to remembrance of God in guarding against Satan's efforts to destroy community through intoxicants. Thus recovery programs provide the tools for expanding the Qur'an's discussion of substance use from a reason to avoid substance use to the solution if one is struggling through addiction. God and community can prevent substance use; God and community are the treatment for addiction.

Placing addiction within a personalized framework of *tawhid*, *taqwa*, and *al-nas* is only possible when communities are strong and there are no forces that comprehensively distance people from God. A personalized approach presumes that people in addiction are just believers who have strayed from the path and need to be brought back again. Their actions impact the members of their communities, and the more distanced from God they become, the more damage may be done to their communities. Thus, out of compassion for those struggling with addiction and out of obligation to maintain *al-nas*, communities reach out to draw people away from their addictions and back into relationship with God.

SOCIO-ECONOMIC INJUSTICE, HIV, AND ADDICTION

For the vast majority of people struggling with HIV and addiction throughout the world, such strong and engaged communities are rarely the reality. Instead, their lives are restricted and marginalized by socio-economic injustices, leaving them consistently unable to secure the resources and/or access the services they need. Moreover, these socio-economic injustices often erode precisely the community infrastructure that people in addiction would otherwise turn to for support.

For Waheedah, these socio-economic injustices were reflected primarily in the form of the United States' anti-drug policies. Over the last twenty-five years, these policies have waged a full spectrum attack, pushing mass incarceration rather than drug treatment, which brings with it a slew of "invisible punishments"[9] that have systematically eroded family and community infrastructure in poor communities of color (Mauer, 2006, 162, 177). Currently, more than one out of every hundred adults is confined in an American jail or prison, with the daily jail/prison census exceeding 2.3 million (Pew Center on the States, 2008, 5). This four-fold jump in prison population is the direct result of increased policing, prosecution, and sentencing for drug-related crimes (Mauer, 2006, 91).[10] When released, poor men and women of color face a series of laws and regulations that make it nearly impossible for them to get jobs, find housing, get financial assistance, and support their families.[11]

Waheedah's entrapment in these socio-economic injustices was further exacerbated by her HIV diagnosis. By targeting people at risk of HIV, anti-drug policy has dramatically increased the number of people with HIV behind bars: each year, one in four people with HIV passes through a correctional facility (Hammett, Harmon, and Rhodes, 2002, 1791). Once incarcerated, people with HIV face a devastating combination of inadequate health care and HIV stigma. The hallmarks of for-profit prison health care are frequent lapses in medication, poor access to emergency care, and fees for medical visits/prescriptions, all of which compromise people's abilities to take care of themselves. Moreover, many of the steps people with HIV take to protect their health run the risk of breaking their confidentiality. So Waheedah, like many people with HIV, "dared not tell anyone for fear of being shunned, rejected, stigmatized and left alone." For months, Waheedah spoke to no one about her HIV status. And once she began to receive information from John Bell, she hid his handouts in the only safe place she had: her Qur'an. If Waheedah had not met John Bell while she was incarcerated, her steps after release would have been almost guaranteed. Once released, people with HIV are generally sicker than when they entered prison. And they have no referrals for medical care, housing, or drug treatment. Delay in receiving HIV medication means a swift deterioration in the immune system; lack of housing means living in a shelter or on the streets; and lack of drug treatment leads to high rates of relapse, and can hasten the road back to prison. According to a June 2002 study by the Bureau of Justice, two-thirds of people will be re-arrested within three years of their release.[12]

A STRUCTURAL QUR'ANIC APPROACH TO ADDICTION

Within this context of socio-economic injustice and community-wide HIV stigma, people struggling with HIV and addiction may also be viewed as the *mustad'afun*. The structures marginalizing their lives stand in direct opposition to *tawhid*, threatening the wholeness of *al-nas*. In the United States, anti-drug policy has ensured that poor people of color like Waheedah are arrested, sentenced, and incarcerated for a problem that requires the support of the community, not distancing from it. And when released, people are stripped of their voting rights, economic benefits, employment opportunities, housing options, and the right to educational loans. Excluded from society's traditional means of sustaining themselves, the options that remain are precisely those factors that put people at greatest risk of HIV: continued drug use, drug dealing, and sex work for money. And the cycle continues – people again get arrested, sentenced, and incarcerated, further disrupting their families and communities, further entrenching a deep moral disorder (Fournier and Carmichael, 1998, 214–217).

Standing in solidarity with people struggling with HIV and addiction provides a new orientation for understanding the Qur'anic verses on intoxicants. Consider again the verses offering the final prohibition of intoxicants:

> Believers, intoxicants and games of chance, idols and divining arrows, are abominations devised by Satan. Avoid them, so that you may prosper. Satan seeks to stir up enmity and hatred among you by means of intoxicants and gambling, and to keep you from the remembrance of God and from your prayers. Will you not abstain from them? (Q. 5:90–91)

When substance use is understood as a personal problem, verses 5:90–91 will only be read as a prohibition of intoxicants. But if one looks at these verses from the structural context presented here, what do verses 5:90–91 say about the lives of people struggling with HIV and addiction? Substance use is characterized as an "abomination devised by Satan" because it can create hatred among people and divert people from God. But for people struggling with addiction and HIV, substance use is not the cause of the hostility in their communities, nor is it the cause of their distance from God. Both of these defining characteristics of Satan's coercions are caused by the socio-economic injustices that marginalize the lives of people with HIV. Regardless of whether a person is using intoxicants or not, enmity and hatred still exist because of the destruction of communities through socio-economic injustices and community-wide HIV stigma.

Thus a personalist understanding of verses 5:90–91 is insufficient in the midst of structures that marginalize people struggling with HIV and addiction. Instead, verses 5:90–91 provide a broad principle for Satan's coercions: anything that destroys community and alienates people from God. Furthermore, these verses call for active resistance in face of all threats to God and community: "Will you not abstain from them?" This is the same mandate presented earlier in discussing *tawhid*, *taqwa*, *al-nas*, and *mustad'afun*: the duty to follow God's path and establish justice; the charge to forbid evil and command good.

In the context of HIV and addiction, forbidding evil necessitates a multidimensional approach appropriate to the socio-economic injustices that people are living through. For Waheedah and other people with HIV in the United States, this protection must include legislative work to repeal unjust sentencing laws and "invisible punishments"; advocacy work to funnel money allocated for policing and prisons into community restoration projects like recovery programs, education, jobs, and housing; and comprehensive HIV education focused on countering transmission myths and HIV stigma.[13] But simply removing laws, shifting around money, and clarifying HIV treatment information will not undo all of the disorder that people with HIV are living through. Waheedah is part of a community that has endured a twenty-five-year assault, leaving it totally fractured if not almost dissolved. Funds and laws on their own will not establish justice if there is no community for these funds and laws to reach.

Thus commanding good requires a much more comprehensive project of building community and fostering hope. A critical first step in this project is the creation of safe spaces for those struggling with HIV and addiction. This approach may seem too incremental to people not immersed in the crises created by socio-economic injustices and HIV stigma, but this step is necessary because people are all too often starting with nothing. These smaller networks of people form the building blocks of vibrant community infrastructure; without them, there can be no hope for creating a *tawhidi* society. As this community-building work progresses, it is important to emphasize that community-building work is not and cannot be seen as separate from policy-reform work. Just as these communities will be centers for reflecting on the trauma of incarceration, so, too, must they be centers for devising strategies to challenge the socio-economic injustices marginalizing the lives of people struggling with HIV and addiction. To position community-building work as detached from policy-reform work would introduce more divisiveness into an already dehumanizing system. Moreover, without the direction of people who are struggling with HIV and addiction, legislative work, advocacy work, and education will all lack the nuanced approach necessary to be truly transformative. But through creating supportive communities that are inclusive of people who are struggling with HIV and addiction, everyone can begin the critical work of unraveling the layers of socio-economic injustice. And as a partnership of all people, these communities can become the living embodiment of a *tawhidi* society.

Only when people have this genuine support of a community, only when people believe that they can create the lives they want to live, will the promise of a future beyond HIV and addiction become real. Waheedah's own process of HIV acceptance is testament to this. When she was released from prison, she immersed herself in a supportive community of activists, and became a leader in the struggles against HIV and addiction in Philadelphia. Her role within this community has been critical for bringing her closer to God and prayer. As she felt the holistic support of this community, HIV's hold on her began to lift. And because she saw the Philadelphia jail policies that marginalized her life begin to change, she was also able to begin to envision a life for herself beyond addiction.

In this context of real community and hope, the personalist understanding of the Qur'anic verses on intoxicants may re-emerge as relevant within the HIV/addiction discourse. The mandate to "avoid intoxicants, so that you may prosper" offers a structure for protecting these growing communities and people's devotion to God. But all community members, whether struggling with HIV and addiction or not, are never absolved from the insights gleaned through a structural reading of the verses on intoxicants. The insidious coercions of Satan waged through power imbalances and arrogance remain forces to resist. Unless actively combated, these forces will thwart efforts to realize a *tawhidi* society. Thus, all people are continually challenged to pursue lives imbued with *taqwa*. And through living this responsibility to themselves, their communities, and God, they all become for ever part of the struggle to establish the just order of God's creation.

ON LIVING A QUR'ANIC APPROACH TO HIV AND ADDICTION

How does one begin this project of community-building which is so crucial for transforming the forces that marginalize the lives of people struggling with HIV and addiction? What does it mean to work alongside people in the stark reality presented in this paper? Where people's lives are messy? Where so much pain has accumulated over the years? Where, despite that, people have found ways to cope, or at least survive?

Commanding good and forbidding evil often seem like two distinct mandates. Individuals need to be supported; laws and policies need to be challenged. But for people struggling with HIV and addiction, the individual pain and the bad policies are one and the same. Both must be addressed simultaneously. To begin, you only need to step close to people, to earn their trust. With this trust, it is possible to work with people to ensure that their immediate needs are met. With this trust, it is possible to strategize with people to help them get their lives back. With this trust, it is possible to work together for the realization of a *tawhidi* society in a time of HIV. It is not necessary to enter this work with answers; you only need to be willing to walk with people to figure them out.

I still remember Waheedah's interview for TEACH Outside. She was so eager to get involved with activist work, fighting for the rights of people like herself who were struggling with HIV and addiction. Worried that Waheedah could easily get overloaded in those first months after being released from prison, my colleague, John Bell, hesitated before telling her softly, "We've been waiting for you." In the five years I have known Waheedah, she has continued to work tirelessly to transform the systemic issues impacting the lives of people with HIV. And over these years, we have been joined by so many others, all struggling forward in their own ways: educating their communities, working with young people, reconciling with their families, starting new families . . . We have won; we have failed; we have done what we can. And we have woken up to try again another day. If there is to be any hope of healing the deep wounds that have been inflicted upon *al-nas*, it is this work, in all its joy and its pain, that marks the path forward.

The hope created through this work guides the life that Waheedah and so many others know today. It is this life that Waheedah calls all who hear her struggle to grasp, claim, embrace, caress, salute, and assert.

BIBLIOGRAPHY

American Psychiatric Association 1994. *Diagnostic and Statistical Manual of Mental Disorders.* 4th edn. Washington, DC, American Psychiatric Association.

Boutwell, Amy and Josiah D. Rich 2004. "HIV infection behind bars." *Clinical Infectious Diseases*, 38: 1761–1763.

Bureau of Justice. *Prison Statistics.* At http://www.ojp.usdoj.gov/bjs/prisons.htm (accessed April 22, 2007).

Cook, Michael 2000. *Commanding Right and Forbidding Wrong in Islamic Thought.* Cambridge, Cambridge University Press.

Dannin, Robert 2002. *Black Pilgrimage to Islam.* Oxford, Oxford University Press.

Engineer, Asghar Ali 1990. *Islam and Liberation Theology: Essays on Liberative Elements in Islam.* New Delhi, Sterling Publishers Private Limited.

Esack, Farid 1997. *Qur'an, Liberation and Pluralism: An Islamic Perspective on Interreligious Solidarity Against Oppression.* Oxford, Oneworld Publications.

Fournier, Arthur M. and Cynthia Carmichael 1998. "Socioeconomic influences on the transmission of human immunodeficiency virus infection – The hidden risk." *Archives of Family Medicine*, 7: 214–217.

Gätje, Helmut 1996. *The Qur'an and Its Exegesis.* Oxford, Oneworld Publications.

Hammett, Theodore M., Mary Patricia Harmon, and William Rhodes 2002. "The Burden of Infectious Disease Among Inmates of and Releases from US Correctional Facilities, 1997." *American Journal of Public Health*, 92: 1789–1794.

Hasnain, Memoona 2005. "Cultural approach to HIV/AIDS harm reduction in Muslim countries." *Harm Reduction Journal*, 2: 23–31.

Ibn Kathir, Al-Hafiz 2006. *The Exegesis of the Grand Holy Qur'an*, Vols I, II and III. Trans. Muhammad Mahdi al-Sharif. Beirut, Dar al-Kotobi al-Ilmiyah.

Jackson, Sherman A. 2005. *Islam and the Blackamerican: Looking Toward the Third Resurrection*. New York, Oxford University Press.

Kahf, Mojha 2005. "The Muslim in the Mirror." In Saleemah Abdul-Ghafur (ed.), *Living Islam Out Loud: American Muslim Women Speak*. Boston, Beacon Press, 130–138.

Karic, Enes 2007. "Intoxicants." In *Brill Online: Encyclopedia of the Qur'an*. At http://www.brillonline.nl.ezp1.harvard.edu/subscriber/uid=1478/entry?entry=q3_SIM-00226 (accessed April 22, 2007).

Kueny, Kathryn 2001. *The Rhetoric of Sobriety: Wine in Early Islam.* Albany, NY, State University of New York Press.

Maddow, Rachel 2002. *Pushing for Progress: HIV/AIDS in Prisons.* Washington DC, National Minority AIDS Council.

Mauer, Marc 2006. *Race to Incarcerate*. Revised and updated. New York, The New Press.

Mauer, Marc and Meda Chesney-Lind (eds) 2002. *Invisible Punishment: The Collateral Consequences of Mass Imprisonment*. New York, The New Press.

McLellan, A. Thomas, David C. Lewis, Charles P. O'Brien, and Herbert D. Kleber 2000. "Drug Dependence, A Chronic Mental Illness: Implications for Treatment, Insurance, and Outcomes Evaluation." *Journal of the American Medical Association*, 284: 1689–1695.

Pew Center on the States, Public Safety Performance Project 2008. "One in 100: Behind Bars in America 2008." At www.pewcenteronthestates.org/uploadedFiles/8015PCTS_Prison08_FINAL_2-1-1_FORWEB.pdf (accessed April 17, 2008).

Rahman, Fazlur 1989. *Major Themes of the Qur'an*. Minneapolis, Bibliotheca Islamica.

—— 1996. "Islam's Origins and Ideals." In Nimat Hafez Barazangi, M. Raquibuz Zaman, and Omar Afzal (eds), *Islamic Identity and the Struggle for Justice*. Gainsville, University Press of Florida, 11–18.

Shari'ati, Ali 1986. *Jihad and Shahadat: Struggle and Martyrdom in Islam.* Ed. Mehdi Abedi and Gary Legenhausen. Houston, TX, Institute for Research and Islamic Studies.

Travis, Jeremy 2002. "Invisible Punishment: An Instrument of Social Exclusion." In Marc Mauer and Meda Chesney-Lind (eds), *Invisible Punishment: The Collateral Consequences of Mass Imprisonment.* New York, The New Press, 15–36.

Valverde, Mariana and Kimberley White-Mair 1999. "'One day at a time' and other slogans for everyday life: The ethical practices of Alcoholics Anonymous." *Journal of the British Sociological Association,* 33: 393–410.

van Bommel, Abdulwahid 1997. "Quality or Sanctity of Life." In Hendrik M. Vroom and Jerald D. Gort (eds), *Holy Scriptures in Judaism, Christianity and Islam: Hermeneutics, Values and Society.* Amsterdam, Rodopi B. V., 205–214.

Weinberg, Darin 2000. "'Out There': The Ecology of Addiction in Drug Abuse Treatment Discourse." *Social Problems,* 47: 606–621.

AFTERWORD: IDEALS, REALITIES, AND ISLAM: THOUGHTS ON THE AIDS PANDEMIC

Kecia Ali

This volume is a landmark achievement in the struggle against the spread of HIV and AIDS among Muslims. Rather than languish at the level of platitudes, the essays collected here acknowledge the existence of the pandemic and take seriously the challenges it poses. All the contributors share the goals of avoiding new infections and supporting those with the disease, yet they, and the people whose lives and ideas they discuss, disagree profoundly over matters of policy, ethics, law, medicine, and theology. Some of these differences of opinion are predictable from personal trajectories, others are traceable to intellectual commitments, but they cannot be meaningfully categorized as "more" and "less" Islamic. Muslims have different bedrock assumptions and life experiences that affect how we understand and practice Islam. We all agree about the Oneness of God, but not about how God punishes sexual transgressions, or indeed what kinds of relationships constitute transgression. In reflecting on the foregoing chapters, I will highlight some areas we can work on together despite disagreements, and some things that bring diverging views into sharp relief. I will conclude with some thoughts of my own on the value of idealism as we struggle to respond as Muslims to the AIDS pandemic.

PREVENTION

Measures to limit the spread of HIV and to care for those affected need not – indeed, must not – depend on resolving core disagreements; the situation is too urgent for that. In a situation of immediate peril, one may do what is necessary to prevent harm and alleviate suffering. Mohammad Hashim Kamali frames the problem in religious terms: the campaign for "AIDS awareness is about protecting at least two of the essential values of the Shari'ah (those of life and lineage)." Muslims therefore must combat the destructive power of HIV infection and AIDS through education and prevention campaigns. Since Muslims widely accept the concepts of "essential values" and "avoiding harm" that are central to Islamic legal and ethical thought, leaders and activists can effectively ground their support for certain best practices in these shared values.

There are two possible problems with appealing to principles like preventing harm. First, invoking these principles must not be an authoritarian attempt to justify one's actions with reference to a dehistoricized and timeless Islam. Rather, their use should be understood as a respectful and creative continuation of the long tradition of Muslim engagement with social issues. Second, and more importantly, real-life conditions sometimes make harm avoidance strategies difficult to implement. For example, in potentially risky situations condom use is, in Malik Badri's words, "the lesser of two evils." Yet even if Muslim intellectuals, clerics, lay thinkers, and popular preachers can overcome ideological resistance to agree on the religious legitimacy of condom use, practical obstacles remain. One common obstacle is the social and ethico-religious taboo that aligns discussing condom use with admitting sin. Another is the lack of bargaining power of economically dependent women to insist that their husbands or sex partners use condoms – a problem exacerbated by the aforementioned taboo, as insistence on condoms can be viewed as an accusation of immoral conduct.

COLLABORATION

This brings me to my second point: in seeking to prevent harm, you may have to help or collaborate with those you disapprove of, or disagree with. Although the majority of Muslim authorities find sex before marriage or outside of marriage abhorrent under any circumstances, accepting and even advocating condom use in such cases does not mean approving of these acts. Similar issues arise when considering needle exchange programs: injecting drug use is undoubtedly personally damaging as well as religiously illicit. But providing clean needles, like condoms, is not condoning behavior, only seeking to minimize real damage – necessary, if distasteful, in preventing HIV transmission.

Not only must we be willing to help those individuals whose actions we disapprove of, we must be willing to act in collaboration with those with whom we disagree on matters of morality. These agreements at the lowest common denominator will not eclipse important disagreements on broader questions. Muslim thinkers differ with each other on key moral issues, like same-sex intimate relationships, and the views of Muslim authorities and ordinary Muslims do not always coincide. Sex-worker advocates and popular preachers may agree that condom use is better than the alternative, but will otherwise disagree on how to approach prostitution as a social fact. Prevention campaigns are likely to run into serious obstacles when trying to agree on a "message" for the general public. Should one advocate abstinence? Regular HIV testing? Perhaps a starting point is distinguishing between widely held but demonstrably false beliefs – such as the disastrous view that sex with a virgin can cure an afflicted person – and matters about which reasonable individuals can disagree – such as the morality of certain types of sexual encounters and relationships. The former ought to be debunked; the latter, debated.

Effective strategies to reduce the transmission of HIV and the severity of AIDS must function despite the existence of illicit or unethical relations, but should where possible set the stage for longer-term improvements. In the short term, prevention strategies must be able to operate without massive changes in social and familial dynamics. Context-specific, locally grounded initiatives such as that dealing with intravenous drug use in Lahore's Heera Mandi, described by Chris Byrnes, provide care for infected and ill people and work to reduce transmission rates even if they cannot end endemic poverty, alter urban economic structures, or prevent discrimination. Ideally, strategies of response can themselves begin the process of transformation by instituting and practicing new forms of community engagement. Kate Long's essay on storytelling as a tool for response suggests the possibilities inherent in complicated, individual, and intensely local mechanisms for doing theology. While one cannot end the pandemic through theologizing, transformations in ideals are also necessary in moving from preventive strategies to reduce transmission and assist people living with AIDS to attempts to end the pandemic entirely.

TRANSFORMATION

It is possible to mitigate some of the effects of injustice by palliative measures and best-practice compromises, but a long-term commitment to profound change will be essential to eradicate the disease. Here is where the disagreements that exist between collaborators will become more apparent, and where those who can agree on minimizing harm will differ sharply. I side unabashedly with those who envision egalitarian gender and economic relationships in the world, who see a moral and religious obligation to combat oppression, poverty, and violence – indeed, who see poverty itself as both violent and oppressive.

Poverty also has a disproportionate impact on women's lives, increasing the urgency of moving toward gender equality in social and intimate contexts. As Kabir Bavikatte and others point out, HIV infection is not merely a byproduct of "freely chosen sexual immorality" but reflects both socio-economic and gendered marginalization. As Clara Koh puts it, "gender inequality meets with poverty to amplify women's risk of infection." Women who engage in sex work are vulnerable, but so are married women. Badri may be correct that "[i]n a perfectly Islamic society there would be no sexually transmitted diseases," but married women infected by husbands who stray cannot be faulted for deviating from his corrective of "an Islamically rooted message of abstention from sex outside marriage."

Still, the focus on blamelessness may be only a tempting distraction from harder questions about suffering and justice. Is human suffering always bad? Is it worse when undeserved? Does it serve some divine purpose? Should it always be eliminated? Taking these questions out of the abstract and into contact with the reality of people living with HIV or dying due to AIDS related illness makes people's divergent positions on suffering quite clear. Theodicy – why suffering exists – is a complex matter, as Abdulaziz Sachedina shows; we ought to take it seriously. Badri writes that "Human anguish is a Divine test to wipe out sin and to elevate the spiritual position of the suffering person," but other contributors sharply disagree.

Several essays in this volume offer provocative paths toward core questions not only of human suffering but also of economic justice, commanding right and forbidding wrong, and other matters that take ethics and justice beyond individual actions; these essays offer conceptual, textual, and theological arguments. My own inclination when confronted with any problem is to read texts. But I read and write about books professionally and, I suspect, am somewhat out of the main current of humanity in terms of my attachment to the written and published word. So perhaps texts are not always the key. Still, the (in)significance and (ir)relevance of the written word coexists with the unavoidable presence and real weight of ideas in daily life. Scott Siraj al-Haqq Kugle and Sarah Chiddy note that a viable response to HIV and AIDS is one that does not remain in the realm of "moralizing" but "takes seriously the lived experience of people living with HIV." Yet lived experience is also experience that is understood. Even people whose first response to a crisis is not to find a relevant religious text, do think. People do not simply "live" things; even those who do not think about theology for a living have very real ideas about who God is and what God does. And they think about HIV and AIDS too.

IDEAS AND IDEALS

Idealism has gotten a bad rap lately. Critics dismiss it as the province of starry-eyed romantics and disconnected ivory-tower theorizers. Moral absolutists earn scorn for being both uncompromising and unrealistic. But a powerful and persuasive vision of how things should be is an important step towards a better world. A vision hobbled by imagining achievable, incremental improvements to the current global socio-political climate will be incapable of the soaring imaginative leap necessary to inspire profound transformation. Even as we struggle to come to terms with and confront reality, we need to envision our ideal world unbounded by seemingly bedrock elements of the human condition: poverty, hunger, massive social inequalities, racism, sexism, violence.

Let me be clear: I am not advocating a willful and continual refusal to see the world as it is. Self-delusion is destructive in an individual and devastating in the hands of policy makers and community leaders. It is patently obvious to anyone who has worked with drug users that arguing against needle exchange programs because "Muslims are forbidden to use drugs" does not solve any problems. The causes of drug use are complex, as are patterns of addiction, and there are no simple or easy solutions. But a world in which people do not turn to drugs out of alienation or unhappiness, or where they reject them from a powerful commitment to religious prescriptions, is worth striving for, and not only to prevent further HIV transmission through injecting drug use.

As for sex, the predominant route of HIV transmission in most of the world, seeking its total abolition is not only absurd but also undesirable. In the context of AIDS we often focus on disease and risk, the dangers of sex. Religious leaders sermonize about debauchery, sin, illicitness. Advocates for gender justice highlight the possibilities of coercion, domination, and force in intimate relationships. Despite several references by contributors to this volume to Islam as a religion that values sexual fulfillment, only Badri concretely and positively describes sex as an integral component of Muslim life, albeit an idealized and romanticized life. And yet "worshipful pleasure," as Kugle and Chiddy put it, is part of the Muslim heritage. Can one link worship and justice, bodily pleasure and spiritual connection? What might an ethic of sexual justice look like, an ideal to motivate and direct a project of transformation?

There are a few non-negotiable elements in my view. Sex should be as fully consensual as possible. Males and females should be held to the same standards of virginity, chastity, and faithfulness. Sex should take place when mutually desired, be mutually pleasurable, and be both physically and emotionally safe for all involved. Sexual conduct should occur in reciprocally committed, mutually faithful relationships with uninfected partners or, when one partner is living with HIV or AIDS, with full disclosure and adequate, consistent attention to preventing transmission. Partners should agree about mechanisms for disease prevention such as condoms. If there is no agreement, the partner who wishes to take precautions should prevail. Condoms should be widely and inexpensively available and broadly accepted. Safe and reliable contraception should be freely accessible. If one partner desires to avoid conception and the other does not, the partner who desires to prevent or delay childbearing should prevail. Children are too precious and too demanding to be brought into the world without agreement by both parents. Finally, as often as possible sex should be erotic rather than by rote. Sex should sometimes allow participants to glimpse transcendence, experiencing a broadening of consciousness beyond the confines of the self. Even when sex does not achieve these heights, it should still embody care, tenderness, and recognition of another human being as a meaningful subject. Sex should be about connection, not merely climax.

This statement of principles grants concessions to the status quo. I wanted to write simply "Sex should be fully consensual" but found myself unable to make that bald statement in a world of unequal power relationships. My affirmation that there should be no gendered double standard sidesteps polygamy only through leger-demain: the phrase "same standards" can be read as "within mar-riage," meaning virginity for both men and women before marriage and subsequent faithfulness to one's spouse(s). There are cir-cumstances in which polygamy can be reasonable, desirable, or appropriate, but it undeniably makes women vulnerable in critical ways. This list also falls into what Sindre Bangstad notes are the "particular weaknesses" of "'Western' prevention models, based" in large part "on liberal notions of individual bodily and sexual autonomy (defined as the ability to exercise and negotiate 'safe sex' practices)." I recognize the problem, but am not sure how to fix it, or even if it is fixable. Sometimes approximations are the best one can do. Full and free liberal notions of consent may be a chimera, but for sex to be union, there must at the outset be two autonomous beings.

Sexual justice is necessarily entwined with legal justice, eco-nomic justice, and gender justice. Legal disabilities (e.g., discrimi-natory regulations for marriage) and economic realities (women's inability to support themselves financially) reinforce each other. Additionally, gender discrimination manifests not only in concrete realities but also in social ideas and ideals. Sexual injustice obstructs social and individual harmony. Yet the attainment of a fully just soci-ety is not a prerequisite for all forms of sexual flourishing. Good sex can be transformative. It can embody radically egalitarian modes of relating to other human beings as means rather than ends, as fellow possessors of the divine spark. This is, of course, a more difficult thing to achieve in the face of concrete material deprivation, if only because privacy is a commodity in short supply in most households. If we insist on the equal dignity of each human being and truly believe that human worth is measured only in piety, then we must work for a world where non-commercialized sexual connection and response is available to everyone, not only those who have two-storey homes and locks on the master bedroom door. Sexual generosity does not have to cost anything.

Ultimately, viable Islamic responses to HIV and AIDS require fundamental shifts in both thinking and behavior. We must first envision an ideal without being bogged down by thinking about feasible, minute improvements, and then think about how to achieve it. In the process, we must balance long-term transformation and short-term palliation. There is a place for idealism that is not willfully blind to reality, but that refuses to have its vision constrained by present injustice. One of the earliest and most enduring elements of Islam's call to humanity has been the demand to take seriously the transformative power of the human conscience. This book represents a significant response to that call.

NOTES ON CONTRIBUTORS

Kecia Ali received her PhD from Duke University and teaches historical and contemporary aspects of Islam in the Department of Religion at Boston University. Her own research centers on early Islamic law and gender discourses in classical and modern Muslim contexts. She is the author of *Sexual Ethics and Islam: Feminist Reflections on Qur'an, Hadith, and Jurisprudence* (Oneworld, 2006) and a forthcoming study of marriage in early Islamic jurisprudence. Professor Ali is currently completing a biography of Imam ibn Idris al-Shafi'i.

Malik Badri is a psychologist who trained at the American University of Beirut and the University of Leicester in England. He has served on the faculties of various universities including the University of Riyadh, American University of Beirut, University of Jordan, and the International Islamic University in Kuala Lumpur. Professor Badri is the author of a number of publications, including *The AIDS Crisis – Natural Product of Modernity's Sexual Revolution*.

Kabir Sanjay Bavikatte is based in Cape Town and works as an environmental and human rights lawyer with Natural Justice, an organization focusing on the rights of indigenous people. He has lived in India, Brazil, and Guyana, and worked as a lawyer, teacher, and activist focusing on a range of issues including the rights of street children, religious minorities, LGBT communities, and sex workers. Kabir has an abiding interest in exploring the interface between spirituality and activism and a passion for adventure sports.

Sindre Bangstad is a Norwegian social anthropologist who has specialized in the study of contemporary Muslim communities in Cape Town. His PhD dissertation from Radboud University/The International Institute for the Study of Islam in the Modern World (ISIM) in the Netherlands, *Global Flows, Local Appropriations: Facets of Secularisation and Re-Islamization Among Contemporary*

Cape Muslims, was published by Amsterdam University Press in the Netherlands in 2007.

Caitlin Yoshiko Buysse has a Masters in Theological Studies from Harvard Divinity School, where she specialized in Islamic Studies. She received her undergraduate degree in Religious Studies from Northwestern University, and has studied abroad several times, including a Buddhist Studies program in Kyoto, Japan, and an Arabic program in Rabat, Morocco. Caitlin also studied in Sri Lanka as a Fulbright scholar, working on issues of charity and economic justice in relation to the 2004 tsunami.

Chris Byrnes has a Masters degree from Harvard University where he studied religion and politics with a concentration in Islamic Studies. His work deals primarily with conflict transformation, religious pluralism, and theologies of social justice. He has studied in India, Pakistan, Spain, and Lebanon, and earned his Bachelor's degree in Physics and Religious Studies from Denison University in Granville, Ohio.

Farid Esack is a South African Muslim theologian who cut his teeth in the South African struggle for liberation. He studied in Pakistan, the United Kingdom, and Germany and is the author of *Qur'an, Liberation and Pluralism*, *On Being a Muslim*, and *An Introduction to the Qur'an* (all published by Oneworld). He has published widely on Islam, Gender, Liberation Theology, Interfaith Relations, Qur'anic Hermeneutics, and AIDS. Professor Esack served as a Commissioner for Gender Equality in South Africa and has taught at a number of universities in Europe, the United States, South Africa, Pakistan, and Indonesia. He is the Deputy Moderator of Peace for Life and a founder of Positive Muslims.

Trad Godsey graduated with a BA in Asian Studies from Samford University in 2005 and with a Masters in Theological Studies from Harvard Divinity School in 2008. His focus of study is the contemporary Islamic world. His main interests include constructions of masculinity, HIV/AIDS and Islam, Muslim-Christian relations, and contemporary, lived religion. He is currently pursuing a PhD in Religious Studies.

Mohammad Hashim Kamali is professor of law at the International Islamic University of Malaysia. He is the author of *Freedom of*

Expression in Islam (1994), *Islamic Commercial Law* (2000), and *Principles of Islamic Jurisprudence* (2003). A former Dean of the International Institute of Islamic Thought and Civilisation (ISTAC), he is currently the CEO and Chairman of the Hadhari Institute for Advanced Islamic Studies of Malaysia. He studied law at Kabul University and did his PhD in Islamic and Middle Eastern law at the University of London.

Clara Koh is a researcher with the United Nations Development Fund for Women (UNIFEM) in Banda Aceh, Indonesia. Her project concerns working within an Islamic framework to strengthen women's rights in Aceh's legal reform. Clara is a graduate of the Master of Theological Studies program at Harvard Divinity School.

Scott Siraj al-Haqq Kugle is a research scholar in comparative religious and Islamic studies. He has taught courses at universities in the USA and South Africa on Islamic scripture, ethics, and mysticism. His recent research at the Institute for the Study of Islam in the Modern World in the Netherlands focused on Islamic constructions of gender and sexuality. He earned a PhD in Religious Studies with a specialization in Islam from Duke University in 2000 and has published three books including *Sufis and Saints' Bodies: Corporeality and Sacred Power in Islamic Culture* (University of North Carolina Press, 2007), which considers how the human body is imagined in Islamic culture. He has published in the *Encyclopedia of Islam*, the *Encyclopedia of the Qur'an*, and the *Encyclopedia of Islam and the Muslim World*.

Kate Henley Long received her Bachelor of Arts in Religion from Mount Holyoke College in 2004 and her Master of Divinity in 2008 from Harvard University. Also a dancer and choreographer, Long's current work focuses on the performing arts as a location for theological inquiry about embodied experience. She resides, studies, and choreographs in Cambridge, Massachusetts.

Marina Mahathir headed the non-governmental Malaysian AIDS Council for twelve years from 1993 until 2005. She has also been involved in several AIDS NGOs, sat on several UN expert panels, represented Asia Pacific AIDS NGOs on the UNAIDS Programme Coordinating Board, and spoken at the United Nations General Assembly. Currently she is a member of the Steering Committee of the Asia Pacific Leadership Forum on HIV and Development, as well as Chair of the AIDS Society of Asia and the Pacific (ASAP) Working Group on the 9th International Congress on AIDS in Asia and the Pacific (ICAAP).

Laura McTighe is the former director of Prison Services for Philadelphia FIGHT (a Philadelphia-based AIDS advocacy organization), where she spent five years living and working alongside people with HIV who were formerly incarcerated. In her research and organizing work, Laura continues to focus on the socioeconomic injustices fueling the AIDS crisis. She completed a Masters in Islamic Studies at Harvard Divinity School and works in Philadelphia with faith communities who are struggling to respond to the HIV and prison crises impacting their members.

Peter Piot is UNAIDS Executive Director and Under Secretary-General of the United Nations. He earned a medical degree from the University of Ghent, a PhD in Microbiology from the University of Antwerp, Belgium, and was a Senior Fellow at the University of Washington in Seattle. In 1976, Dr. Piot co-discovered the Ebola virus in Zaire. In the 1980s he launched and expanded a series of collaborative projects in Africa, including Project SIDA in Kinshasa, Zaire, the first international project on AIDS in Africa. Dr. Piot is the author of sixteen books and more than five hundred scientific articles. He has received numerous awards for scientific and societal achievement, and was made a Baron by King Albert II of Belgium in 1995.

Abdulaziz Sachedina is Frances Myers Ball Professor of Religious Studies at the University of Virgina, Charlottesville. He has studied in India, Iraq, Iran, and Canada, and obtained his PhD from the University of Toronto. He has been conducting research and writing in the field of Islamic Law, Ethics, Biomedical Ethics, Inter and Intrafaith Relations and Theology (Sunni and Shiite) for more than two decades. Dr. Sachedina's publications include: *Islamic Messianism* (SUNY, 1980); *Human Rights and the Conflicts of Culture*, co-authored (University of South Carolina, 1988); *The Just Ruler in Shiite Islam* (Oxford University Press, 1988); *The Prolegomena to the Qur'an* (Oxford University Press, 1998); *The Islamic Roots of Democratic Pluralism* (Oxford University Press, 2002); *Islamic Biomedical Ethics: Theory and Practice* (Oxford University Press, 2008).

Nabilah Siddiquee received her Master's degree in Middle Eastern Studies from Harvard University, where she researched Moroccan Family Law and women's human rights. She earned her Bachelor's degree in History and Near Eastern Languages and Civilizations at Yale University, and has studied Arabic at the American University in Cairo and Yarmouk University in Irbid, Jordan. Her current interests are in international law and human rights, focusing on the Middle East and South Asia.

ENDNOTES

Introduction

1. Some details were changed in the original publication "to honour the family's request for anonymity."

Chapter 1

1. An earlier rendition of this article first appeared as "Can God Inflict Unrequited Pain on His Creatures? Muslim Perspectives on Health and Suffering" in John R. Hinnells and Roy Porter (eds), *Religion, Health and Suffering* (London, Kegan Paul International, 1999).

2. The "preserved tablet" is also regarded as the repository of destiny upon which "the pen" writes. In this sense the Qur'an was sent to the tablet as an event which was to occur in the future. Both these notions of the Tablet as containing the laws of God as well as the knowledge of destiny are also found in the Torah where the Book of Jubilees 3:10 speaks of the laws relating to the "purification of women after childbirth being written on tablets in heaven". See A. J. Wensinck, *The Muslim Creed* (London, Frank Cass & Co. Ltd., 1965), pp. 188ff.

3. There are different versions of this tradition in Muslim sources. The shorter version in *Sahih al-Bukhari*, vol. 7, p. 409, Hadith no. 608 simply states the first part of the tradition in the section on leprosy. On the other hand, *Sahih al-Tirmidhi* (Beirut, Dar al-Fikr, 1983), vol. 3, p. 306, Hadith no. 3320 mentions the detailed version which ends with the declaration by the Prophet: "There is neither contagion nor jaundice. God created every person and then decreed his term, his sustenance and his afflictions (*a'ib*)."

4. Whether in Shi'ism there is a concept of "redemptive" suffering, comparable to Christianity, is taken up in Mahmoud Ayoub, *Redemptive Suffering in Islam: A Study of the Devotional Aspects of "Ashura" in Twelver Shi'ism* (The Hague, Mouton Publishers, 1978). However, the author never connects mourning rituals for the martyrdom of al-Husayn, including the so-called self-flagellation, with a process of "redemption" or "self-mortification" in Shi'ite Islam. In some works by Western Christian authors a connection has been drawn between this Shi'ite practice and Christian monastic tradition, where self-flagellation was regarded as necessary process of self-mortification. See, for instance, Sir Lewis Pelly, *The Miracle Play of Hasan and Husayn*, 2 vols (London, W. H. Allen & Co., 1879). My own studies in Shi'ite literature on martyrology has not found any support for this interpretation.

5. This skeptical attitude is not limited to any particular school of thought in Islam, but is often part of the culture, sometimes without any reference to the aforementioned belief in God's sole power of healing.

Chapter 2

1. Bukhari, *Sahih, Kitab al-Tibb*, "a strong (*qawiyy*) believer is preferred and better liked by God than a weak (*da'if*) believer", vol. 7:222, Hadith no. 1, does not mention the exception. The exception is recorded in the version reported by Ibn Maja, *Sunan, Kitab al-Tibb*, vol. 2:1137, Hadith no. 3426.
2. This Hadith is discussed in considerable detail by Nabilah Siddiquee elsewhere in this volume.

Chapter 3

1. The concept of the "Islamization of knowledge", which gained wide currency among Muslim intellectuals in the 1980s (Sardar, 2004, 194–203), and once drew on support and funding from Muslim regimes as varied as those of Saudi Arabia, Pakistan, Iran, and Malaysia, was developed by the Indonesian-Malaysian scholar Syed Mohammed Naquib al-Attas in his *Islam and Secularism* (1978). The reviews of Badri's book in the *American Journal of Islamic Social Sciences* (Watanabee, 1998), and in the *Muslim World Book Review* (Hoffmann, 1998) illustrate his appeal to scholars who subscribe to the "Islamization of knowledge" notions. Scholars who adhere to this paradigm may be referred to as a "community of interpretation," sharing as they do certain fundamental epistemological interpretations and ideological preferences.
2. Qutb was an Egyptian civil servant. As a leading member and ideologue of the Muslim Brotherhood, he was gradually radicalized through his personal experiences of the torture and repression of the Brotherhood by the Nasserist state, and was executed in 1966. His writings have been important inspirations for the salafi-jihadi strand of contemporary Islamist thought. See Qutb (1978, 183–185) for his comments on modern "Western" sexual moralities. Mawdudi (1903–1979), a Pakistani scholar, founded the Islamist Jama'at i-Islami of Pakistan. His writings influenced Qutb, and have also had an important impact on Islamist thought.
3. Khalid El-Roayheb (2005) is among the authors who have argued that attitudes towards homosexuality in the Muslim world have to be seen in historical and social contexts. In fact, he argues that Islamic cultures in the period 1500 to 1800 lacked a specific concept of homosexuality, in which event current tendencies towards homophobia in different parts of the "Muslim world" must be seen as reflecting a thoroughly modern development.
4. It should be recalled that classical *fiqh* (Islamic law) texts were often open and discursive texts which did not offer final and conclusive solutions. It was therefore, paradoxically, largely the codification of Shari'ah law as an expression of the will of the state under the influence of Westernization, which brought about the modern situation in which Islamic commandments are seen by Muslims as authoritative, final, and unequivocal.

5. Both Moosa and El Fadl see this as a lamentable impoverishment of the rich intellectual tradition in Islam. There can be little doubt that Muslim intellectuals who subscribe to an "Islamization of knowledge" for the most part share the epistemic closedness which Moosa and El Fadl point to. But one could be forgiven for thinking that both Moosa and El Fadl overstate their case somewhat. Muslim public intellectuals such as they themselves and Abdolkarim Soroush, Mohammed Arkoun, Farid Esack, Fazlur Rahman, Hassan Hanafi, Abdullahi Ahmed an-Naiʿm, Amina Wadud, Asma Barlas, Saʿdiyya Shaikh, and others, point to the existence of a rich contemporary intellectual tradition in Islam, even if the locations from which these intellectuals speak (more often than not secular "Western" universities) are different than for the ancients.

6. See www.islamonline.net/livedialogue/english/guestcv.asp?hGuestID=Z0lr7w.

7. FIMA, of which IMA-SA is an affiliate, was established in 1981, and is based in Illinois in the USA. Their yearbooks for 2002, 2003, and 2004 all featured articles by Badri.

8. The acronym AIDS is, according to Badri, a misnomer: it should instead be "Gay Related Immune Deficiency" (GRID) (ibid., 271).

9. With regard to Haitians originally having been infected by North American male homosexuals, there is considerable support in the literature for this. Among the first Haitians to have come down with opportunistic infections related to HIV were a significant number of homosexual and bisexual Haitian men who had had sexual contact with North American men either in the USA or in Haiti, or in both places. However, none of them had ever been to Africa (Farmer, 1992, 127–128).

10. "Reparative therapy" has come under much criticism among psychiatrists and psychologists internationally, since its claim to success has so far not been backed up by any reliable and valid empirical studies. The American Psychiatric Association (APA) approved a position statement opposed to such therapy in 2000, and recommended that psychiatric practitioners refrain from engaging in attempts to alter patients' sexual orientation.

11. www.islamonline.org/livedialogue/english/Browse.asp?hGuestID=ZlbGS0.

12. It is worth recalling that Mawdudi and Qutb were not opposed to all facets of "Western" modernity. Like many later Islamists they identified technological and scientific progress with "Western" modernity, and fully endorsed the adoption of this part of it by Muslim societies. Badri seems, however, to be somewhat more ambivalent on this point. Unlike early Islamist intellectuals like Qutb and Mawdudi, who failed to realize the extent to which technological and scientific progress (to which in their visions Muslims ought to aspire) sets in motion epistemological and normative changes (think of the impact of the introduction of the pill, and the internet), which cannot easily be cordoned off from religious life, Badri seems to have realized this, and is consequently highly ambivalent with regard to modern media such as television, for instance. Yet his vision for society and morality, as well as his reflections on "traditional" and "early" Muslim society as a template for contemporary Muslim societies, are thoroughly modern and epistemologically intimately linked to the "Western" modernity which he finds so reprehensible.

13. After Frantz Fanon (1925–61), the author of *Black Skins, White Masks* (Fanon, 1967), who argued that "the native" could only salvage his own humanity

through a dialectical inversion of the colonialist image and representation of himself.

14. In Uganda this has changed in recent years, due to an ideological shift in the direction of neo-conservatism and evangelical Christianity in government circles in the USA, which provides much funding for the Ugandan government's AIDS prevention programs through PEPFAR and USAID. This has meant that promotion of condoms has been replaced by a promotion of abstinence, and acceptance of sex workers has been replaced by moral condemnation, in spite of scientific evidence from the US suggesting that abstinence programs do not lead to safer-sex practices among young people there. Developments in Uganda have been detailed by Epstein (2005), and a Human Rights Watch report from 2005 (HRW, 2005).

15. Despite several attempts and correspondence with the university, the editors have not been able locate any record of a Dr. Qandil as an instructor at Harvard University or to ascertain whether he was at any stage affiliated with the university.

16. Macfie (2002, 43), in a review of literature on Orientalism, points out that it was widely believed among Christians in Europe in medieval times that Muslims promoted homosexuality, prostitution, and adultery.

17. It should of course also be noted that the fundamental epistemological premise of Said's book, namely that the colonial enterprise in the Arab world was intimately linked to the academic production of knowledge by Orientalists, was relatively poorly argued by Said, and he may therefore not have been quite as innocent of the misreadings of his work as was previously thought. In referring to Orientalism in the singular Said also suggested a much greater uniformity among Orientalist academics and authors of different nationalities and persuasions than was warranted by historical facts.

18. El-Haj (2005, 42), for instance, has recently argued that the very act of writing about Occidentalism(s) as a parallel of Orientalism(s) is problematic due to the fact that Occidentalism(s) does not stand in the same relationship to power and histories of knowledge as Orientalism(s) does. In other words, it seems as if El-Haj thinks that "othering" is somehow more defensible when it cannot be linked to, or is not underwritten by, colonial power and its exercise. Interestingly, Said himself in an interview referred to a phenomenon he termed "Occidentosis", and described the idea that "all the evils in the world come from the West" as "Orientalism in reverse" (Viswanathan, 2005, 221).

19. Global attitudinal surveys conducted in recent years, such as the University of Michigan's World Values Survey, have suggested the greatest differences in attitudes between individuals in Muslim and "Western" societies are in the fields of sexual mores, and family and marital values. Cf. Ebrahim (2006).

Chapter 4

1. The meaning of the word *fāhishah* will be discussed in further detail below.
2. Here, Goldziher references Khatīb al-Baghdādi.
3. Biographical information here on Ibn Māja is partially referenced from Suhaib Ḥasan Abdul Ghaffar, *Criticism of Hadith among Muslims with Reference to Sunan Ibn Maja*, 2nd edn (London, Ta-Ha Publishers Inc., 1986). Biographies

of Ibn Māja can be found in the works of Hāfiz Abu Ya'la al-Khalīli, Ibn al-Jawzī, Shams al-Dīn al-Jazāri (d. 711/1311), and Ibn Hajar, as well as in Ibn Khallikān's (d. 681/1282) *Wafayāt al-A'yān*.

4. These numbers are slightly different in Hashim Kamali's book, which cites 4,341 total *ahādīth*, and 1,329 unique *ahādīth* in Ibn Māja's collection.

5. There is another version of this hadith related by Tabarāni on the authority of Ibn 'Abbās, which is not included in any of the six authoritative collections. The translation of this version is the following: "Five (actions) entail five (consequences): Whenever a people break their covenant, their enemy will be given power over them. Whenever they judge by other than what Allah has revealed, poverty becomes rampant among them. Whenever shameful deeds (*al-fāhishah*) become prevalent among them, death becomes rampant in their midst. Whenever they measure falsely, they are denied (the harvest of plants), and will suffer famine. Whenever they refuse to pay zakāt, they will be deprived of rain." See Al-Sayed Ahmad al-Hashimi, *Selection of Prophetic Hadiths & Muhammadan Wisdoms*, translated by Salma al-Houry (Beirut, Dār al-Kutub al-Ilmīyya).

6. Other references to the crimes of the people of Lut and their punishment are found in the following verses: *al-A'rāf* (7), 80–84; *Hud* (11), 77–83; *al-Hijr* (15), 58–77; *al-Anbiya* (21), 74–75; *al-Shu'arā'* (26), 160–174; *al-Naml* (27), 54–58; *al-'Ankabūt* (29), 28–35; *al-Saffāt* (37), 133–138; and *al-Qamar* (54), 33–39.

7. Among early Meccan surahs, relevant passages, in chronological order, include: 105; 91:11–15; 85:17–20; 73:15–16; 79:15–26; 89:6–14; 53:50–54; 69:4–12; 51:24–46.

8. It is worth noting that Muhammad Asad's translation of the word "*fitna*" renders a different meaning to the verse: "And beware of that *temptation to evil* which does not befall only those among you who are bent on denying the truth, to the exclusion of others, and know that God is severe in retribution" (*al-Anfāl* (8), 25).

Chapter 5

1. Some parts of this article first appeared in the International Islamic University of Malaysia Law Journal (M.H. Kamali, "Protection Against Disease: A Shari'ah Perspective on AIDS," *International Islamic University of Malaysia Law Journal*, vol. 5 (1995), 1–20.

2. Some jurists have in fact argued that the Shari'ah is, from beginning to end, premised on the elimination of *darar*. Cf. Jamil Muhammad Mubarak, *Nazariyyat al-Darar al-Shar'iyyah* (Cairo, Dar al-Wafa'li'l-Taba'ah wa'-Nashr, 1408/1988), 38.

3. Muslim jurists have usually divided the welfare of the people into three categories: necessities (*daruriyyat*), needs (*hajiyyat*), and luxuries (*kamaliyyat* or *tahsiniyyat*). The Muslim state must seek to fulfill these interests in this order of priority. The necessities are further divided into five basic values – *al-daruriyyat al-khamsah*: the protection of religion, life, intellect, lineage or honor, and property.

Chapter 6

1. In using the term "feminist" to describe this broad spectrum of activities, it must be said that not all Muslim women (and men) want to be labeled as such, nor should this label give credence to the notion that gender activism is a property of the West (Cooke, 2001, ix). Rather, I use this term to connote any person or movement that seeks to undermine all forms of structural patriarchy, be they imperialist, economic, environmental, religious, or social.
2. Moghadam does indicate that women's rights discourse in Iran combines religious argumentation with international conventions, such as UN-CEDAW.

Chapter 7

1. As of December 2006, the Ministry of Health reported a total of 70,300 cases in Malaysia.
2. In December 2005, Malaysia's parliament passed amendments to the Federal Territory Islamic Family Laws, which, among other things, loosened procedures for polygamy, dropping requirements for justice for first wives, and gave men certain rights that were previously exclusive to women.
3. When Malaysia gained independence in 1957 as a federation of nine states (later thirteen states, plus the Federal Territories of Kuala Lumpur and Labuan), all laws except for those governing the Islamic religion and property came under federal jurisdiction. The rulers of the nine states became heads of religion in their respective states, and each state could then pass Islamic personal laws through its own state legislature. As a result, there are variations in the laws across the country. In the states of Kelantan and Terengganu, the ruling opposition Islamic party passed what is known as the *hudud* laws, based on very strict interpretations of the Shariah.
4. In Malaysia, four states have decided to implement mandatory premarital HIV testing for Muslim couples. Although this is not the policy of the Federal Ministry of Health, these states have been able to do this through the state Islamic religious departments, over which the federal government has no control. Procedures for testing vary from state to state, and, thus far, no evidence has been established that proves the efficacy of these tests in reducing the number of infections in these states.
5. Surah 4, verse 34: "Men are the protectors and maintainers of women, because God has given the one more (strength) than the other, and because they support them from their means. Therefore the righteous women are devoutly obedient, and guard in (the husband's) absence what God would have them guard. As to those women on whose part ye fear disloyalty and ill-conduct, admonish them (first), (Next), refuse to share their beds, (And last) beat them (lightly); but if they return to obedience, seek not against them means (of annoyance): For God is Most High, great (above you all)." This Surah has been used to justify men beating their wives, but Abdullah Yusuf Ali maintains that "Imam Shafi'i considers this inadvisable, though permissible, and all authorities are unanimous in deprecating any sort of cruelty, even of the nagging kind" (A. Y. Ali).
6. There have been controversies about US government policy on funding for HIV/AIDS programmes in developing countries, particularly under the

President's Emergency Plan for AIDS Relief (PEPFAR). Conditions attached to funding require recipients to promote abstinence over safer sex and prohibits any form of harm reduction programmes for prevention of HIV among drug users, such as needle exchange programs.

Chapter 8

1. UNIFEM and UNAIDS have partnered to form the Gender and HIV/AIDS Portal (genderandaids.org), a resource for determining and addressing the gendered pandemic. See also the publication, *AIDS as a Gender Issue: Psychosocial Perspectives*, edited by Loraine Sherr (London, Taylor & Francis, 1996), for a comprehensive collection of early articles specifically related to the gendered nature of the AIDS pandemic.
2. WHO's fact sheet no. 249, "Women and Sexually Transmitted Infections" claims that women are more vulnerable than men to contracting STIs for biological, cultural, and socio-economic reasons (www.who.int/mediacentre/factsheets/fs249/en).
3. See Sida's May 2007 publication, *AIDS and Gender Relations: Men Matter! AIDS, Gender, and Masculinities*, which provides a non-religious approach to reforming masculinity to cope with the AIDS pandemic.
4. Carole Campbell writes about the gendered nature AIDS has taken on in *Women, Families, and HIV/AIDS* (Cambridge, Cambridge University Press, 1999). She elaborates on the difficulty of addressing men and notions of masculinity in relation to AIDS and education. Sexual health has largely been the burden of the women, due to the ineffectiveness of addressing men's problematic role in all of this. Campbell's work also points to the problems men incur because of denial and resistance to appearing weak and vulnerable.
5. See Leila Ahmed's *Women and Gender in Islam: Historical Roots of a Modern Debate* (New Haven, Yale University Press, 1992). Her work is pivotal for understanding the role Islam played in both continuing and reforming pre-Islamic traditions vis-à-vis women.
6. www.uu.nl/content/tbvSAGA18–01–2005tekstkamana.doc.
7. From a study, "Clients of Sex-Workers in Different Regions of the World: Hard to Count", found at sti.bmj.com.
8. www.uu.nl/content/tbvSAGA18–01–2005tekstkamana.doc.

Chapter 9

1. *Shaz* literally means "rare" and *luti* is a reference to what is commonly referred to as the "people of Lot", i.e., the men who sexually attacked Lot's visiting male guests who, according to the Qur'an, were angels sent by God.
2. *Surah al-Ahzab* (33:50–52) directly addresses the question of sexual relationships outside of marriage with slaves and concubines, explicitly allowing this for the Prophet (and implicitly allowing it for other believers) while contrasting such women to those formally married.
3. This alternative and progressive Islamic perspective is presented in more detail in Kugle, "Sexuality and Sexual Ethics in the Agenda of Progressive Muslims,"

in Omid Safi (ed.), *Progressive Muslims: on Gender, Justice and Pluralism* (Oxford, Oneworld Publications, 2003) and also Kugle, "Sexual Diversity in Islam" in Vincent Cornell, Virginia Gray Henry-Blakemore, and Omid Safi (eds), *Voices of Islam*, vol. 5 (New York, Praeger Press, 2007).

4. For narratives about the effeminate men or *mukhannathun* in Medina during the era of the Prophet, Rowson cites classical Islamic sources such as al-Khalil ibn Ahmad, *Kitab al-'Ayn* (Baghdad, Dar al-Rashid, 1980), al-'Ayni, *Umdat al-Qari* (Beirut, Muhammad Amin Damaj, 1970) and Abu'l-Faraj al-Isfahani, *Kitab al-Aghani* (Cairo, 1905–1906).

5. The Qur'an does assume a heterosexual norm among its listeners. This does not automatically mean that the Qur'an forbids homosexuality or condemns homosexuals, but that the Qur'an assumes that sexual desire between men and women is the social and statistical norm, and that addressing and regulating this desire is the basis for establishing a moral society.

6. This phrase occurs in *Surah al-Nur* 24:31, as discussed above. A similar verse can be understood to speak of lesbian women when it says, "of the women, those not reproducing who do not wish for intercourse" in *Surah al-Nur* 24:60.

7. It is beyond the scope of this paper to provide such explanation, but readers are urged to examine Kugle's work elsewhere, as well as the work of Canadian scholar Amreen Jamal (Kugle, 2003, 2007; Jamal, 2001).

8. For further elaboration of one of these terms – *fāhishah* – see Nabilah Siddiqee's paper elsewhere in this volume.

9. Al-Shami, Salih Ahmad (ed.), *al-Jami' Bayn al-Sahihayn* (Damascus: Dar al-Qalam, 1995) 3:505–520 is an invaluable tool for such research.

10. Researchers in pre-Islamic and early-Islamic Arabic literature have uncovered a wealth of examples. Salah al-Din Munajjad has documented that same-sex practices existed among both men and women in pre-Islamic Arabia. For an in-depth discussion of this, see al-Din Munajjad (1975).

11. In the Maliki, Shafi'i, Hanbali, and Ja'fari schools of law, corporal punishment meant stoning to death for a perpetrator who had already been legally married to a woman and one hundred lashes for an unmarried perpetrator. The Hanafi and Zahiri schools opposed inflicting death and argued for a punishment at the ruler's discretion that could not exceed ten lashes. The legal arguments which led to varied decisions about sodomy are complex, involving the question of whether sodomy is a legal issue related to any verses in the Qur'an and which hadith are authentic and authoritative in the matter. See Schmitt (2001).

12. Yip uses this term to refer to someone who identifies as either homosexual or bisexual or queer, but for whom male-with-male sexual intimacy is an important part of their sexual fulfillment (Yip, 2004).

13. Bertozi et al. produce a table in a document entitled "Disease Control Priorities in Developing Countries" (2nd edn, 2006), 334 (http://files.dcp2.org/pdf/DCP/DCP18.pdf), which shows that receptive anal intercourse represents the highest risk per exposure (at less than or equal to 3.0%). Jay Levy in his recent book *HIV and the Pathogenesis of AIDS* (2007) provides an updated version of the table that shows an approximation of 1.0% HIV transmission for receptive anal, still the highest percentage among sexual modes (Levy, 2007, 37).

Chapter 10

1. The emphasis on silence, taboos about sex and sexuality, and its negative consequences for the AIDS pandemic are by no means limited to Muslim cultures. These tendencies are both common to many traditional cultures and bear striking similarities to other major world religions such as Roman Catholicism. For a more extensive explanation of my point of departure, please see n. 2.

2. My concern about Islamic responses to HIV and AIDS arises largely from my experience in the tradition-grounded and ideal-focused religion of Catholicism. Much of my own work – scholarly as well as vocational – falls into the realm of negotiating the tension between Catholic ideals and the realities of modern life. This work includes issues surrounding reproductive choice, condom use, and ministry to gay and lesbian Catholics, all of which are issues considered "taboo" in Catholic communities and non-negotiable from the perspective of Catholic religious ideals. As with HIV and AIDS in Muslim communities, however, I believe that such realities cannot be ignored by responsible people of faith despite the fact that in addressing them, certain taboos may be violated. I find the approach of dealing with these issues within both a practical and a theological framework to be useful and seek to apply a similar methodology in this paper. I do not think that the difficulty of addressing HIV and AIDS is unique to Islam, or that Islam is in any way uniquely "at fault" for failing to respond sufficiently to the pandemic. Muslim responses to HIV and AIDS is one case among many in which religiously-minded communities have the capacity to use their particular theological traditions to respond in new and creative ways to complicated social realities.

Chapter 14

1. TEACH Outside was founded in 2000; Waheedah was a graduate of the Fall 2003 class.

2. Waheedah is a Sunni Muslim, having followed Warith Deen Muhammad's break with the Nation of Islam after the death of his father, Elijah Muhammad, in 1975. Today, the vast majority of Black Muslims in the United States are followers of Sunni Islam, though Louis Farrakhan did revive the Nation of Islam in 1977 and retains a significant Nation of Islam membership among Black people. For a more detailed exploration of the Black Muslim community in the United States, see Dannin (2002) and Jackson (2005).

3. Mohja Kahf discusses this issue in her own work with a battered Muslim woman who was convinced that Islam supported her husband's right to beat her. "She would not leave [her old worldview] without Islam. She had to take Islam with her to make a new life, a new way of thinking about life as a woman alone in the world" (2005, 135).

4. Because Waheedah, like most of the Muslims I have worked with, practices Sunni Islam, this paper explores the Qur'an's guidance on substance use, not the texts or theologies of the Nation of Islam.

5. For a more detailed exploration of the responsibility to command good and forbid evil in Islamic thought, see Cook (2000).

6. While *khamr* is the most common word for intoxicant in the Qur'an, the Qur'an at times also uses the word *sakar* for intoxicant and the word *sukara* for

intoxication (Kueny, 2001, 1–24). In discussing *khamr*, the Qur'an specifically mentions wine and drunkenness. But over the years *khamr* has been understood to encompass *any* intoxicants, including drugs like crack and heroin (Karic, 2007).

7. For a more detailed exploration of the transmission and interpretation of these verses, see Ibn Kathir (2006).

8. The *Diagnostic and Statistical Manual of Mental Disorders*, the other major classification system for psychiatric illnesses, uses nearly identical criteria in its definition of substance dependence (American Psychiatric Association, 1994).

9. In his chapter "Invisible Punishment: An Instrument of Social Exclusion," Jeremy Travis defines invisible punishment as the laws and regulations that diminish the rights of those convicted of crimes, including restrictions on voting rights, employment possibilities, educational loans, public housing funds, welfare assistance, and drivers' licenses. Travis names the punishments "invisible," because they operate totally independently of the criminal justice system, are not proportional to a person's crime, and are generally indefinite restrictions for which former prisoners have no course of redress. Nearly all of these punishments are imposed exclusively on people with felony drug convictions (Travis, 2002, 15–36).

10. Drug-related sentencing reforms include longer sentences, Mandatory Minimum sentences for drug offenses, and 3-Strikes Laws, where a person automatically faces life imprisonment after the third conviction. These reforms have ensured that people are serving longer sentences for mostly nonviolent crimes that could arguably be better addressed through drug treatment programs. About eighty percent of people in US prisons report histories of addiction; only about ten percent of them are receiving drug treatment (Maddow, 2002, 25).

11. For a more detailed exploration of the war on drugs, see Bureau of Justice, and Mauer 2006.

12. For a more detailed exploration of the impact of the war on drugs on people with HIV, see Boutwell and Rich (2004).

13. This aspect of HIV educational and prevention work is the focus of Memoona Hasnain's article, "Cultural Approach to HIV/AIDS Harm Reduction in Muslim Countries." She discusses how gender inequality, stigma/discrimination and ignorance/misinformation fuel the spread of HIV in Muslim countries. Focusing on how religion defines culture and thereby gives meaning to individuals' lives, she advocates a project of comprehensive HIV education and prevention work rooted in the cultural infrastructure of Muslim countries. Citing examples of HIV work in Uganda and Senegal, she argues for the proof that education and prevention campaigns initiated by religious leaders can have a dramatic impact on people's understanding of HIV and willingness to use harm reduction tools like condoms and needle exchange programs, thus halting the spread of HIV (Hasnain, 2005, 23–31).

INDEX

The Crucifixion and the Qur'an
A Study in the History of Muslim Thought

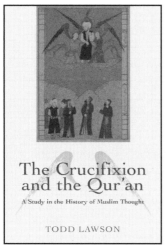

The Crucifixion
and the Qur'an

A Study in the History of Muslim Thought

TODD LAWSON

This innovative work is the first book devoted to the issue of the crucifxion of Jesus as approached by the Qur'an.

Arranged along historical lines, and covering various Muslim schools of thought, from Sunni to Sufi, *The Crucifixion and the Qur'an* will fascinate anyone interested in Christian-Muslim relations.

9781851686360 - HB £30.00/$50.00
9781851686353 - PB - £19.99/$29.99

Todd Lawson is Associate Professor at the Department of Near and Middle Eastern Civilizations, University of Toronto. He is the author of *Reason and Inspiration in Islam: Theology, Philosophy and Mysticism in Muslim Thought.*

"With admirable lucidity the book takes us chronologically through all the main interpretations of the key verse where crucifixion is explicitly mentioned."

Michael Carter - *Professor of Medieval Studies and Arabic, University of Sydney*

"This important, thought-provoking book harbingers fruitful new trajectories for conversations between Christians and Muslims."

Asma Afsaruddin - *Associate Professor of Arabic and Islamic Studies, University of Notre Dame.*

Browse all our titles at www.oneworld-publications.com

Islam: Past Present and Future

Hans Küng Islam
Past, Present & Future

9781851686124 - PB - £19.99/$29.95

In this extraordinarily comprehensive book, Hans Küng gives an in-depth account of Islam, explaining why "peace between religions" is imperative.

Providing a masterful overview of Islam's 1,400-year history, Küng's critically acclaimed bestseller examines its fundamental beliefs and practices, outlines the major schools of thought, and surveys the positions of Islam on the urgent questions of the day. Deft and assured this essential reference work is now available in paperback for the first time.

Dr. Hans Küng is President of the Foundation for a Global Ethic (Weltethos). From 1960 until his retirement in 1996, he was Professor of Ecumenical Theology and Director of the Institute for Ecumenical Research at the University of Tübingen. He is a scholar of theology and philosophy and a prolific writer.

"A brilliant treatment of Islam and its beliefs by a brilliant theologian." **Washington Times**

"A magnificent 'tour de force' by our greatest living theologian" **Lord George Carey,** *former Archbishop of Canterbury, 1991-2002*

Browse all our titles at www.oneworld-publications.com